FRENCH
Countryside Cooking

NOURISH

EAT WELL, LIVE WELL

FRENCH COUNTRYSIDE COOKING
DANIEL GALMICHE

First published in the UK and USA in 2021 by Nourish,
an imprint of Watkins Media Limited
Unit 11, Shepperton House, 83–93 Shepperton Road
London N1 3DF

enquiries@nourishbooks.com

Recipes in this book have been previously published in
Revolutionary French Cooking by Daniel Galmiche.

Managing Editor: Ella Chappell
Editors: Nicola Graimes, Wendy Hobson,
Sophie Elletson and Dan Hurst
Cover Design: Francesca Corsini
Interior Design: Karen Smith
Photography Art Direction: Manisha Patel
Commissioned Photography: Yuki Sugiura
Food Stylists: Daniel Galmiche with Aya Nishimura
Prop Stylist: Wei Tang
Production: Uzma Taj

Typeset in Archer
Printed in China

A CIP record for this book is available from the
British Library

ISBN: 978-1-84899-390-7 (Hardback)
ISBN: 978-1-84899-391-4 (eBook)

10 9 8 7 6 5 4 3 2 1

Publisher's note
While every care has been taken in compiling the recipes
for this book, Watkins Media Limited, or any other
persons who have been involved in working on this
publication, cannot accept responsibility for any errors
or omissions, inadvertent or not, that may be found in
the recipes or text, nor for any problems that may arise
as a result of preparing one of these recipes. If you are
pregnant or breastfeeding or have any special dietary
requirements or medical conditions, it is advisable to
consult a medical professional before following any of
the recipes contained in this book. Ill or elderly people,
babies, young children and women who are pregnant or
breastfeeding should avoid recipes containing raw meat
or fish or uncooked eggs.

Notes on the recipes
Unless otherwise stated:
• Use free-range eggs and poultry
• Use medium eggs, fruit and vegetables
• Use fresh ingredients, including herbs and chillies
• Do not mix metric and imperial measurements:
   1 tsp = 5ml   1 tbsp = 15ml   1 cup = 250ml

nourishbook.com

FRENCH
Countryside Cooking

Inspirational dishes from the forests,
fields and shores of France

DANIEL GALMICHE

CONTENTS

RECIPE KEY

You will find one, or several, of the above symbols marked on each recipe in this book. They are used to denote when the ingredients in each recipe are in season and at their best. Eating seasonally is both more sustainable and the resulting food will taste better, so do take them into account when planning what you are going to cook.

DEDICATION

THIS BOOK IS DEDICATED TO TWO VERY SPECIAL AND IMPORTANT PEOPLE – MY WIFE, CLAIRE, AND MY SON, ANTOINE. WITHOUT THEM IN MY LIFE, AND THEIR TREMENDOUS SUPPORT, I WOULD NOT BE ABLE TO DO WHAT I DO. THEY BOTH LOVE FOOD, THEY HAVE ENDLESS PATIENCE AND THEY ARE FUN TO BE WITH. THEY ALSO UNDERSTAND WHAT I DO FOR LIVING, WHICH MAKES IT SO MUCH EASIER FOR ME WHEN I AM SO OFTEN AT WORK. SO THIS COOKBOOK IS FOR YOU GUYS, WITH ALL MY LOVE – ALWAYS.

FOREWORD

We are all becoming increasingly aware of the importance of being close to the natural world. As chefs, we can draw enormous inspiration from the bountiful number of delicious things to be found within easy reach as we stroll through a woodland or orchard, or by a lake or river. But there is also something else that happens to us as we allow the sounds, smells and feelings of the great outdoors to envelope our senses. We are revived, nourished and healed.

Heading out into the countryside is something we can all do, and Daniel has grouped the recipes into environments from meadows to farmyards and from orchards to rivers, so whatever you can get access to there will be something to inspire you in this book. His cooking style shows respect for both tradition and innovation, mixed with enthusiasm and curiosity about the whole gamut of ingredients.

I have enjoyed several countryside walks with Daniel over the years; we have always been good friends, especially when our businesses were not many miles apart. When he was head chef at Cliveden, I would occasionally take a break from the Fat Duck, drive the short distance and we would walk, talk and swap ideas and thoughts about many things, but inevitably our conversations would turn to food. Our cooking styles are very different but I recognized a kindred spirit – warm, energetic and completely caught up in the romance of cooking and the pleasures of the table.

In a strange twist of fate, I now live in rural France whilst Daniel lives in the rolling Chiltern Hills of England so we don't get to see each other as much now. But reading this book took me right back to those days of hanging out with him.

In the pages that follow you'll get a taste of what Daniel is all about and experience his brilliant cooking and infectious enthusiasm for anything to do with food.

Heston Blumenthal

FOREWORD

Daniel is not only a great professional, a Michelin star chef, but a friend who happened to live in the same region as I do – the rugged Jura Mountains, not too far from elegant, hilly Burgundy – two renowned food and wine regions. For this reason, I may understand Daniel's cooking better than most because he was brought up as I was, hunting for wild game, gathering wild mushrooms, wild asparagus, herbs, plants and berries in the immense forests of Franche-Comté. He worked with the paysans, helping them to gather their harvests, and at the village fromagerie, helping to make the famous Comté cheese. All this prepared him for the years to come.

He learnt from his great aunt, Maman Galmiche, from a young age; this made him respect how much labour goes into working the soil: the planting, growing and harvesting. All through the process, this "apprenticeship" made him understand the seasons, the love of food and people. The knowledge grows and then you are ready for the next stage, learning your trade. This is what Daniel has done. You can sense it, feel it and taste it in his cooking. You can see his passion coming through, hence his success running four different restaurants, all gaining a coveted Michelin star.

But here, in this book, Daniel shows who he really is, where he comes from and where it all started: at home with Maman Galmiche in his beloved Franche-Comté.

Back in the late 80s, when Daniel and I were two of only 32 Michelin-star chefs, we met in England during some demonstrations and spent a few evenings reinventing gastronomy. But really I got to know Daniel in Singapore in the 90s, when I was a guest chef at the prestigious Raffles Hotel. I was there doing a week-long promotion with my team, creating many of my signature dishes from my two-Michelin-star Le Manoir aux Quat'Saisons. My god that was tough! I remember taking a few hours off and heading to his restaurant L'Aigle D'Or, part of the Duxton Hotel where Daniel was the resident chef. So, whilst talking about food, new techniques and ideas we tasted seven or more of his new dishes. It was a divine experience, reconnecting with an old friend and enjoying the most delicious food. This sealed our friendship.

I have huge respect for the man and the craftsman, his talent, his passion, his style of cooking and also the love he has for the produce, for nature and his peers.

A man of my own heart.

Raymond Blanc

INTRODUCTION

I could almost have started this book with a story:

Once upon a time in Franche-Comté, a young boy was walking through the kitchen at his great aunt's house. Suddenly he stopped in his stride, looked up and shouted,

"When I grow up, I want to be a cuisinier."

He was five years old. At that time, nobody thought anything about it and life went on as usual. But, some time later ...

... that young boy did, indeed, become a chef. And I am sure you know who I am talking about.

I have always enjoyed my profession and, after many years, I still love it. It's challenging, exciting and fun. It gives me the chance to work with some fabulous people – dedicated, knowledgeable and hard-working – some with considerable experience and others young and eager to learn and experiment, always keen to try new ideas.

BACK TO MY ROOTS

But that is moving ahead. From as long ago as I can remember, I was surrounded by gourmands. Food was very important in our house, and I learnt all the time from my mum – for I watched her constantly. Mum was passionate about food, always testing, asking me what I thought, or calling Dad to make him try this sauce or that new dish. She went to so much trouble to cook for all of us and was always totally focused. She hated it when something wasn't right, even to the point of starting again from scratch if it was for the Christmas dinner, or another special day, and she was not happy with the dish.

The style of cooking reflected the classic cuisine of France, but even more it followed the traditional style of Franche-Comté. All the time, we followed the seasons and enjoyed the freshest produce. Dad hunted, so Mum cooked whatever was in season, with fresh vegetables from our garden and fruit from the orchard. To this day, my favourite dish is *gibelotte de lapin*, farm rabbit casserole – a delight.

When I was 15, I went to catering college for a year, and after that I began a three-year apprenticeship to learn the skills of my craft. That was really hard work – with the long hours, strict discipline and so much to learn. You had to stay focused every moment, which was very tiring at times. But that is something that never changes in a good kitchen. Dedication, focus, discipline and passion are vital if you want to be a good chef, and if you want to be successful.

Once I qualified, I clearly remember the first day I started work. It was in the Luxeuil-les-Bains Hotel, Beausite. The chef just put three large boxes of spinach leaves in front of me, showed me how he wanted it prepared and off I went. And I've never looked back. I loved cooking from the start, even though it was tough – like cleaning the stove, and replacing the coal early in the morning, in winter, when you were punished for not coming up to scratch. Luckily for me, though, that was the last winter before the coal-fired stove was replaced with a modern version.

When I finally emerged into the culinary world of France, I was imbued with the classic principles of French cuisine and I applied them rigorously. I strove for perfection in everything and honed my skills and experience in restaurants in France, Britain, Singapore and Portugal – among other places. Having settled in Britain in 1986, I gained a Michelin star in four different restaurants, and then was finally appointed executive head chef at The Vineyard in 2009.

FRENCH BRASSERIE COOKING

If I felt very fortunate to have advanced my career to such a level, I felt even more so in 2010 when I was offered the opportunity to publish my first book. As soon as we set to work on my *French Brasserie Cookbook*, I knew exactly what I wanted the concept to be and what I wanted the recipes to look like. This book would represent my childhood memories of cooking: using the seasons, featuring local specialities, the grandma way. I wanted it to be totally French, very regional and to paint a picture of the way we cooked in my home in Franche-Comté.

Setting the idea in a broader context, I had always believed that brasserie cooking had developed from that very same style of home cooking but that the link hadn't been made completely, and when I researched the idea I found that to be true. So the project not only allowed me to revisit so many of the recipes from my childhood, but also gave me the chance to learn so much more about where brasserie food originally came from, when it was created and why it has become so popular.

It is difficult to describe the emotions when you actually hold your first book in your hands. And what I love in particular is all the positive feedback. It pleases me enormously that you are out there cooking my recipes and enjoying them, so please do continue to cook – and to tell me all about your successes.

LOOKING BACK ... LOOKING FORWARD

When I came to think about a new book, I decided a complete change of perspective was needed. *French Brasserie Cookbook* was a book focused on my roots in French cooking – looking back to recapture the past traditions of my childhood (with some modern twists along the way, of course). But things have changed in cooking in France, as it has in countries around the world, and I wanted to reflect those changes.

So, I realized during the Covid-19 lockdown that what was going to be important to people was the return to simplicity. In fact, one of the few upsides of the pandemic is that people have started to spend more time in the kitchen; we have rediscovered the pleasure of cooking for ourselves and our family, of sharing food, and are seeking out recipes and cookery books. So, I decided to revise *Revolutionary French Cooking*, to make it simpler and more in line with what I feel people are looking for right now. Initially, the issue was getting access to any produce, then later, for some, accessibility to good-quality produce, knowing where it came from and who made it; it seemed people were starting to think differently.

Lockdown coincided, for me, with a move to the countryside – a week before it started! When we arrived in our new home amidst the farms, hills and fields, it immediately reminded me of France and of my childhood. The time and space lockdown provided gave me the opportunity to reflect on what was happening all over the country, and how it was changing the way we eat. Then I started walking in nature every day, as a lot of us did, and ideas started to form. Like many of us, I imagine, I became even more aware of the seasons and the produce they bring and felt even more gratitude and respect for the work of farmers. The end of summer snuck in and autumn started approaching.

Being amongst the goodness of the harvest this year made me certain: we had to return to basics. The first thing I wanted to look at in this book were the chapter titles, which instantly came knocking and opened my memory draws – orchards, woodlands, hedges, meadows, streams and farmyards – and they transported me straight away to the exact spots I needed to go to collect the ingredients. I hope they will do the same for you and that they will evoke your own memories of picking berries with your grandfather or foraging for mushrooms as a child.

The beauty of seeing nature blooming, the change of colours and scents in the air, the orchards in transformation, the hedges getting thicker with new shoots, the field where barley will grow and change from pale green to gold as the sun helps it on its way to the harvest, the mill where it will be crushed to that beautiful flour we need to make our bread. The orchard flowers are taken away by the wind and tiny fruits start to appear; patience will be needed to see them becoming those lovely reddish apples that we'll crunch into after picking them. The grass is lush in the fields and young lambs appear, playing, free.

The garden too has plenty to say at harvest time: not only are the roses and other flowers starting to open, but the vegetables are almost ready and I am very much looking forward to eating them.

Then it's end of August and you can already smell autumn. The leaves have dried and the early morning mist transforms the scenery into magical moments. What a sight! No wonder it is so many people's favourite season; I know it is mine.

The famous 12 August date that starts the grouse shooting season has passed, which will go on until February, when all the different game seasons finish.

But that is not all. Here come the wild mushrooms, the root vegetables, the figs, apples, pears. The walnuts have just been harvested and are now drying, which attracts some small visitors: the squirrel family. I saw one running on the top of the wooden fence outside the window; it was in a great hurry under lashing rain, yet still, up and down it went all day, soaked to the bone, gathering huge walnuts in its tiny paws. I realized that not only was it going against weather and time in order to gather as many as it could before nightfall, but also that it was stealing from our neighbour's outdoor store and was trying to get as many as it could before being caught! It took them one by one to its hiding place where it could feed the family all through winter. We are lucky, we have four seasons and the next is never far away but for a squirrel, there is really only one and it knows it. Time is precious – and so is food.

So autumn and winter will pass, and then there's what will come soon after: asparagus, peas, cabbages, artichokes, leeks and so on as the months pass and take us into spring. Then, before you know it, we will be in summer with so many fruits and abundant choices. We are so lucky that it is all provided for us by Mother Nature, and we all know we need to look after her better, to protect her so we can look forward to the next time around, the next celebration, the next family gathering, the next joy of cooking a meal for those we love, the next banquet!

Look for the best produce you can, go to farmers' markets, use your local butcher and fishmonger, get your groceries direct from the farm (they are delivering more and more now). This is the best and often the cheapest produce. Supermarkets are still there for essentials but we need to support our farmers and local businesses and try to be sustainable for the generations to come.

DEHYDRATING FOOD

Intensity of flavour has to be the number one reason for dehydrating foods. Although, of course, it originated in ancient times as a simple but effective means of preserving foods through the lean winter months, now it's more about the fact that taking out the water not only means bacteria can't grow, it also produces some radical transformations, concentrating both taste, texture and goodness. Plus, it still means you don't have to waste any seasonal gluts but can instead easily transform all kinds of foods into handy storecupboard items, from fruit strips that make a great lunch-box snack to dried mushrooms to sprinkle into a risotto to intensify the flavour.

Of course, drying food will never replace freezing, as that does a better job of retaining the taste, appearance and goodness of fresh food. But dehydrating is easy, costs virtually nothing, needs no special equipment – and still gives you a huge range of flavoursome and densely textured treats to enjoy.

SUN-DRIED PRODUCE

Not surprisingly, the original dehydrator was the sun! And you'll still see fruit, vegetables or herbs spread out on cloths or wooden trays in a sunny courtyard or barn roof when you are on holiday in hotter climes. In Portugal, Spain or even Madagascar, you might come upon rows of flattened fish laid out to dry, a traditional practice as popular as salting or smoking.

Drying food in hot countries is virtually effortless. In cooler, more humid areas, it can be more challenging. If you are not careful, food can go mouldy on the drying tray, so techniques have to be different. Reindeer meat in Scandinavia, for example, is pickled in salt water before being dried in the spring sunshine when the air temperature is below zero, while in Iceland, shark meat is also dried in sub-zero temperatures. But commercial dehydrators don't need sunlight. They push hot air around the food to dry it quickly and conveniently whatever the weather.

As in many professional kitchens and sometimes at home, we use dehydrators. A subtle, sweet celery leaf sprinkled with sugar can become as transparent and fragile as glass to finish a terrine. Slices of pancetta, gently oven-crisped, then finished in the dehydrator, are perfect crumbled over a pea velouté, roasted poultry, risotto or even roast pork. A few blanched, dried mushrooms can be blitzed to a dust to flavour soup or an oeuf en cocotte.

DEHYDRATING AT HOME

But you don't need a commercial dehydrator, and you don't need to live in the land of eternal sunshine either – though wouldn't that be nice! In our house back in France, drying ingredients was a seasonal affair. Every autumn, wooden boxes lined with newspaper would appear in the boiler room, perched on the top of the boiler, and gradually be filled with our harvest of mushrooms. The boiler room was always the warmest part of the house. Not surprisingly, our dogs soon realized this and selected it as their winter bedroom – sensible creatures! That memory makes me smile as it is so fresh in my mind.

Newspapers, by the way, are ideal for absorbing moisture from drying foods and I still use them today. I dry foods in my glass greenhouse – the sun's heat on the enclosed space dries foods such as tomatoes perfectly. I also dry herbs, especially basil and tarragon, and use them to flavour oils, but I do that in the microwave. Just spread out the separate leaves on a sheet of paper towel, lay another sheet on top, then microwave on high for three or four 30-second bursts, watching carefully.

Mostly, however, I dry foods in my ordinary oven on a very low setting. I usually make use of the time control, then I can just leave it alone to do its own thing for long periods without interruption. It's quicker to dry food in an oven than by sun-drying or even using a dehydrator, and you only need a couple of oven trays and a thermometer.

It's true you can only make small quantities in an oven, but I think that can be an advantage. It means you can experiment with plenty of different foods and there's no risk of making the effort to dry a large quantity of something you later decide you don't like!

You can dry most foods, apart from those with a high water content, such as cucumbers, as they are likely to spoil before the process is finished. Fruits tend to go crisp more quickly than vegetables, but you can dry most things in 8–12 hours. Good vegetables to start with are onions, garlic and peppers. For fruits, try apples, peaches, apricots or pears.

HOW TO DEHYDRATE FOOD IN YOUR OVEN

- Ensure equipment, surfaces and hands are clean.
- Only fresh, good-quality food will give the best results. Wash it, then pat dry with a paper towel.
- Prepare the food as though you were cooking it, so you might peel and core an apple, remove the stone from a plum, trim the fat off meat. Then leave them whole, or cut into thin slices or strips.
- For foods like apple that tend to go brown, add ½ tbsp of vinegar or lemon juice to 250ml/9fl oz/1 cup of water, then dip the slices as you cut.
- Blanch hard fruits or vegetables in a saucepan of boiling water for a few seconds, then refresh in iced water and pat dry.
- Fruits like apples, peaches and rhubarb will keep their flavour if you poach them first in a light syrup.
- You could marinate meats in olive oil and vinegar, then toss with seasonings before dehydrating.
- Put food in a single layer, not overlapping, on a lined baking sheet or a wire rack in the oven (or the racks in your hydrator). Put a drip tray under meat. Items with similar drying times can be mixed on a rack.
- Switch on the oven to 45–70°C/115–150°F/gas ¼ or less, depending on the recipe. If your oven doesn't go below 70°C/150°F/gas ¼, don't worry. Set it to its lowest temperature but leave the oven door slightly open, enough for the air to circulate and keep a constant temperature.

- Turn the tray every 30 minutes or so if you can until the food is completely dry. That will be about 4–5 hours for beetroot (beets), onions and peppers; 6–8 hours for garlic; 8–10 hours for apples, mushrooms and pears; 10–12 hours for apricots, peaches and potatoes.

Most dried foods will last well, so keep them in sterilized, airtight jars in a cool, dark, dry place – then you can enjoy intriguing your friends at your next dinner party.

DEHYDRATED PUMPKIN CRISP

This makes an easy introduction to drying so do have a go at making this delicious sprinkle for your next risotto.

Start by preheating the oven to 70°C/150°F/gas ¼ and lining a large baking sheet with baking paper. Then, simply grate the flesh of 100g/3½oz of peeled butternut squash or pumpkin into long spaghetti-like strips straight over the baking sheet. Bake for 4½ hours, turning halfway through. The strands will stick together in a net-like shape and go dry and crisp. Simply break them over the dish to serve. They'll keep in an airtight container for up to a month.

Follow the same recipe using strips of grated carrot or parsnip for delicious versions of the crisp. Or why not try making a batch of each and breaking a colourful selection to finish off your dish.

SOUS-VIDE COOKING

I am sure everyone is familiar with using *sous-vide* – a vacuum – as a way of storing food, as we see vacuum-packed food all over the place, from spices and coffee to cured meats and rice. It is a great way of packing food for transport. But, although it has been around for a while now and is used a lot in professional kitchens, you may not be so familiar with cooking *sous-vide*.

In my restaurant, we sometimes use this method, and we have a professional vacuum-pack machine that seals the food ready to go in a special water bath. It's usually a great way of cooking, although I have to confess it has gone wrong once or twice and given us all a good laugh – although laughter is not quite the reaction if it happens in the middle of a busy service! If a bag is not sealed properly – or the cling film (plastic wrap) isn't tied securely if you are trying it at home – and no one notices in time, it can cause a mini disaster, and you could find yourself with an empty bag or a chicken breast swimming in water. So just watch those knots and tie them tightly!

WHY WOULD YOU PREPARE FOOD THIS WAY?

So what are the advantages of cooking in this way? Well, to start with, you can prepare dishes one or two days ahead and keep them refrigerated, or portioned up and frozen ready to cook when you need them. Imagine how useful that would be when you have a party coming up and you can spread the preparations so you have less to do on the day.

Then there's the fact that, when prepared this way, the food develops some beautiful flavours as it cooks in its own juices, with all the flavours locked in. As nothing is lost, there's an intensity of flavour in the finished dish.

Then we come to temperature, which is critical in *sous-vide* cooking. When you cook *sous-vide*, you can cook at a low temperature, around 70°C/158°F.

This is important because meat, in particular, can be adversely affected when cooked at very high temperatures as the collagen fibres within the meat can become tough. This is less important with fish but it can still happen. So to keep the meat tender, it is recommended that you cook at less than 70°C/158°F. This makes this style of cooking perfect for the cheaper cuts of meat and also for offal. Many people don't like to cook offal in case they overcook and ruin it, but with *sous-vide* cooking that's not a problem because the cooking method is so gentle. You'll be sure to get perfectly tender results every time.

SOUS-VIDE COOKING AT HOME

So how can you try out *sous-vide* cooking at home without a professional vacuum-packing machine? I will show you how to cook a chicken breast, and you can use the same procedure for other foods. Just glance through the recipe options in the book that I've listed on page 19 and you'll see how versatile the technique is.

Firstly, make sure you use cling film (plastic wrap) and not "food wrap". Cling film is perfect for cooking as it can withstand the necessary temperatures, whereas food wrap will not.

- Put four layers of cling film (plastic wrap) on your work surface. Place a boneless chicken breast in the centre of the cling film, then roll it tightly, pressing out the air to each side as you roll. Make a knot in one end, then press the air out the other side before you knot that end. This will give you a partial *sous-vide*.
- Of course, you cannot keep the product as though it had been properly vacuum-packed because you have not created a full vacuum. Therefore you need to treat the parcel as you would any non-vacuumed product and store it properly in the refrigerator or freezer for the recommended time only. If you follow your common sense, then you'll be fine.
- For most *sous-vide* dishes, there are two alternative cooking methods: boiling and

steaming. To boil, place the parcel in a saucepan large enough to hold it comfortably, then just cover it with water. Put the pan on a medium heat and bring the water up to 70°C/158°F. Keep it at that temperature for the time indicated in the recipe, which will depend on the size of the portion. A 180g/6¼oz chicken breast will take about 20 minutes; if it is stuffed, it will take a further 5–10 minutes.

- Alternatively, you can steam the parcel. Put a large saucepan of water on to simmer, with a steamer insert on top. Put the chicken in the steamer, cover and cook for 20–25 minutes.
- When the food is ready, just cut off one end of the cling film (plastic wrap), push the meat through and pat it dry on a paper towel or a clean dish towel.
- Next, to regain the crisp skin, heat a non-stick frying pan (skillet) over a medium heat and pan-fry the chicken, skin-side down, for a minute or so until crisp and browned. Then serve it with a lovely sauce, or *jus*.

Just as a reminder, if you only want to prepare the parcel in advance, make sure you do keep it refrigerated and for a maximum of 2 days. Do not cook it in advance.

Since some meats have a stronger texture, I usually wrap them in cling film (plastic wrap) in the same way but cook them as a confit, in hot fat. This method is suitable for chicken leg meat, or the dark meat from poultry or game birds.

Now you understand the technique of *sous-vide* cooking, I hope you'll try some of my recipes, such as Sous-Vide Little Gems with Ewes' Cheese (see page 139), Pork Loin with Mushrooms, Figs and Chestnuts (see page 202) or Pancetta-Wrapped Monkfish with Carrot and Mandarin Purée (see page 114).

QUAIL SALAD – OR PERHAPS A POUSSIN

Quail is the quickest and easiest option if you want to try out cooking *sous-vide* at home, or this recipe

will work equally well with poussins, which are readily available in the supermarket. This is one example of when it is best if you cook the legs as a confit as the texture of the meat is different. Simply wrap 2 quail legs and 2 quail breasts separately in cling film (plastic wrap), as described in the general instructions on page 18. Cook the legs very gently in goose or duck fat for 40 minutes until the meat is super tender and falls off the bone. When the legs are almost cooked, steam the breasts very gently for about 4 minutes until tender and cooked through. You can test the meat by piercing through the cling film with a sharp knife and the juices should run clear.

Once unwrapped, heat a non-stick frying pan (skillet) over a high heat, add the breasts, skin-side down, and brown for 2 minutes, then turn them over and cook for a further 2 minutes. Deglaze the pan with a splash of white wine vinegar and a little salt and pepper, stirring to remove any caramelized bits stuck to the bottom.

I make a delicious salad to serve with the quail by tossing together a handful of rocket leaves, a handful of pea shoots and a few red chicory (Belgian endive) leaves. Then I sprinkle over some shredded tarragon leaves and a quartered boiled new potato. That's just enough per person. Cut the legs and the breasts in half, then put on top of a pile of fresh salad. As an extra bonus, you could finish the dish with a quail's egg per portion, boiled for just 2½ minutes so the yolk is perfectly runny.

SMOKING FOOD

I am a big fan of smoked foods, particularly meat, as I just love those smoky flavours, and although smoking was developed as a way of preserving food, I think it is more about the wonderful flavours it creates. Originally – going back to ancient times – people used to hang their kill to dry in their caves. Since there was no way out for the smoke from the fire, they noticed that both the flavour and the preserving qualities were improved by the smoke ... and so it began!

Since then, smoking foods, usually over wood smoke, has become popular in many regions of the world and has developed commercially. In particular, smokehouses were built on farms to preserve meat – well away from the farm buildings to avoid fire spreading if an accident happened – and on the coast, to be handy for the fishermen landing their catch.

The first commercial smoker in the UK was set up in Scotland in 1939. Much later, when I worked in Scotland, there was a small smokehouse just down the road from us, which I used to drive past every day. Those memories will stay with me for ever as I can still vividly recall the delightful smell of the burning wood.

Where I come from in Franche-Comté, smoking foods has always been a speciality and the technique is still very much alive today. On market day, I often used to go shopping with my mum or my sister, Dolores. They were both really good cooks – although that goes without saying in my family as we are all enthusiastic gourmands. Anyway, you will see that in this book, I like to use products from my home area and one of those is Morteau, a rather delicious smoked sausage. We often bought this from the market, along with smoked pork shoulder, bacon or neck. To serve with it, Mum used to make a lovely sauerkraut with turnip instead of cabbage – that day was one we looked forward to.

We serve some smoked dishes in my restaurant. My friend, John, has supplied our smoked salmon, haddock and mackerel for the last 20 years and, trust me, he is very good at it! I also love to use some smoked ingredients, like smoked paprika and, of course, Morteau sausage. But we also do some smoking ourselves; my particular favourites are smoked beetroot (beets), which has a wonderful earthy flavour, to serve as a side dish or as part of a salad, and smoked duck, a meat that seems perfect to prepare in this way.

FOODS FOR SMOKING

All kinds of poultry and meat can be smoked, creating a range of products from spiced pastrami to smoked bacon. Smoked fish ranges from cod or haddock to salmon, herring or mackerel. Tofu and cheeses absorb fabulous flavours in the smoker, as do nuts, vegetables like peppers and beetroot (beets), and fruit such as prunes, which are often smoked while drying. Then there are smoked teas, like lapsang souchong, and even whisky. It is important to remember, though, that not all methods of smoking act as a preservative.

HOT AND COLD SMOKING

Whatever their size, smokers create heat and smoke by burning wood chips or sawdust, or they may have gas burners. In the UK, oak or alder are the woods of choice in most smokehouses, as well as beech and fruit-tree woods, such as apple. In the US, corncobs are popular, while in New Zealand, they like to burn the wood from the manuka tree. Some smokers also have steam coils to create humidity and maintain the correct temperature, which is obviously crucial or the results will be dry and flavourless.

Hot smoking uses both smoke and heat in a wood-fired oven, a smoke-roaster or even a barbecue. The temperature reaches 52–80°C/125–176°F so, at the higher temperatures, the food is cooked as well as absorbing the smoky flavours.

Cold smoking does not cook the food as the temperature of 20–30°C/62–68°F only imparts the wood-smoke flavour, so many cold-smoked foods are cured in brine first. For our smoked recipes, I'm using a method based on a Chinese technique known as tea smoking, as a combination of rice, tea and sugar is used to create the smoke. We'll then cook our smoke-flavoured foods afterwards. (I decided that the Icelandic tradition of smoking fish over dried sheep's dung was perhaps not one to try at home!)

HOW IT'S DONE

I hope you will try this method. You can buy smokers in pre-packed sets and there is a vast range of different wood chips available online for you to try. However, I would recommend you use my tea-smoking option first as you can simply adapt your steamer or wok.

Just one reminder. Be careful of the heat and smoke, especially when disposing of the smoking ingredients as they'll stay hot for a while even after you take them off the heat.

- You need a steamer with a lid, or a wok with a lid and a metal rack, and some kitchen foil.
- Your smoking mixture is 100g/3½oz/½ cup basmati rice, 2 tablespoons of green tea and 2 teaspoons of caster (superfine) sugar.
- Prepare the food as if you were going to cook it, so trimmed, stoned, left whole or sliced.
- Put a large piece of kitchen foil, shiny-side down, in the bottom of a steamer or wok. Put the rice, tea and sugar on the foil, cover with a steamer insert or wire rack, then put on the lid. Put over a medium heat for about 5 minutes until the mixture starts smoking.
- Quickly lift the lid and put the food onto the rack. Put the lid back on, turn the heat down to low and smoke for the time recommended in the recipe; that's about 5 minutes for chicken or duck pieces.
- Lift out the food and put on a plate to rest.
- Wrap the smoking ingredients in the foil and discard them carefully.

Leave the food to cool, or continue to cook, following the recipe instructions, then savour those stunning flavours. Try smoking a cod fillet following the method below, or try Smoked Duck and Lentils with Lavender (see page 177).

FENNEL-SMOKED COD WITH WARM BEAN SALAD

When you smoke fish with herbs such as fennel, the subtle scent permeates the fish to complement the lovely smoky flavour. Try this simple cod recipe.

Add a pinch of dried fennel to the smoking mixture in the foil-lined wok, then put in the smoker 2 very fresh pieces of cod, skin-side down, season with salt and pepper, cover and smoke for 5 minutes. Remove them from the smoker and brush the skin with a little olive oil. Heat a frying pan (skillet) over a medium heat and pan-fry the cod, skin-side down, for about 5 minutes until the skin is wonderfully crisp and golden. Flip it on the other side and cook for 2 minutes to finish it off. Cool and discard the smoking ingredients.

The perfect partner would be a warm white bean salad. Gently warm 300g/10½oz cooked white beans in a pan with 1 or 2 diced oven-dried tomatoes and a chopped garlic clove. Take off the heat and stir in 2 teaspoons of chopped parsley leaves, drizzle with a little extra virgin olive oil and top with your smoked cod fillet to serve. You are in paradise! Can I join you for dinner?

BASIC
RECIPES

In this chapter, you will find a few basic recipes that are essentials in many of my dishes, like a home-made stock and a salad dressing. Plus, I've selected some recipes that are perfect to serve with the main courses in this book. Complex dishes are complemented most effectively by the simplest accompaniments, and if they are carefully created using the best ingredients, then you really cannot go wrong.

CHICKEN STOCK

MAKES 2l/70fl oz/8 cups
PREPARATION TIME 10 minutes, plus at least 1
    hour cooling
COOKING TIME 2–2½ hours

2kg/4lb 8oz chicken wings or bones,
    or 2 chicken carcasses
1 thyme sprig
2 carrots, peeled and halved lengthways
1 small handful of parsley stems
1 small onion, unpeeled and halved
6 black peppercorns

l Put all the ingredients in a large, heavy-based
saucepan over a high heat. Add 4l/140fl oz/16
cups of cold water, bring to the boil, then skim off
any foam that rises to the surface. Turn the heat
down to low and leave to simmer, uncovered, for
2–2½ hours until the liquid has reduced by half.

2 Remove from the heat and pass through a sieve
(strainer), using a ladle to help you, then leave to
cool for at least 1 hour.

3 If you want to freeze the stock, divide the
cooled stock into small plastic tubs with lids,
leaving some space for it to expand, and pop the
containers in the freezer for up to 4 weeks.

BEEF OR VEAL STOCK

MAKES 2l/70fl oz/8 cups
PREPARATION TIME 15 minutes, plus at least 1
    hour cooling
COOKING TIME 3 hours 40 minutes

1.25kg/2lb 12oz beef bones from roast beef or
    veal bones
2 tbsp olive oil
1 thyme sprig
2 parsley sprigs
2 carrots, peeled and halved lengthways
2 onions, peeled and quartered
1 celery stick, chopped
1 garlic bulb, unpeeled and halved crossways
6 black peppercorns
2 bay leaves

l Preheat the oven to 200°C/400°F/gas 6. Put
the bones in a baking tray and roast for 20
minutes, stirring occasionally, until golden
brown. Transfer the bones to a large, heavy-based
saucepan, add all the remaining ingredients and
cook over a medium heat for 10 minutes.

2 Add 4l/140fl oz/16 cups of cold water and bring
to the boil over a high heat. Skim off any foam
that rises to the surface, then turn the heat down
to low and simmer, uncovered, for 1 hour.

3 Top up the water to the previous level, then
return to the boil and simmer for a further
2 hours until the liquid has reduced by half.
Remove from the heat and pass through a sieve
(strainer), using a ladle to help you, then leave to
cool for at least 1 hour.

4 If you want to freeze the stock, divide the
cooled stock into small plastic tubs with lids,
leaving some space for it to expand, and pop the
containers in the freezer for up to 4 weeks.

NOTE AND VARIATION
Using Beef Stock: Most chefs use veal jus rather
than beef stock as it can be too strong. Use the

bones from your Sunday roast to make a good stock, or substitute a shop-bought veal jus.

For Lamb Stock: Use lamb instead of beef bones. Leave to cool, then chill. Lift off the layer of fat from the surface, then use or freeze as above.

FISH STOCK

MAKES 2l/70fl oz/8 cups
PREPARATION TIME 10 minutes, plus 30 minutes
   soaking and at least 1 hour cooling
COOKING TIME 2¼–2¾ hours

1.25kg/2lb 12oz fresh fish bones, flesh removed
1 small handful of parsley stems
1 onion, unpeeled and quartered
1 thyme sprig
1 celery stick, halved
6 black peppercorns

l Put the fish bones in a large bowl, cover with cold water and leave to soak for 10 minutes, then rinse thoroughly using a sieve (strainer). Repeat 3 times.

2 Put the bones in a large, heavy-based saucepan with all the remaining ingredients and cover with 4l/140fl oz/16 cups of cold water. Bring to the boil over a high heat, then skim off any foam that rises to the surface. Turn the heat down to low and leave to simmer, uncovered, for 2–2½ hours until the liquid has reduced by half.

3 Remove from the heat and pass through a sieve (strainer), using a ladle to help you, then leave to cool for at least 1 hour.

4 If you want to freeze the stock, divide the cooled stock into small plastic tubs with lids, leaving some space for it to expand, and pop the containers in the freezer for up to 4 weeks.

VEGETABLE STOCK

MAKES 1.5l/52fl oz/6 cups
PREPARATION TIME 15 minutes, plus at least 1
   hour cooling
COOKING TIME 2¼ hours

2 tbsp olive oil
1 celery stick, chopped
1 thyme sprig
1 spring onion (scallion), chopped
1 handful of parsley stems, chopped
1 garlic clove
2 carrots, peeled and halved lengthways
2 new potatoes, halved
6 black peppercorns
2 button mushrooms, halved

l Warm the oil in a large, heavy-based saucepan over a medium heat. Add all the remaining ingredients, partially cover, and cook for 10 minutes. Add about 3l/105fl oz/12 cups of cold water and bring to the boil over a high heat, then turn the heat down to low and leave to simmer, uncovered, for 2 hours until the liquid has reduced by half.

2 Remove from the heat and pass through a sieve (strainer), using a ladle to help you, then leave to cool for at least 1 hour.

3 If you want to freeze the stock, divide the cooled stock into small plastic tubs with lids, leaving some space for it to expand, and pop the containers in the freezer for up to 4 weeks.

MAYONNAISE WITH VARIATIONS

MAKES **200ml/7fl oz/scant 1 cup**
PREPARATION TIME **10 minutes**

2 egg yolks
1 tbsp French mustard
a squeeze of lemon juice
150ml/5fl oz/scant ⅔ cup sunflower oil or
    grapeseed oil
sea salt and freshly ground black pepper

l Beat together the egg yolks and mustard in a bowl. Add a few drops of lemon juice and season with salt and pepper. Gradually drizzle in the oil, a little at a time, whisking continuously until the mayonnaise thickens.

2 For the variations, stir the additional ingredients into the mayonnaise, then whisk in 2 tablespoons of hot water to help bind the ingredients.

VARIATIONS (pictured above)
For Chilli Mayonnaise: Add 1 long red chilli, deseeded and finely chopped
For Tarragon Mayonnaise: Add 1 tbsp tarragon vinegar, 1 tsp chopped tarragon leaves
For Garlic Mayonnaise: Add 2 garlic cloves, finely chopped

FRENCH DRESSING

MAKES **about 150ml/5fl oz/scant ⅔ cup**
PREPARATION TIME **5 minutes**

2 tsp Dijon mustard
2 tbsp white balsamic vinegar
60ml/2fl oz/¼ cup olive oil or sunflower oil
60ml/2fl oz/¼ cup extra virgin olive oil or
    sunflower oil
sea salt and freshly ground black pepper

l Whisk together the mustard, vinegar and 2 tablespoons of water in a small bowl, then whisk in the olive oil and extra virgin olive oil until you have quite a thick, glossy liquid.

2 Season with salt and pepper to taste before drizzling over salad.

CHICORY & RADISH SALAD

SERVES **4**
PREPARATION TIME **10 minutes**

2 large heads of chicory (Belgian endive), halved
    lengthways and leaves separated
12 English radishes, thinly sliced
3 tbsp chopped parsley leaves
1 tbsp Chardonnay vinegar
3 tbsp extra virgin olive oil
sea salt and freshly ground black pepper

l Toss the chicory (Belgian endive) leaves, radishes and parsley together in a bowl.

2 Whisk together the Chardonnay vinegar and oil in a small bowl and season with salt and pepper. Drizzle the dressing over the leaves and toss together to combine.

REDUCED BALSAMIC VINEGAR

MAKES **about 4 tbsp**
COOKING TIME **12 minutes**

125ml/4fl oz/½ cup balsamic vinegar

1 Pour the vinegar into a small sauté or frying pan (skillet), put over a medium heat and bring to a gentle simmer.

2 Turn the heat down to low heat and cook for 10 minutes until the liquid has reduced by half and is thickened and syrupy.

CROÛTONS

SERVES **4**
PREPARATION TIME **5 minutes**
COOKING TIME **5 minutes**

25g/1oz unsalted butter
2 tbsp olive oil
2 small slices of sourdough bread, crusts removed and cut into 1cm/½in cubes
sea salt and freshly ground black pepper

You can cut the bread into whatever size or shape croûtons you fancy, just make sure that you cook them until golden brown on each side, without allowing them to burn.

1 Heat a large frying pan (skillet) over a medium heat. Add the butter and oil and when the butter is foaming, add the cubes of bread and fry for 45–60 seconds on each side until golden brown.

2 Drain on paper towel and season with salt and pepper.

TOMATO & DEEP-FRIED CAPER SALAD

SERVES **4**
PREPARATION TIME **10 minutes**
COOKING TIME **1 minute**

4 large beef tomatoes, thinly sliced
1 red onion, very thinly sliced
100g/3½oz jar baby capers
about 170ml/5½fl oz/⅔ cup vegetable oil
135ml/4½fl oz/generous ½ cup extra virgin olive oil
1 tbsp good-quality sherry vinegar
1 small handful of basil leaves, torn
sea salt and freshly ground black pepper

1 Put the tomatoes and red onion on a serving plate and season with salt and pepper. Open the jar of capers, strain off 2 tablespoons of the liquid and leave to one side. Take out half the capers and pat them dry very carefully on paper towel.

2 Put the vegetable oil in a small saucepan over a medium heat until just shimmering. Be careful not to overheat the oil, it must not be smoking but needs to be hot enough to fry the capers. Carefully add the capers to the hot oil and fry for 30 seconds until nice and crisp – again, make sure you don't leave them frying for too long as they just need to be crisp. Drain on paper towel.

3 To make the dressing, whisk together the reserved caper liquid, the extra virgin olive oil and sherry vinegar, then pour over the tomatoes. Scatter the deep-fried capers over the top, then finish with freshly torn basil leaves.

CREAMED MASHED POTATOES

SERVES 4
PREPARATION TIME 30 minutes
COOKING TIME 55 minutes

1kg/2lb 4oz floury potatoes, such as Desiree,
    unpeeled
100ml/3½fl oz/scant ½ cup full-fat milk
100ml/3½fl oz/scant ½ cup double (heavy) cream
2 garlic cloves, sliced
2.5cm/1in piece of horseradish, peeled, or 2 tsp
    wasabi (Japanese horseradish) paste
sea salt and freshly ground black pepper

l Put the potatoes in a large saucepan, cover
with cold water and add a pinch of salt. Bring
to the boil over a high heat, then turn the heat
down to low, partially cover with a lid and
simmer for 30–40 minutes, or until completely
cooked through.

2 Meanwhile, preheat the oven to 200°C/400°F/
gas 6. Drain the potatoes, then put them on a
baking sheet and bake for 10 minutes. Remove
from the oven and as soon as they are cool
enough to handle, peel the potatoes, then pass
them through a sieve (strainer), using a ladle
to help you. Cover with a lid and leave to one
side but do not let them go cold or the mash will
be gluey.

3 Put the milk, cream and garlic in a saucepan
over a medium heat and bring to the boil. Pour
half the mixture into the potatoes, mix well, then
gradually add the remaining liquid, stirring
all the time. Season with salt and pepper to
taste, then grate 2 teaspoons of the horseradish
directly over the mash so you get all the juices.
Alternatively, sprinkle with the wasabi (Japanese
horseradish) paste. Serve hot.

SWEDE BOULANGÈRE

SERVES 4
PREPARATION TIME 15 minutes, plus making the stock
COOKING TIME 55 minutes

a little butter, for greasing
2 large swede (rutabaga), about 500–600g/1lb 2oz–
    1lb 5oz each, peeled and cut into 5mm/¼in slices
2 large white onions, sliced
2 garlic cloves, finely chopped
2 thyme sprigs, leaves picked
500ml/17fl oz/2 cups Chicken Stock
    (see page 24)
sea salt and freshly ground black pepper

l Preheat the oven to 200°C/400°F/gas 6 and
lightly butter a shallow baking dish large enough
to hold about 1.5l/52fl oz/6 cups. Bring a large
saucepan of salted water to the boil over a high
heat, add the swede (rutabaga) and boil for 4–5
minutes, then drain and spread out on a clean
tea towel to dry. Leave to cool slightly before
building your *boulangère*.

2 Spread a layer of swede (rutabaga) in the
bottom of the prepared dish, followed by a
layer of the onions and a sprinkling of garlic
and thyme leaves. Season with a little salt and
pepper. Repeat with as many layers as will fit in
the dish, but finish with a layer of swede. Press
down lightly.

3 Put the stock in a saucepan over a medium
heat and warm slightly, then pour it over the
boulangère. The stock should not cover the last
layer of swede (rutabaga) as the swede will sink
down slightly as the dish cooks.

4 Bake for 45–50 minutes, then check to see that
the swede (rutabaga) is tender when pierced with
the tip of a knife. If not, return it to the oven for a
further 5 minutes and check again until the knife
slides easily into the vegetables. Serve hot.

THAI-STYLE PILAU RICE

SERVES 4
PREPARATION TIME 10 minutes, plus making the stock
COOKING TIME 25 minutes

4 tbsp olive oil
1 large onion, diced
4cm/1½in piece of root ginger, peeled and diced
1 long red chilli, deseeded and finely diced
1 lemongrass stalk, split lengthways
200g/7oz/1 cup basmati rice
400ml/14fl oz/scant 1⅔ cups Vegetable Stock
  (see page 25)
40g/1½oz unsalted butter, chopped
grated zest and juice of 1 lime
sea salt and freshly ground black pepper

1 Preheat the oven to 150°C/300°F/gas 2. Heat an ovenproof frying pan (skillet) over a medium heat, add the oil and onion and fry for 3 minutes until just softened, then add the ginger, chilli and lemongrass and fry for a further 3 minutes until softened but not coloured.

2 Turn the heat down to low and add the rice. Fold in gently, then sweat for 3–4 minutes. Add the stock, turn the heat up to high and bring to a simmer. Season with salt and pepper, dot the butter over the top of the rice, then cover with a *cartouche* (see page 232) or partially cover with a lid and transfer to the oven for 12–14 minutes.

3 Check to see if the rice is tender and the liquid has all been absorbed. If the rice is not quite tender, return it to the oven for a further 5 minutes, then check once more. Remove the *cartouche*, discard the lemongrass, then season the rice with the grated lime zest and juice, and salt and pepper to taste. Serve hot.

TOMATO COULIS

MAKES 800ml/28fl oz/scant 3½ cups
PREPARATION TIME 20 minutes
COOKING TIME 40 minutes

12 ripe tomatoes
2 tbsp olive oil
1 red chilli, deseeded and chopped
290g/10¼oz jar roasted peppers, drained and
  finely chopped
1 small shallot, finely chopped
50g/1¾oz/⅓ cup strawberries, hulled
4 garlic cloves, crushed
a pinch of caster (superfine) sugar
a pinch of smoked paprika
4 tbsp white balsamic vinegar
2 large basil leaves
sea salt and freshly ground black pepper

1 With a sharp knife, cut a small cross on the bottom of each tomato, then put them in a heatproof bowl and cover with boiling water. Leave for 30 seconds, then lift them out with a slotted spoon and put in a bowl of iced water. Lift the tomatoes out, then peel off and discard the skins. Cut the tomatoes into quarters, remove and discard the seeds, then roughly chop the flesh.

2 Heat a sauté pan over a high heat and add the tomatoes, oil, chilli, peppers, shallot, strawberries and garlic. Turn the heat down to low and sweat for 4–5 minutes until softened.

3 Add the sugar and paprika, then stir in the vinegar and deglaze the pan by stirring to remove any caramelized bits stuck to the bottom. Cover with a *cartouche* (see page 232) and cook over a low heat for 30–35 minutes, or until you have a very soft purée.

4 Transfer to a blender, add the basil and blitz to a fine purée, or use a hand-blender. Pass through a fine sieve (strainer), using a ladle to help you, and season with salt and pepper to taste.

SAVOURY SHORT PASTRY

MAKES enough for a 28cm/11¼in tin
PREPARATION TIME 15 minutes, plus 2 hours chilling

125g/4½oz unsalted butter, softened to room
    temperature and roughly diced
250g/9oz/2 cups plain (all-purpose) flour, plus extra
    for dusting
a pinch of salt
1 egg yolk
3 tbsp milk or water

1 Put the butter, flour and salt in a mixing bowl
and rub together with your fingertips until you
have a crumbly, powdery texture. Add the egg
yolk and milk or water and continue working the
pastry until the ingredients are combined and
the texture is smooth. Turn out the pastry onto
a lightly floured work surface and knead for 1–2
minutes until silky smooth.

2 When the pastry is ready, either wrap it in a
clean dish towel or put it on a plate, cover with a
clean dish towel and leave in the refrigerator for 2
hours before using – this will relax the dough and
make it easier to use.

SWEET SHORT PASTRY

MAKES enough for a 20cm/ 8in tin
PREPARATION TIME 10 minutes, plus 20 minutes
    chilling

grated zest of ½ blood orange
90g/3¼oz unsalted butter, softened
a pinch of salt
65g/2¼oz/heaped ½ cup icing (confectioners') sugar
25g/1oz/¼ cup ground almonds
1 egg
175g/6oz/heaped 1⅓ cups plain (all-purpose) flour

1 Beat together the orange zest, butter, salt, sugar,
ground almonds and egg in a bowl until light and
fluffy, then sift in the flour and fold through. As
soon as the dough is formed, stop! You don't want
to work this pastry at all.

2 Wrap the pastry in cling film (plastic wrap) and
put in the refrigerator for 20 minutes, then bake
as directed in the recipe.

BEURRE NOISETTE

MAKES 125ml/4fl oz/½ cup
COOKING TIME 5 minutes

125g/4½oz unsalted butter
2 tsp lemon juice
sea salt and freshly ground black pepper

1 Heat a frying pan (skillet) over a medium-high
heat, add the butter and cook for a few minutes
until it turns a nutty golden brown.

2 Add the lemon juice, swirl to combine, then
remove from the heat immediately. Season with
salt and pepper.

CHILLI CRÈME ANGLAISE

MAKES 1.4l/48fl oz/5½ cups
PREPARATION TIME 20 minutes, plus 30 minutes
  infusing and at least 1 hour chilling
COOKING TIME 15 minutes

1l/35fl oz/4 cups full-fat milk
1 long red chilli, halved lengthways and deseeded
1 vanilla pod, halved lengthways and seeds
  scraped out
8 egg yolks
200g/7oz/heaped ¾ cup caster (superfine) sugar

1 Put the milk in a saucepan over a low heat.
Add the chilli and vanilla seeds. Whisk, then
throw in the vanilla pod as well. Bring to the
boil, then remove from the heat, cover with
cling film (plastic wrap) and leave to infuse at
room temperature for 30 minutes.

2 Meanwhile, whisk together the egg yolks
and sugar in a large bowl. Strain the chilli milk
through a fine sieve (strainer) into the egg yolk
mixture and mix well, then pour it back into the
saucepan. Put over a medium heat and cook for
5–8 minutes, stirring continuously (otherwise you
will get scrambled eggs!) until it starts to thicken.
You will be able to tell when the crème anglaise is
ready if, when you run two fingers down the back
of the spoon, the two lines don't immediately
join. If the custard starts to scramble, don't panic
– you can rescue it by pouring the mixture into
a food processor and blitzing it until it regains a
smooth, thick texture.

3 Strain once more into a clean bowl and mix
for a few minutes to cool the custard down, then
put it in the refrigerator to chill for at least 1 hour
before using. It will keep in the refrigerator for
about a week.

REAL VANILLA ICE CREAM

SERVES 4
PREPARATION TIME 10 minutes, plus 20 minutes
  infusing and at least 3 hours freezing
COOKING TIME 10 minutes

115ml/3¾fl oz/scant ½ cup full-fat milk
1 vanilla pod, split and seeds scraped out
3 egg yolks
200ml/7fl oz/scant 1 cup double (heavy) cream

1 First make a sabayon (see page 233). Put the
milk, vanilla pod and vanilla seeds in a saucepan over a low heat and bring just to a simmer.
Remove from the heat, cover with a lid and
leave to infuse for 20 minutes. Remove the
vanilla pod, wash and pat dry with paper towel.
(You can add the pod to a jar of sugar to make
your own vanilla sugar.)

2 Whisk together the egg yolks and warm milk
in a heatproof bowl set over a saucepan of gently
simmering water, making sure the bottom of
the bowl does not touch the water. Heat for 5–8
minutes, stirring continuously, until thickened.
Remove from the heat and whisk continuously
until the mixture cools completely.

3 Whip the cream until it forms soft peaks, fold
it into the sauce, then pour into a 500ml/17fl oz/
2 cup freezerproof container. Cover with cling
film (plastic wrap) and put in the freezer for at
least 3 hours until firm.

CHAPTER 1
FROM WOODLAND
& FOREST

In this first chapter, you immediately know what to look for, from mushrooms during the autumn to game during the hunting season. At the edge of the woods and forests, wild apples and hazelnuts are often found, along with wild garlic and edible moss. Nature made it all available for us; we just have to know where to look and what to do with it. And respect that some things are not available right now and we need to be patient and wait until next time around. The anticipation makes it all the more exciting.

CHICKEN, LEEK & WILD MUSHROOM PARCELS

SERVES 4
PREPARATION TIME 20 minutes, plus
    making the stock and 30 minutes
    marinating
COOKING TIME 1 hour

270g/9½oz unsalted butter
2 boneless skinless corn-
    fed chicken breasts, about
    180g/6¼oz each, cut into
    2cm/¾in cubes
grated zest and juice of 1 lemon,
    plus 1 whole lemon
2 tbsp Greek yogurt
2 tsp finely chopped tarragon
    leaves
1 small young leek, green part cut
    in half lengthways and then into
    slices, white part reserved for
    something else
200g/7oz mixed wild or
    shiitake mushrooms
1 tbsp sunflower oil
2 x 270g/9½oz packs fresh filo
    pastry, cut into 16 x 22cm/
    6¼ x 8½in rectangles
1 egg, beaten
2 tbsp sherry vinegar
200ml/7fl oz/scant 1 cup Chicken
    Stock (see page 24)
200ml/7fl oz/scant 1 cup
    whipping cream
sea salt and freshly ground black
    pepper

I wanted to try a twist on a *pithivier*, a puff pastry torte, and I decided filo pastry would make it both unusual and lighter. I am sure you will find this fun – especially when you get to eat the delicious results.

1 To make the clarified butter, put 250g/9oz of the butter in a saucepan over a very low heat. Leave for 30 minutes until the butter has melted and the solids have fallen to the bottom. Set aside.

2 Mix the chicken, lemon zest and juice, yogurt and half the tarragon in a non-metallic bowl. Marinate in the refrigerator for 30 minutes.

3 Bring a saucepan of water to the boil, add the leek, return to the boil and blanch for 1 minute. Lift out using a slotted spoon and refresh in iced water, then lift out and pat dry with paper towel. Add the mushrooms to the boiling water, blanch for 1 minute, then lift out, refresh and pat dry.

4 Heat a large, non-stick frying pan (skillet) over a high heat. Add the remaining butter and the oil and when foaming, add the mushrooms and sauté for 2 minutes. Add the leek and chicken and sauté for a further 2 minutes until starting to colour. Remove from the pan and leave to cool at room temperature.

5 Preheat the oven to 180°C/350°F/gas 4. Cover the filo with a clean damp dish towel and work quickly with one piece at a time. Lay a sheet of filo onto the work surface, brush lightly with clarified butter, then grate a little lemon zest over the top. Lay a second sheet over the top and brush with butter as before, then season with a little salt. Put another sheet on top, brush with butter and grate over a little lemon zest. Finish with a fourth sheet, then a little pepper. Beat the egg and 1 tablespoon of water to make an egg wash. Brush the edges of the pastry with the egg wash, then spoon a quarter of the chicken onto the bottom half of the pastry. Gently fold the pastry over the filling, press the edges together and tuck them under to seal and form a parcel. Put on a baking sheet and put in the refrigerator while you make 3 more parcels, then brush the outsides with the clarified butter. Bake for 20–25 minutes until golden and crisp.

6 Meanwhile, return the frying pan (skillet) to a medium heat, add the sherry vinegar and deglaze by stirring to remove any caramelized bits stuck to the pan. Add the stock and cream, turn the heat to low and simmer for 10 minutes until there is 200ml/7fl oz/scant 1 cup of sauce thick enough to coat the back of a spoon. Add the remaining tarragon and season to taste. Spoon the sauce over the parcels to serve.

RABBIT TERRINE WITH ONION MARMALADE

SERVES 12–14

PREPARATION TIME 35 minutes, plus
at least 10 hours chilling

COOKING TIME 10 hours overnight
cooking, plus 2 hours

16 small rabbit legs, about 3kg/6lb
8oz total weight

2 tbsp olive oil, plus extra
for brushing

4 thyme sprigs

12 silverskin baby onions, peeled
and cut in half

8 spring onions (scallions)

6 rabbit fillets, about 300g/10½oz
total weight

1 tsp roughly chopped flat-leaf
parsley leaves

sea salt and freshly ground black
pepper

FOR THE ONION MARMALADE

2 tbsp olive oil

1kg/2lb 4oz large white onions,
cut in half and thinly sliced

175g/6oz/heaped ¾ cup caster
(superfine) sugar

200ml/7fl oz/scant 1 cup
cider vinegar

500ml/17fl oz/2 cups dry
white wine

2 tbsp white balsamic vinegar

1 thyme sprig

1 Preheat the oven to 70°C/150°F/gas ¼. Put the rabbit legs on a baking sheet, season with salt and pepper, drizzle with the oil, then scatter over the thyme and cover with baking paper. Cook in the oven overnight, or for at least 10 hours. The next day, remove the baking sheet from the oven and leave to one side.

2 Turn the oven up to 160°C/315°F/gas 2½. Put the baby onions and spring onions (scallions) on a baking sheet, brush with oil and roast for 20 minutes. Remove the spring onions and leave to one side, then roast the baby onions for a further 25 minutes. Remove from the oven and leave to one side, then turn the oven down to 70°C/150°F/gas ¼.

3 Put the rabbit fillets on a baking sheet, season with salt and bake for 12 minutes so they remain soft, then set aside. Take the leg meat off the bone and put in a large bowl. Strain the cooking juices through a fine sieve (strainer) into a saucepan. Bring to the boil, then turn the heat down to medium and simmer for 10 minutes until reduced by two-thirds. Shred the leg meat using two forks, then stir in the parsley and reduced liquid.

4 To assemble the terrine, cover the base and sides of a 24 ×10cm/ 9½ × 4in and 8cm/3¼in deep terrine dish with cling film (plastic wrap), letting it hang over the sides. Cover the base with some of the rabbit leg mixture, then lay the baby onions along the centre of the terrine at regular intervals. Cover with more of the rabbit leg mixture, then lay half of the fillets side by side along the centre. Put half the spring onions (scallions) on either side of the fillets and cover with more rabbit leg mixture. Repeat with the remaining fillets and spring onions, then cover with the remaining rabbit leg mixture. Fold the cling film over the terrine to cover it completely, then put a 1–2kg/2lb 4oz–4lb 8oz weight, such as a bag of sugar, on top. Leave in the refrigerator to chill for at least 10 hours, or overnight.

5 To make the onion marmalade, put the oil in a saucepan over a medium-low heat, add the onions and cook gently for 15 minutes until softened but not coloured. Meanwhile, dissolve the sugar in the cider vinegar in a bowl. Add the vinegar solution to the pan with the wine, balsamic vinegar and thyme. Bring to the boil over a medium-high heat, then turn the heat down to medium and cook for a further 15 minutes, stirring occasionally, then turn the heat down to low and cook for about 10 minutes until the liquid becomes thick and syrupy. Leave to cool completely, discard the thyme, then pour into a sterilized jar and seal. Serve the terrine with the onion marmalade. The marmalade can be stored in the refrigerator for up to 2 months.

GAME, CHESTNUT & SULTANA TERRINE

SERVES 6–8
PREPARATION TIME 45 minutes, plus
3–4 hours marinating, cooling
and 2 days chilling
COOKING TIME 1 hour

35g/1¼oz/heaped ¼ cup sultanas
(golden raisins), such as
Muscatel
3 tbsp Madeira
2 pheasant breasts and legs, about
200g/7oz total weight, skinned,
boned and cut into large dice
4 partridge breasts and legs, about
200g/7oz total weight, skinned,
boned and cut into large dice
300g/10½oz pork fat from the
belly, minced (ground)
80ml/2½fl oz/⅓ cup Manzanilla or
other dry sherry
¾ tsp sea salt
½ tsp freshly ground black pepper
12 slices of smoked streaky bacon
2 eggs
100ml/3½fl oz/scant ½ cup double
(heavy) cream
½ tsp dried tarragon
35g/1¼oz cooked whole chestnuts,
roughly chopped
chargrilled warm toast and mixed
leaf salad, to serve

Game birds, such as pheasant and partridge, are a seasonal favourite of mine. I've combined these two in this terrine and, to add to the autumn theme, I've added chestnuts, with their lovely earthiness, as well as sultanas (golden raisins) for a touch of sweetness. You can buy ready-cooked and peeled chestnuts in the supermarket, which are wonderfully easy to use. I find that Muscatel sultanas give the best flavour. Make sure you follow the timings as you don't want a dry terrine, which can easily happen if bird game is overcooked.

1 Put the sultanas (golden raisins) in a bowl with the Madeira and leave to soak while you prepare the pheasant and partridges. Put the pheasant and partridge leg meat into a food processor and pulse to a coarse mince. Put the mince in a bowl with the diced pheasant and partridge breasts and minced (ground) pork fat, and mix well. Add the soaked sultanas and any Madeira left in the bowl, the sherry, salt and pepper and mix once more. Cover and leave to marinate in the fridge for 3–4 hours.

2 Preheat the oven to 140°C/275°F/gas 1. Line the base and sides of a 24 x 10cm/9½ x 4in and 8cm/3¼in deep terrine dish (preferably cast iron) with a double layer of cling film (plastic wrap). Line with the bacon, allowing both ends to overhang the sides. Leave to one side.

3 Whisk the eggs, cream and tarragon until combined. Using a spatula, gradually mix them into the meat, then stir in the chestnuts. Spoon the mixture into the prepared terrine and press down until even. Fold the overhanging bacon over the top to cover, then fold over the cling film (plastic wrap) and cover with the terrine lid.

4 Put the terrine in a deep roasting dish and pour in enough just-boiled water to come two-thirds of the way up the sides of the terrine. Bake for 1 hour, then check to see if it is cooked by inserting a thermometer into the centre. It should read about 68°C/154°F. If the terrine is not ready, carefully return it to the oven for a further 15 minutes. Alternatively, you can insert a knife into the terrine and it should come out hot and dry if the terrine is ready.

5 Remove the terrine from the roasting dish, take off the lid and top with a piece of baking paper and a heavy weight, about 1–2kg/2lb 4oz–4lb 8oz. Leave to cool completely at room temperature. Once cold, cover and leave in the refrigerator for a couple of days before serving to allow the flavours to develop. Serve in thick slices with chargrilled toast and a mixed leaf salad.

VENISON BOURGUIGNON WITH DARK CHOCOLATE & STAR ANISE

SERVES 4
PREPARATION TIME 20 minutes,
   plus making the stock and at
   least 3 hours marinating
COOKING TIME 2 hours 25 minutes

800g/1lb 12oz venison haunch, cut
   into large cubes
1l/35fl oz/4 cups red wine, such as
   French Southern Rhône
2 thyme sprigs
3 garlic cloves, crushed with the
   blade of a knife
1 star anise
3 tbsp Cognac
100ml/3½fl oz/scant ½ cup olive oil
2 tbsp plain (all-purpose) flour
600ml/21fl oz/scant 2½ cups Beef
   Stock (see page 24)
1 bouquet garni, made with 1 thyme
   sprig, 1 parsley sprig and 1 bay
   leaf, tied with kitchen string
2 carrots, peeled, halved
   lengthways and cut into chunks
12 silverskin onions
30g/1oz dark organic chocolate,
   70% cocoa solids, grated
100g/3½oz thick pancetta, diced
2 handfuls of mixed seasonal wild
   mushrooms, such as girolles,
   horn of plenty and chanterelles
1 handful of flat-leaf parsley leaves,
   roughly chopped
sea salt and freshly ground black
   pepper

Venison is a great alternative to beef and, during hunting season, which lasts from autumn to the end of winter, this is a perfect dish to make. Venison is also a very lean meat and full of goodness, as deer eat only the best there is available. Their diet is superb and you can almost say they are difficult when it comes to choosing what's on offer! This version of the French classic is finished with dark chocolate, providing a hint of tobacco and bark which combines beautifully with the earthy flavour of the wild mushrooms and woody aroma of the star anise. To bring the dish together you need to use a robust red wine such as one from the Southern Rhone region that also has a hint of spice and chocolate; all in all a magical combination. I like to serve it with roughly mashed buttered swede (rutabaga) or turnips.

1 Mix together the venison, wine, thyme, garlic, star anise and Cognac in a large bowl. Cover with cling film (plastic wrap) and leave to marinate in the refrigerator for at least 3 hours. Drain the venison through a colander into a bowl, reserving the flavoured marinade.

2 Heat 4 tablespoons of the oil in a large, flameproof casserole dish over a medium heat. Add the venison and cook for at least 20 minutes until very well coloured on all sides but not burnt. Season with salt and pepper, then sprinkle in the flour and cook, stirring, for a further 2–3 minutes until the meat is lightly coated. Add the stock and the reserved marinade and bring to the boil, skimming off any foam that rises to the surface. Add the bouquet garni, carrots and onions, turn the heat down to low, partially cover and simmer for 1 hour 50 minutes, stirring occasionally, until the meat is very tender and the sauce has become rich and silky.

3 Five minutes before the venison is ready, remove 2 ladles of the sauce into a bowl. Whisk in the chocolate until melted and combined. Return the chocolate-flavoured sauce to the casserole dish, stir together well, then cover with a lid and turn off the heat.

4 Heat the remaining oil in a frying pan (skillet) over a medium heat. Add the pancetta and fry for 2–3 minutes until just coloured, then stir in the wild mushrooms and fry for a further 1–2 minutes until just tender. Add to the venison and stir through. Season with salt and pepper to taste, then stir in the parsley, taking care not to break up the venison, and serve.

LAMB SWEETBREAD & WILD MUSHROOM VOL-AU-VENTS

For a while now I've wanted to cook lamb sweetbreads in a puff pastry case and here it is. This is a very tasty dish but it's best to ask your butcher to prepare the sweetbreads for you as they can be a bit fiddly. Serve two per person for a generous portion with vegetables of your choice. Mine would be pan-fried courgettes (zucchini), steamed spinach or red chard.

SERVES 4
PREPARATION TIME 15 minutes
COOKING TIME 25 minutes

500g/1lb 2oz all-butter puff pastry
2 tbsp plain flour (all-purpose),
    plus extra for dusting
1 egg, beaten
300g/10½oz prepared lamb
    sweetbreads
40g/1½oz unsalted butter
2 tbsp olive oil
1 tbsp very fine dry breadcrumbs
300g/10½oz mixed wild or button
    mushrooms
4½ tbsp whipping cream
1 tbsp chopped chives
sea salt and freshly ground black
    pepper
vegetables of your choice, such as
    pan-fried courgettes (zucchini)
    or steamed spinach or red chard,
    to serve

1 Preheat the oven to 190°C/375°F/gas 5 and line a baking sheet with baking paper. Roll out the pastry on a lightly floured work surface and cut out 8 x 9cm/3½in diameter x 5mm/¼in thick rounds. Put 4 of the pastry rounds on the prepared baking sheet. Using a 7.5cm/3in cutter, cut out a circle in the remaining rounds, leaving an outer ring. (Use the cut-out circles for another recipe.) Brush the top of the rounds with beaten egg, making sure the egg does not go over the edge, then lay a pastry ring neatly on top of each one. Carefully brush with egg, then bake for 20 minutes, turning halfway, until risen and golden.

2 While the pastry cooks, bring a saucepan of salted water to the boil. Add the sweetbreads and cook for 1½ minutes, then refresh in a bowl of iced water, pat dry and remove the skin. Cut the sweetbreads into large cubes. Toss in the flour to coat and tap off any excess.

3 Heat a large frying pan (skillet) over a medium heat. Add half the butter and oil and when the butter is foaming, add the sweetbreads and fry for 4–5 minutes, or until golden brown and crisp. Add the breadcrumbs, toss to combine and cook for a further 1 minute until the crumbs are crunchy, then drain on paper towel.

4 When the vol-au-vent cases are cooked, turn the oven down to 100°C/200°F/gas ½. Lift off the centre top layer to of each vol-au-vent to make a hollow. Keep them warm in the oven, with the door ajar, while you finish the filling.

5 Heat the remaining butter and oil in the cleaned frying pan (skillet) over a medium heat. When the butter is foaming, add the mushrooms and fry for 1–2 minutes until softened. Add the cream and bring to the boil, then after 2–3 minutes when it starts to coat the mushrooms, add the cooked sweetbread mixture and the chives, toss to combine and season with salt and pepper to taste. Spoon the mixture into the cooked vol-au-vent cases and serve with your favourite vegetables.

CASSEROLE OF AUTUMN VEGETABLES WITH PEARS & CEPS

SERVES 4
PREPARATION TIME 30 minutes,
    plus making the stock
COOKING TIME 1 hour 10 minutes

80g/2¾oz unsalted butter
1 tbsp sunflower oil
200g/7oz carrots, peeled and cut
    into 2cm/¾in chunks
200g/7oz swede (rutabaga), peeled
    and cut into 2cm/¾in chunks
2 firm pears, peeled, cored and cut
    into 8 wedges
2 large shallots, cut into thick rings
40g/1½oz dried ceps or porcini,
    soaked in 150ml/5fl oz/scant
    ⅔ cup warm water
2 thyme sprigs
200g/7oz celeriac (celery root),
    peeled and cut into 2cm/¾in
    chunks
12 garlic cloves, unpeeled
200g/7oz butternut squash, cut
    into 2cm/¾in chunks
4 small new potatoes, such as
    Charlotte or Ratte, scrubbed and
    each cut into 3 pieces
125ml/4fl oz/½ cup Chicken or
    Vegetable Stock (see page 25)
1 tbsp chopped flat-leaf
    parsley leaves
sea salt and freshly ground black
    pepper

At home, I often make casseroles and it is very much the way my mother likes to cook. It is not by accident that I have chosen pears and ceps; not only do I love them but they bring so much to the casserole with their superb flavour and texture.

1 Heat a large, flameproof casserole dish over a medium-high heat. Add 20g/¾oz of the butter and the sunflower oil and when the butter is foaming, add the carrots. Immediately turn the heat down to medium, partially cover and cook for 12–15 minutes, stirring occasionally, until the carrots just start to soften around the edges but not colour. Add the swede (rutabaga), cover again with the lid and cook for a further 10–12 minutes, stirring occasionally.

2 Meanwhile, heat a large, non-stick frying pan (skillet) over a medium heat. Add 20g/¾oz of the butter and when foaming, add the pears and shallots and cook for 8–10 minutes until just tender and starting to caramelize.

3 Using a small slotted spoon, remove the ceps from their soaking water, taking care not to stir the bowl, then put on paper towel and pat dry. Strain and reserve the soaking water. Add the ceps to the pan with the pears and shallots, then stir in the thyme sprigs and sauté for a further 3–4 minutes over a medium-low heat until the ceps have softened. Season well with salt and pepper, remove from the heat and leave to one side.

4 Add another 20g/¾oz of the butter to the casserole dish with the celeriac (celery root) and garlic, partially cover and cook for 8–10 minutes, stirring occasionally, until slightly softened. Add the butternut squash and potatoes and cook for a further 8–10 minutes, stirring occasionally. Turn the heat up to high, remove the lid and add the remaining butter, the stock and reserved cep water, making sure there is no sediment from the ceps in the water. Cook for 5–8 minutes until the liquid has reduced enough to just coat the vegetables; do this quickly so that the vegetables don't overcook. Remove the casserole dish from the heat, add the pear mixture and parsley, stir gently to combine and heat through, then serve hot.

WARM CHOCOLATE COOKIES WITH COCONUT ICE CREAM

When you are cooking with chocolate, the choice of chocolate is very important. Here I have chosen chocolate with 60% pure cocoa – not over-bitter, as a lot of people don't like that, but instead one that is a touch richer, with hint of tobacco leaf, bark and spices coming through to give a thoroughly modern twist. The warm cookies have a soft, cake-like texture.

SERVES 4
PREPARATION TIME 25 minutes, plus at least 3 hours freezing
COOKING TIME 15 minutes

FOR THE COCONUT ICE CREAM
3 egg yolks
115ml/3¾fl oz/scant ½ cup coconut milk
4 tbsp toasted desiccated (shredded) coconut
200ml/7fl oz/scant 1 cup double (heavy) cream

FOR THE CHOCOLATE COOKIES
100g/3½oz unsalted butter, plus extra for greasing
150g/5½oz dark chocolate, 60% cocoa solids, broken into pieces
2 eggs, separated
55g/2oz/¼ cup caster (superfine) sugar
75g/2½oz/scant ⅔ cup plain (all-purpose) flour
a pinch of salt

1 To make the ice cream, first make a sabayon. Whisk together the egg yolks and coconut milk in a heatproof bowl set over a saucepan of gently simmering water, making sure the bottom of the bowl does not touch the water. Whisk for 5–8 minutes until thickened. Remove from the heat, add the desiccated (shredded) coconut and whisk continuously until the mixture cools completely.

2 Whip the cream, using an electric whisk, until soft peaks form, then fold it into the sabayon. Pour into a 500ml/17fl oz/2 cup freezerproof container. Cover with cling film (plastic wrap) and put in the freezer for at least 3 hours until firm.

3 To make the cookies, preheat the oven to 220°C/425°F/gas 7. Lightly grease two 12-hole mini tart tins. Melt the chocolate and butter in a small saucepan over a low heat, stirring occasionally.

4 Meanwhile whisk together the egg yolks and sugar in a large mixing bowl, using an electric whisk, for about 5 minutes until pale, thick and doubled in volume.

5 As soon as the chocolate has melted, fold in the flour with a wooden spoon or spatula until combined. You must be very careful when doing this and work quite quickly. Pour the chocolate mixture slowly into the egg mixture and fold together.

6 Whisk the egg whites with the salt in a large clean bowl until soft peaks form, then fold them into the chocolate mixture. Spoon the cake mixture into the prepared tart tins, half-filling each hole, to make 12–18 cookies. Bake for 5–6 minutes until risen and slightly firm to the touch. Remove from the oven and turn out onto a wire rack to cool until just lukewarm, then serve with the coconut ice cream.

CHAPTER 2
FROM FIELD & PASTURE

Where we live in the Chiltern Hills, we are surrounded by fields and pastures. I appreciate my surroundings more every day and feel lucky to be amongst them. From my window I can follow the seasons, from the changes of the wind as it travels through the barley like ocean waves, to the different smells, to the sound of the young lambs during the lambing season. Even the sudden jump of a deer when sensing my presence as I walk through the high grass in the early morning.

BEEF CARPACCIO WITH BEEF TARTARE & WASABI CREAM

The dish carpaccio was first created in 1950 by Giuseppe Cipriani for the Comtesse Amalia Mocenigo, who had been advised by her doctor that she should eat her meat raw. At the same time, works by the famous 15th-century painter, Vittore Carpaccio, were being exhibited. His paintings almost always contained large areas of red in varying tones, and this reminded Cipriani of meat, and so he gave his dish the name carpaccio. Although other meats and fish, particularly tuna, can be used for carpaccio, this dish is made with tender beef fillet. I have given it a modern twist by serving it with a piquant wasabi (Japanese horseradish) cream accompanied by beef tartare seasoned with capers and shallot, and some tiny, delicate croûtons, fresh chives and rocket (arugula).

SERVES 4

PREPARATION TIME 25 minutes, plus 2–3 hours freezing and making the croûtons

350g/12oz beef fillet, trimmed
3 tbsp olive oil
100ml/3½fl oz/scant ½ cup whipping cream
1 tsp wasabi (Japanese horseradish) paste
3 tbsp finely chopped chives
40g/1½oz very small Croûtons (see page 27)
sea salt and freshly ground black pepper
1 handful of rocket (arugula) leaves, to serve

FOR THE TARTARE
2 tsp finely diced shallot
1 tsp chopped parsley leaves
1 tsp tomato ketchup
1 tsp chopped capers
1½ tsp olive oil
150g/5½oz beef fillet, trimmed and very finely chopped

1 To make the carpaccio, lay two pieces of cling film (plastic wrap), about 30 x 20cm/12 x 8in, on top of each other to form one sheet of cling film. Put the beef fillet in the centre, then drizzle with 1 tablespoon of the oil and wrap in the cling film to form a tight cylinder. Put in the freezer for 2–3 hours, or until firm but with a slight softness when pressed.

2 Meanwhile, prepare the tartare. Mix the shallot, parsley, tomato ketchup and capers in a bowl. Season with salt and pepper, then drizzle in the remaining oil, stirring continuously. Finally, stir in the chopped beef and season with salt and pepper to taste. Cover with cling film (plastic wrap) and chill until ready to serve.

3 Just before serving, gently whisk together the cream and wasabi (Japanese horseradish) paste in a bowl until soft peaks form. Cover with cling film (plastic wrap) and leave at room temperature.

4 Take the beef out of the freezer and remove the cling film (plastic wrap). Using a very sharp knife, cut it into very thin slices and lay over serving plates, spreading the slices out. Work quickly, as the beef will soon defrost and it is much easier to work with them when still slightly frozen.

5 Season with salt and pepper to taste, sprinkle with the chives, croûtons and a drizzle of oil, and serve with the tartare, wasabi (Japanese horseradish) cream and some fresh rocket (arugula) leaves.

HEIRLOOM BEETROOT 'TAGLIATELLE' & CARPACCIO

Heirloom beetroot (beets) comes in fantastic colours – from ruby red to vibrant yellow – and its earthy, nutty flavour goes really well with the freshness of the chervil. Try not to overcook the beetroot though, as it will break when you cut it into thin slices. It should be soft but with a slight crunch. You could scatter some small crispy lardons over the top instead of the goats' cheese, if you like, and serve with some crusty bread.

SERVES 4
PREPARATION TIME 25 minutes
COOKING TIME 1½ hours

4 heaped tbsp sea salt, plus extra
    to season
4 beetroot (beets), different
    colours if possible
100ml/3½fl oz/scant ½ cup
    beetroot (beet) juice
1 tbsp good-quality balsamic
    vinegar
2 tbsp extra virgin olive oil
a few chives, cut into 5cm/2in
    pieces
½ tbsp chervil leaves
1 handful of yellow frisée lettuce
1 handful of lamb's lettuce
100g/3½oz soft goats' cheese
    log, such as Ste Maure, rind
    removed, crumbled
freshly ground black pepper
crusty bread, to serve (optional)

1 Preheat the oven to 160°C/315°F/gas 2½. Take a 50 x 30cm/20 x 12in piece of foil and sprinkle the sea salt over the centre in a thick layer. Put the beetroot (beets) on top of the salt, then fold the foil over and scrunch the edges to make a parcel. Put the parcel on a baking sheet and roast for 1½ hours until the beetroot is just tender when pierced with the tip of a knife. Remove from the oven and leave the beetroot, still wrapped in its foil parcel, until cool enough to handle. Open the parcel, discard the salt, then peel the beetroot and leave to one side until ready to use.

2 While the beetroot (beets) are cooking, make the dressing. Pour the beetroot juice into a small saucepan over a medium heat and bring to a simmer, then turn the heat down to low and cook for about 10 minutes until the juice has reduced by just over half to about 2 tablespoons. Whisk in the balsamic vinegar and season with salt and pepper to taste, then leave the mixture to cool.

3 Thinly slice 3 of the cooked beetroot (beets), put on a serving plate and brush with the oil. Season with salt and pepper and scatter the chives and chervil over the top.

4 Using a mandolin or sharp knife, cut the remaining beetroot (beets) into very fine julienne strips to make "tagliatelle", then spoon half the beetroot dressing over the strips. Spoon neat piles of beetroot "tagliatelle" in the centre of the beetroot carpaccio. Toss the frisée and lamb's lettuce in a bowl, spoon the remaining dressing over and toss until the leaves are coated. Scatter the leaves over the top of the beetroot, sprinkle with the goats' cheese and serve with crusty bread, if you like.

JERUSALEM ARTICHOKE VELOUTÉ WITH TRUFFLE OIL & CHIVE CREAM

SERVES 4
PREPARATION TIME 25 minutes,
   plus making the stock
COOKING TIME 30 minutes

25g/1oz unsalted butter
1 shallot, finely diced
600g/1lb 5oz Jerusalem artichokes,
   peeled and chopped
1–1.2l/35–40fl oz/4–4¾ cups
   Chicken or Vegetable Stock (see
   pages 24–25)
400g/14oz white asparagus, peeled
   and woody ends discarded
125ml/4fl oz/½ cup
   whipping cream
1 tbsp finely chopped chives
6 drops of truffle oil
1 baguette, sliced, to serve
sea salt and freshly ground black
   pepper

Jerusalem artichokes are a delightful root vegetable that can be roasted, puréed or served, as here, in a velouté. When cooked this way, with a delicious chive cream, they become beautifully velvety and nutty and make a lovely creamy soup for a special occasion.

1 Melt the butter in a large saucepan over a low heat. Add the shallot and artichokes and cook for 5 minutes, stirring occasionally. Turn the heat up to high, add 1l/35fl oz/4 cups of stock and bring to the boil. Turn the heat down to low and simmer for 10–12 minutes or until the artichokes have just softened.

2 Meanwhile, cut off the asparagus tips and leave to one side. Roughly chop the stems, add to the soup and cook for 4 minutes until just tender. Whip half the cream, using an electric whisk, until soft peaks form.

3 Transfer the soup to a blender, season with salt and pepper and blend until smooth (you may have to do this in batches depending on the size of your blender). Add the whipped cream and blend once more, then pass through a fine sieve (strainer), using a ladle to help you, into the cleaned saucepan. Leave to one side.

4 Whip the remaining cream until soft peaks form, then fold in the chives and half the truffle oil and season with salt and pepper to taste. (You could use a hand-held blender to add the chive cream to the soup at this stage, or keep it separate and serve on top of the soup as below.)

5 Bring a saucepan of salted water to the boil, add the reserved asparagus tips and cook briefly for 2–3 minutes until just tender when pierced with the tip of a knife. Drain and season with the remaining truffle oil and with salt and pepper to taste. Put into four soup bowls.

6 Gently reheat the soup, adding the remaining stock if it is too thick, until bubbles just start to form on the top. Do not allow it to boil. Ladle the soup over the asparagus and top with a spoonful of the truffle oil and chive cream. Serve with slices of baguette.

SWEDE & SQUASH SOUP WITH CARAMELIZED CHESTNUTS

SERVES 4
PREPARATION TIME 20 minutes,
    plus making the stock
COOKING TIME 55 minutes

1 swede (rutabaga), about
    400g/14oz total weight, peeled
    and diced
2 tbsp olive oil
1 butternut squash, about 500g/
    1lb 2oz total weight, peeled,
    deseeded and diced
50g/1¾oz unsalted butter
1 small onion, chopped
1.2l/40fl oz/4¾ cups Vegetable
    Stock (see page 25), plus extra
    for thinning, if necessary
200ml/7fl oz/scant 1 cup
    whipping cream
200ml/7fl oz/scant 1 cup
    full-fat milk
75g/2½oz cooked whole chestnuts
1 tbsp caster (superfine) sugar
2 tbsp extra virgin olive oil
sea salt and freshly ground black
    pepper

I think swede (rutabaga) has been ignored for too long, but I feel it's making a bit of a comeback. It certainly makes a great warming winter soup, which goes brilliantly with the sliced caramelized chestnuts.

1 Preheat the oven to 200°C/400°F/gas 6. Put the swede (rutabaga) in a roasting tray, drizzle over the olive oil and season with a little salt and pepper. Roast for 5 minutes, then add the squash, stir to coat in the oil, then continue to roast for a further 7–10 minutes until they are just beginning to colour around the edges but are not cooked through. Remove from the tray and drain on paper towel.

2 Meanwhile, heat a large saucepan over a medium heat. Add half the butter and the onion and cook for 3–4 minutes until just softened but not coloured. Add the roasted swede (rutabaga) and squash to the pan and toss together, then pour in the stock, cream and milk and bring to a simmer. Turn the heat down to low and simmer gently for about 30 minutes, uncovered, until the vegetables are very soft. The soup must not boil or the cream will curdle.

3 While the soup is cooking, make the caramelized chestnuts. Heat a non-stick frying pan (skillet) over a medium heat. Add the remaining butter and when foaming, add the chestnuts and sugar. Cook for 3–4 minutes, turning once, until the chestnuts start to caramelize but take care they don't burn. Tip the chestnuts onto baking paper and leave to cool and become crisp, then roughly slice them.

4 When the soup is ready, ladle it into a blender and blend until very smooth (you may have to do this in batches depending on the size of your blender), then pass it through a fine sieve (strainer) into the cleaned saucepan; it should be very creamy and velvety. Season with salt and pepper to taste and warm the soup through. If you feel it is a little thick, add some more stock. Serve drizzled with extra virgin olive oil and topped with the caramelized chestnuts.

PUMPKIN & GOATS' CHEESE LASAGNE

SERVES 4
PREPARATION TIME 40 minutes
COOKING TIME 50 minutes

2kg/4lb 8oz pumpkin, skin
    removed and deseeded
100ml/3½fl oz/scant ½ cup
    full-fat milk
500ml/17fl oz/2 cups
    whipping cream
1 rosemary sprig
a pinch of freshly grated nutmeg
300g/10½oz soft goats' cheese
    log, such as Golden Cross, rind
    removed, crumbled
40g/1½oz unsalted butter
2 pinches of toasted pumpkin seeds
1 tbsp toasted pumpkin seed oil
100g/3½oz firm ewes' cheese, such
    as Ossau Iraty, diced
sea salt and freshly ground black
    pepper

FOR THE GOATS' CHEESE & PUMPKIN
SALAD

75g/2½oz lamb's lettuce leaves
1 tbsp toasted pumpkin seeds
50g/1¾oz soft goats' cheese log,
    such as Golden Cross, rind
    removed, crumbled
1 tsp toasted pumpkin seed oil
2 tbsp extra virgin olive oil
1 tbsp Chardonnay vinegar or
    white wine vinegar

This "lasagne" is made with very thin layers of pumpkin, rather than pasta. For me, goats' cheese is perfect with pumpkin, while the addition of pumpkin seeds and a drizzle of pumpkin oil make this a delicate, light and surprisingly lovely meal.

1 Cut a 13 x 7.5cm/5 x 3in rectangle 5cm/2in thick from the pumpkin, then cut it into 12 x 2mm/¹⁄₁₆in slices using a mandolin or sharp knife. Chop the remaining pumpkin (about 750g/1lb 10oz) into bite-sized cubes.

2 Put the cubed pumpkin in a saucepan with the milk, half the cream, the rosemary sprig and the nutmeg and cook over a very low heat for 10–15 minutes until the pumpkin is just tender but with a little resistance. Using a slotted spoon, lift out the pumpkin and leave to one side. Reserve the milk mixture in the pan.

3 Meanwhile, bring a saucepan of salted water to the boil over a high heat. Add the thin slices of pumpkin, a few at a time, and cook for 2–3 minutes until just tender and pliable, then use a slotted spoon to transfer them to a bowl of iced water and leave for 1 minute. Lift out and drain on paper towel, keeping the slices separate, then season with salt and pepper.

4 Return the saucepan containing the milk mixture to a medium heat, add the remaining cream and the goats' cheese. Turn the heat to low and cook, whisking continuously, until the cheese has melted and the sauce thickened to a silky texture. Discard the rosemary sprig.

5 Meanwhile, preheat the oven to 180°C/350°F/gas 4 and grease a 22 x 18cm/8½ x 7in baking dish with the butter. Overlap 4 slices of the pumpkin in the base of the dish. Scatter with half the pumpkin cubes, then add half the toasted pumpkin seeds and pumpkin oil and finish with one-third of the sauce. Repeat with another 4 slices of pumpkin, then the rest of the pumpkin cubes, seeds and oil. Spread another one-third of the sauce over the top, then finish with the remaining pumpkin slices. Add the remaining sauce and sprinkle with the ewes' cheese. Bake for 20 minutes until golden and bubbling, then turn the oven up to maximum and cook for a further 5–8 minutes until golden brown. Leave to rest for 2–3 minutes.

6 Meanwhile, prepare the salad, if you like. Toss the lamb's lettuce, pumpkin seeds and crumbled cheese together in a bowl. In a separate bowl, whisk together the oils and vinegar and season with salt and pepper. Drizzle the salad with the dressing, toss and serve with the lasagne.

RED ONION TARTE TATIN WITH GOATS' CHEESE

SERVES 4
PREPARATION TIME 25 minutes, plus
    30 minutes chilling
COOKING TIME 1 hour

375g/13oz ready-made puff pastry
plain (all-purpose) flour,
    for dusting
200g/7oz/heaped ¾ cup caster
    (superfine) sugar
½ tsp lemon juice
4 thyme sprigs
6 red onions, peeled, root trimmed
    to the level of the base and cut
    into quarters
1 egg, lightly beaten
100g/3½oz soft goats' cheese log,
    such at Ste Maure, rind removed
1 tsp black onion seeds
4 handfuls of pea shoots
1 tbsp extra virgin olive oil
sea salt and freshly ground black
    pepper

This is a twist on the classic tarte tatin as it is made not with fruit, but with onions – deliciously sweet red onions, to be precise – using more or less the same principle and technique. To go with my onion tart, I have chosen goats' cheese, which for me is the perfect partner, and I have also created these as individual tarts, which means they are ideal for serving as a meal for a first course or lunch, and make a lovely dish to serve outdoors, sitting on the terrace or in your garden. My choice of accompaniment would be some fresh salad leaves, or a pea shoot or herb salad, either of which would go well.

1 Roll out the pastry on a lightly floured work surface and cut into 4 discs, each about 20cm/8in in diameter. Put the pastry on a baking sheet, cover with cling film (plastic wrap) and chill in the refrigerator for 25–30 minutes to prevent the pastry shrinking during baking.

2 Meanwhile, preheat the oven to 160°C/315°F/gas 2½. Melt the sugar, lemon juice and 80ml/2½fl oz/⅓ cup of water in a non-stick frying pan (skillet) over a low heat. Increase the heat to medium and cook for 10–12 minutes until it turns a rich golden brown. Divide into four 15cm/6in non-stick cake tins or ovenproof dishes. Put a thyme sprig in the centre of each tin, then put the red onion quarters, rounded-side down, into the caramel; there should be 6 quarters in each pan. Bake for 20 minutes, then remove from the oven and turn the oven up to 190°C/375°F/gas 5.

3 Take the pastry out of the refrigerator and quickly and carefully put the pastry over the top of the onions, pushing the edges down into the sides of the dishes. Brush the tops with the egg wash. This needs to be done really quickly as the pastry will start to melt if you take too long. Sprinkle a little sea salt over the top, then return it to the oven and bake for a further 20–25 minutes until the pastry is golden brown and crisp.

4 Remove the tarts from the oven and leave to cool for a few minutes. Put an upside-down plate the size of the dish on top of the first tart and, holding both the plate and dish, flip it over to unmould the tart onto the plate. Crumble the goats' cheese over the top of the tart and sprinkle with the black onion seeds. Repeat with the remaining tarts.

5 Toss the pea shoots with the extra virgin olive oil in a small bowl, then season with salt and pepper. Serve the tarts as the cheese just starts to melt, with the pea shoot salad served separately.

CELERIAC & APPLE RÉMOULADE WITH CRYSTALLIZED CELERIAC LEAVES

SERVES 4
PREPARATION TIME 25 minutes,
    plus making the mayonnaise and
    20 minutes marinating
COOKING TIME 6–8 hours

leaves from 1 head of celeriac
    (celery root) or celery
1 egg white, lightly whisked
4 tbsp caster (superfine) sugar
1 small celeriac (celery root), about
    500g/1lb 2oz total weight, peeled
1 lemon, halved
grated zest of 1 lime
5 tbsp Mayonnaise (see page 26)
2 tbsp Dijon mustard
1 tbsp whipping cream,
    lightly whipped
1 crisp green eating apple, such as
    Granny Smith, cored
sea salt and freshly ground black
    pepper

What better to have as part of a fresh tray of crudités than a celeriac (celery root) *rémoulade* – well, perhaps, a *rémoulade* with a little freshly cut, crunchy green apple to bring some essential acidity to cut through the richness of the mayonnaise. You'll see what I mean when you try it, as the apples really raise the dish to another level. I have also used the leaves of the celeriac, though if you cannot find celeriac with the leaves attached at your local market or supermarket, just use celery leaves. They are more tender and a touch less bitter but will work fine as they will be sprinkled with caster (superfine) sugar before being dried in an oven and becoming crystallized. It is a fun idea that's worth doing if you have some time to hand, and it really finishes the dish beautifully.

1 Preheat the oven to 70°C/150°F/gas ¼ with the fan switched off. Line a baking sheet with baking paper.

2 Pick all the leaves from the celeriac (celery root), and leave to one side about 24–28 very fine, pale, flat leaves from the centre, then roughly chop the remaining green, slightly firmer leaves. Put the fine leaves in a single layer on the prepared baking sheet, then brush with a little egg white on one side. Sprinkle the sugar lightly over the top of the egg white and put in the oven for 6–8 hours until fully crystallized and dry. Remove from the oven and leave to one side.

3 Quarter the celeriac (celery root) lengthways, then rub all over with a cut lemon to stop it from turning brown. Grate into long strips (you can use a mandolin if you have one, just take care) and put in a bowl with another squeeze of lemon juice. Add the chopped celeriac leaves and lime zest, then add the mayonnaise, mustard and cream and fold together. Cover and leave to marinate in the refrigerator for 20 minutes.

4 Just before the *rémoulade* finishes marinating, cut the apple into fine slices from top to bottom, discarding the end slices that are all skin, then stack the slices back up and cut through into small matchsticks.

5 When ready to serve, fold the apple through the celeriac (celery root) mixture. Pile the *rémoulade* on a plate and carefully put 4–5 crystallized leaves on top. Serve immediately while the leaves are crisp.

LEEK & POTATO TERRINE

This recipe needs a bit of care but I think you will love the result. The recipe contains wild mushrooms and I normally use a summer truffle, but they may be hard to find and quite expensive, so look out for dried *trompette*, or horn of plenty mushroom as it's called in Britain.

SERVES 6–8
PREPARATION TIME 30 minutes, plus
   making the stock and dressing
   and 24 hours chilling
COOKING TIME 30 minutes

a little oil, for greasing
15fl oz/4 cups Vegetable Stock
   (see page 25)
8 baby leeks
1.5kg/3lb 5oz floury potatoes,
   peeled and cut into 12 pieces
15g/½oz dried horn of plenty
   mushrooms
2 leaves of gelatine, about
   4g/⅛oz total weight, soaked
   in cold water
2–5 drops of truffle oil
125–185ml/4–6fl oz/½–¾ cup
   French Dressing (see page 26)
2 tbsp chopped flat-leaf
   parsley leaves
sea salt and freshly ground black
   pepper

1 Oil a terrine mould or 1kg/2lb 4oz loaf tin, then line with three large sheets of cling film (plastic wrap), allowing a long overhang on all sides. Wrap two 500g/1lb 2oz/2¼ cup bags of sugar in two layers of cling film.

2 Bring the stock to the boil in a frying pan (skillet) over a high heat, add the leeks, then turn the heat to low and simmer for 4–5 minutes until just tender. Lift the leeks out of the stock using a slotted spoon and drain on paper towel. Cut in half lengthways and leave to dry.

3 Add the potatoes to the stock a few at a time, return to the boil, then simmer for 10–12 minutes until almost tender; the tip of a knife should just go through with the barest resistance. Lift the potatoes out onto paper towel to dry. Simmer the stock until reduced by half.

4 Put 3–4 pieces of potato directly into the bottom of the terrine, making sure that all the base is covered. Cover the potatoes with half of the prepared leeks, cut-side down, then crumble over half of the dried mushrooms. Repeat with a layer of potatoes, the rest of the leeks, the mushrooms, then a final layer of potatoes.

5 By now the stock should have reduced to about 500ml/17fl oz/ 2 cups. Squeeze out the soaked gelatine and add to the hot stock, whisking until melted. Season with salt and pepper, then strain through a fine sieve (strainer) over the terrine so that the liquid only just covers the potatoes; you don't want it to come too high up. As you pour, press down lightly on the potatoes so there are no air pockets. Fold the cling film (plastic wrap) over the top to cover it completely, then put the prepared bags of sugar down the length of the terrine. Cool, then chill in the refrigerator for 24 hours until totally set.

6 Remove the terrine from the refrigerator and turn it out in its cling film (plastic wrap) wrapping. Cut into thick slices with a very sharp, non-serrated knife, and only then remove and discard the cling film.

7 Add the truffle oil to the French dressing (remember, you only want a few drops of truffle oil as it is very strong), then stir in the parsley and drizzle over the terrine to serve.

WARM WHITE ASPARAGUS SALAD WITH GRAPEFRUIT ZEST VINAIGRETTE

SERVES 4
PREPARATION TIME 25 minutes, plus
    making the mayonnaise
COOKING TIME 20 minutes

1 egg
1kg/2lb 4oz white asparagus,
    peeled and woody ends
    discarded
1 white grapefruit
1 tbsp Dijon mustard
1 heaped tbsp Mayonnaise
    (see page 26)
6 tbsp sunflower oil
1 tsp chopped chervil leaves
sea salt and freshly ground black
    pepper

In France we could almost change our national day to White Asparagus Day. Well, almost, but not quite! But when it comes into season, you will find asparagus on all the tables at home, in restaurants, bistros, brasseries and *auberges* – you name it, it will be on every menu for that short season. I love it, it's just superb. Here, I am serving it with some lovely white grapefruit and a boiled egg and grapefruit dressing that complements the white asparagus perfectly. If you like, you could serve it with some crusty bread and my Chicory and Radish Salad (see page 26).

1 Bring a pan of water to the boil over a medium heat, add the egg, return to the boil, then turn the heat down to low and simmer for 10 minutes. Drain and refresh under cold water, then crack and peel the egg. Finely chop the cooked egg and leave to one side.

2 Divide the asparagus into 4 equal-sized bunches and tie each bunch with kitchen string to secure. Bring a large pan of salted water to the boil over a medium heat, add the bunched asparagus and simmer for 5–8 minutes, depending on the size of your asparagus, until tender but with just a little resistance when pierced with the tip of a knife.

3 Grate the zest from the grapefruit, reserve a pinch and put the rest in a small bowl. Peel the grapefruit, then take out 4 segments, cut each one in half and leave to one side. Juice the rest of the grapefruit, pressing it through a fine sieve (strainer) into the bowl with the zest. Add the mustard and mayonnaise and whisk together until well blended, then whisk in the sunflower oil in a steady stream. Stir in the chopped egg and chervil and season with salt and pepper to taste.

4 Remove the asparagus from the pan and drain briefly on paper towel or a clean dish towel. Remove the string and put the asparagus onto serving plates. Spoon the dressing over the top and finish with the reserved grapefruit segments and a sprinkling of the reserved zest.

PARTRIDGE WITH CELERIAC, TURNIPS & CHESTNUT BOULANGÈRE

SERVES 4
PREPARATION TIME 30 minutes
COOKING TIME 25 minutes

4 partridges, prepared by your
   butcher with a rasher of bacon
   around
80g/2¾oz unsalted butter
3 tbsp sunflower oil
2 garlic cloves, unpeeled, crushed
4 thyme sprigs
200ml/7fl oz/scant 1 cup chicken
   stock (see page 24)
Chestnut Boulangère (see page
   28), just replace the swede
   (rutabaga) with the same
   quantity of celeriac (celery root)
   and turnip
sea salt and freshly ground black
   pepper

Partridge is a game bird which is a little bit underused at home. The game season is from September 1 to February 1 and partridge is widely available at your local butcher at that time of year. This bird is full of flavour but can be tough if too old, so make sure you choose new-season birds. It is always best to hang them for a while to tenderize the meat and bring out the lovely gamey flavour, but beware not to hang for too long as it can become too strong. Choose female partridges, which are more tender, and ask your butcher to prepare them for you – it's so much easier! Partridge really is a 'must try' if you haven't had it before – and it goes beautifully with turnips and celeriac (celery root).

1 Preheat the oven to 180°C/350°F/gas 4 and season the partridge skin with salt. Heat a large ovenproof frying pan (skillet) over a medium heat and add half the butter and the oil. When the butter starts to foam, place the partridges breast-side down in the pan and cook for 2–3 minutes until golden. Turn the partridges, add the garlic and most of the thyme and place in the oven for 6–8 minutes. After 4 minutes, baste them with the butter and oil. Remove from the oven and place in a serving dish. They should be nicely golden on the outside by now, and almost rose-coloured inside. Cover with foil to rest in a warm place.

2 Meanwhile, put the pan back over a medium heat, pour in the chicken stock and deglaze the pan by stirring to remove any caramelized bits stuck to the bottom. Add the remaining butter and thyme, and simmer for 2 minutes, or until the stock becomes slightly thicker and shiny. Make sure you keep enough for the 4 partridges, so do not over-reduce. Check the seasoning. Serve the partridges with the juices from the pan and with the boulangère. Enjoy.

POMME FARCIE
WITH BRAISED
PORK SHOULDER

I love all the less expensive, and often forgotten, cuts of pork, beef or lamb. Here I'm using pork shoulder, which isn't so rare these days, but it's so much better braised than roasted. Be sure to ask your butcher to cut the pork into large cubes and to keep the fat on as it will make the dish much tastier and also keep it moist, which for me is essential. For the best texture, remember to crush the cooked meat partially using a fork – you are not making a rillette so you don't want it too smooth.

SERVES 4
PREPARATION TIME 30 minutes, plus
   making the stock
COOKING TIME 2 hours 25 minutes

20g/¾oz unsalted butter
2 tbsp olive oil
600g/1lb 5oz boneless fatty pork
   shoulder, cut into large cubes
2 small carrots, peeled
   and chopped
2 shallots, chopped
2 garlic cloves, unpeeled,
   lightly crushed
100ml/3½fl oz/scant ½ cup dry
   white wine
500ml/17fl oz/2 cups Chicken
   Stock (see page 24)
4 floury potatoes, such as King
   Edward or Agria, about 200g/7oz
   each, peeled
1 tbsp chopped sage leaves
sea salt and freshly ground black
   pepper
green salad, to serve

1 Preheat the oven to 140°C/275°F/gas 1. Heat the butter with 1 tablespoon of the oil in a large, flameproof casserole dish over a high heat. When the butter is foaming, add the pork, carrots, shallots and garlic and cook for 5 minutes until just beginning to brown. Add the white wine and simmer, deglazing the pan by stirring to remove any caramelized bits stuck to the bottom, until the liquid has reduced by two-thirds. Pour in the stock and bring to a simmer. Reduce the heat to low, partially cover and cook for 2 hours, stirring every 30 minutes until the meat is very tender but not quite falling apart. The sauce should be thick enough to coat the back of the spoon.

2 While the pork cooks, make a horizontal cut along the length of each potato, about one-quarter of the way down, to make a lid. Set its lid next to each potato. Using a teaspoon, scoop out the insides of the potatoes, leaving a 5mm/¼in shell. (You can use the inside flesh for another recipe.) Season the insides with salt and pepper and divide the remaining oil between them. Put the lids back on and tightly wrap in cling film (plastic wrap). Put a large saucepan of water on to simmer, with a steamer insert on top. Add the potatoes to the steamer, cover and cook over a very low heat for 1–1¼ hours until just tender. Turn off the heat, then leave the potatoes in the steamer to cook in the residual heat for 10–15 minutes.

3 When the meat is nearly ready, remove the cling film (plastic wrap) from the potatoes, lift off the lids and turn the potatoes upside-down on a clean dish towel to absorb any condensation. Turn the potatoes over and put in a roasting tin.

4 Remove the pork from the heat, spoon out 100ml/3½fl oz/scant ½ cup of the cooking juices into a bowl and leave to one side. Lightly crush the meat with a fork, stir in the sage and season with salt and pepper. Fill each potato with the mixture, taking care not to break them, cover with the potato lid, then spoon the reserved juices over the top. Put in the oven for 15 minutes until hot and bubbling. Serve with a green salad.

ROAST MARINATED LAMB WITH LIQUORICE

SERVES 4
PREPARATION TIME 10 minutes,
    plus 1 hour soaking and
    overnight marinating
COOKING TIME 20 minutes

1 small stick of liquorice root,
    about 10cm/4in long x 1cm/
    ½in thick
4 small lamb rumps, about
    150g/5½oz each
125ml/4fl oz/½ cup olive oil
20g/¾oz unsalted butter
200ml/7fl oz/scant 1 cup Lamb
    Stock or Chicken Stock (see
    pages 24–25)
sea salt and freshly ground black
    pepper
steamed Swiss chard, to serve

In France, as in Spain, we use liquorice root quite a lot. In fact, I remember as a young boy buying liquorice root and chewing it on my way to school, then keeping it in my bag during lessons and getting it out again to chew on my way back home – great memories! In this recipe, I use it to skewer the lamb rump to infuse the meat while cooking, without the flavour becoming overpowering. The lamb is also really good served with very thin strips or "tagliatelle" of courgette (zucchini) sautéed in olive oil with a little garlic and chilli and finished with some chopped flat-leaf parsley.

1 Put the liquorice in a small bowl of warm water and leave for about 1 hour until it is soft enough to bend easily. Working from the centre of the root towards the end, peel away the outer layer, reserving the peelings. Cut the root lengthways into quarters, leaving the long pieces to dry on a plate.

2 Put the lamb in a shallow bowl and pour over the oil, then add a generous pinch of pepper and the liquorice peelings. Stir to coat, then cover each rump tightly with cling film (plastic wrap), pressing the cling film directly onto the lamb so that there is no air inside. Leave to marinate in the refrigerator overnight to help to tenderize the meat.

3 The next day, preheat the oven to 140°F/275°F/gas 1. Remove the lamb from the marinade and, using a skewer, make incisions through the centre of each piece of meat. Insert a liquorice root piece into each one, pressing them into the lamb.

4 Heat an ovenproof frying pan (skillet) over a medium-high heat. Add the lamb and cook for about 3–4 minutes on all sides, adding the butter when cooking the final side. Transfer the lamb, still in the pan, to the oven and cook for 5–8 minutes, then turn the oven up to 180°C/350°F/gas 4 and cook for a further 4 minutes until cooked but still slightly pink in the centre. Transfer the lamb to a warm plate, cover with foil and leave to rest while you make the gravy.

5 Return the pan that you cooked the lamb in to a high heat and when the juices are bubbling, add the stock and deglaze the pan by stirring to remove any caramelized bits stuck to the bottom. Cook for 5 minutes until reduced by half, then add any resting juices from the lamb and season with salt and pepper to taste. Serve with steamed Swiss chard.

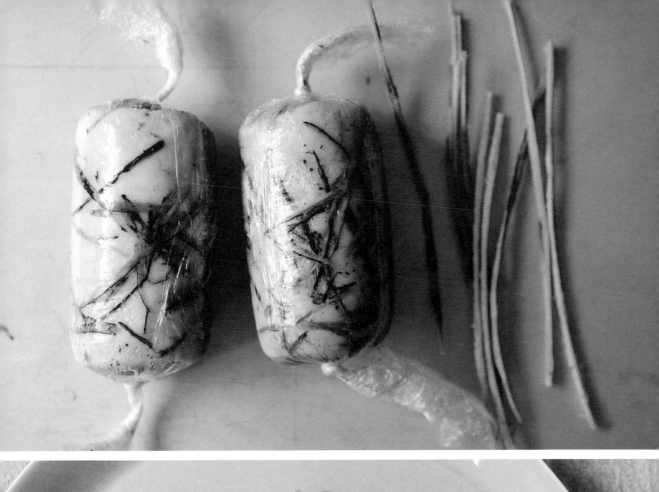

CASSEROLE OF LAMB & POMEGRANATE MOLASSES

SERVES 4
PREPARATION TIME 10 minutes
COOKING TIME 2½ hours

20g/¾oz unsalted butter
2 tbsp sunflower oil
1 onion, roughly chopped
2 garlic cloves, roughly chopped
1kg/2lb 4oz boneless shoulder
 or neck of lamb, cut into
 large cubes
500ml/17fl oz/2 cups Lamb Stock
 or Chicken Stock (see pages
 24–25)
1 rosemary sprig
1 handful of good-quality stoned
 black olives
2 tbsp pomegranate molasses
grated zest of 1 lemon
sea salt and freshly ground black
 pepper
Creamed Mashed Potatoes (see
 page 28), to serve

I think this is my favourite casserole in this book. I like to use lamb shoulder as it has excellent flavour, it's moist and there is just the perfect amount of fat needed for it to be tasty – ask the butcher to trim down the fat if there is too much. I'm pairing it with pomegranate molasses, which is a reduction of pomegranate juice that's taken right down to a thick, syrupy liquid. It's slightly tangy with a delicate sweet and sour accent. Just imagine the aromas in your kitchen when this casserole has been cooking for a couple of hours. Your guests will be wondering and asking questions. But make them wait a little longer until they taste it and all will be revealed. Then you can tell them that the secret ingredient fraternizing with the lamb is pomegranate molasses, which lifts a humble lamb shoulder to new heights.

I Heat a flameproof casserole dish over a medium heat. Add the butter and oil and when the butter is foaming, add the onion and garlic. Reduce the heat to low and cook for 5–8 minutes until slightly soft and translucent but not coloured.

2 Turn the heat up to high, add the lamb and sauté for 12–15 minutes until golden brown on all sides. Add the stock and rosemary and bring to a simmer, then cover with the lid without closing it completely – you just want a little gap so that the condensation does not produce too much liquid – and simmer over a very gentle heat for 1¾ hours, making sure the liquid is just shimmering but not bubbling.

3 Check that the lamb is very tender and the liquid reduced by about half, but no more. If not, then continue cooking for a further 15 minutes and check again. Add the olives and pomegranate molasses and cook for a further 10 minutes until the sauce is lovely and shiny. Add the lemon zest and season with salt and pepper to taste. Serve with deliciously creamy mashed potato.

SLOW-ROASTED SHOULDER OF LAMB WITH GARLIC, BASIL & GINGER

SERVES 4–6
PREPARATION TIME 10 minutes
COOKING TIME 3 hours 40 minutes

1.25kg/2lb 12oz shoulder of
    lamb, either on or off the bone,
    and tied, if boned, at room
    temperature
1 tbsp sea salt
3 tbsp olive oil
4 large basil leaves
8 garlic cloves
5cm/2in piece of root ginger,
    peeled and diced
2 banana shallots
100ml/3½fl oz/scant ½ cup
    Chardonnay vinegar
750ml/26fl oz/3 cups Lamb Stock
    (see page 25)
2 tomatoes, quartered
a few small rosemary sprigs
freshly ground black pepper
fried aubergine (eggplant) and
    courgette (zucchini) slices,
    to serve

You might ask why I have included another recipe for lamb shoulder in this book. Firstly, because it's delicious – that goes without saying. And because, with the neck and the belly, it is the tastiest cut – flavoursome, moist and succulent. These are the cuts we use in the restaurant. You can keep the shoulder on the bone if you want, as it is slowly cooked, and the bone will come out very easily at the end. Here I have used basil, garlic and also ginger, the latter being slightly more unusual with lamb but bringing an exotic touch that goes really well. Then the Chardonnay vinegar brings a welcome sweet acidity. Make sure you brown the lamb well first, then reduce the heat and slow-cook the lamb to perfection.

1 Preheat the oven to 220°C/425°F/gas 7. Season the lamb with the salt and plenty of black pepper, massaging the seasoning into the lamb really well. Put it in a deep-sided, flameproof roasting tray, drizzle with the oil and roast for 25–30 minutes until browned all the over.

2 Add 2 of the basil leaves, the garlic, ginger and shallots to the tray and return to the oven for 5 minutes. Remove the tray from the oven again and put over a low heat. Add the vinegar, which should evaporate more or less immediately, and deglaze the pan by stirring to remove any caramelized bits stuck to the bottom. Add the stock and tomatoes and stir to combine everything, then cover with kitchen foil, leaving one edge open to allow the steam to escape.

3 Turn the oven down to 140°C/275°F/gas 1, return the lamb to the oven and roast for 30 minutes. Remove the foil, baste the lamb and cover again. Repeat after 30 minutes, then remove the foil and cook for a further 2 hours, basting every 30 minutes. The lamb should be lovely and tender, almost falling apart.

4 Remove the tray from the oven, then pour the juices through a sieve (strainer) into a sauté pan. Put over a medium-high heat and cook for 5–8 minutes until thick enough to coat the back of a spoon, stirring continuously. Chop the remaining basil leaves and add to the sauce, then season with salt and pepper to taste.

5 Carve the lamb, spoon over the sauce and top with the rosemary sprigs. Serve with some fried aubergine (eggplant) and courgette (zucchini) slices.

SLOW-ROAST BEEF RIB EYE WITH CARROT & HORSERADISH PURÉE

This is a lovely way of eating beef, and cooking it "low and slow" is an excellent way to get that melting texture. I like to serve this with a carrot purée but with a really gorgeous twist – a little freshly grated horseradish. Make sure that you have a good blender to hand so the purée is very smooth. Just drizzle a lovely beef or red wine sauce on it and it's perfection.

SERVES 4
PREPARATION TIME 20 minutes, plus
    making the stock
COOKING TIME 2½ hours

800g/1lb 12oz rib eye loin of beef,
    trimmed and tied into a joint,
    bone reserved
1 tbsp sunflower oil
1 carrot, peeled and chopped
1 onion, chopped
2 garlic cloves, chopped
2 thyme sprigs
200ml/7fl oz/scant 1 cup dry
    red wine
400ml/14fl oz/scant 1⅔ cups Beef
    Stock (see page 24)
sea salt and freshly ground black
    pepper

FOR THE CARROT PURÉE
80g/2¾oz unsalted butter
1 shallot, chopped
1kg/2lb 4oz carrots, peeled and
    roughly chopped
100ml/3½fl oz/scant ½ cup
    full-fat milk
200ml/7fl oz/scant 1 cup double
    (heavy) cream
2 tbsp finely grated horseradish

1 Preheat the oven to 100°C/200°F/gas ½. Season the beef with salt and pepper. Heat a frying pan (skillet) over a medium-high heat. Add the oil and beef and cook for 10–12 minutes, turning until it is a lovely golden brown on all sides and taking care not to burn it. Put the carrot, onion, garlic, thyme and reserved beef bones in a roasting tray and put the sealed beef on top. Cover loosely with kitchen foil, then roast for 1½–2 hours. Check with a meat thermometer that the temperature in the centre of the beef is 55–60°C/131–140°F, which will give you medium-rare to medium. If you don't have a thermometer, insert the tip of a sharp knife into the meat, then carefully touch it on the inside of your wrist – it should be medium hot.

2 To prepare the carrot purée, heat a saucepan over a medium-low heat. Add half the butter, the shallot and carrots and cook for 10–12 minutes until just tender and the edges are softening but not colouring. Add the milk, cream and horseradish, bring to a low simmer, then cover with cling film (plastic wrap) tightly so that no air escapes. Turn the heat down as low as it will go, and cook for 1½ hours – they will be overcooked and create a delicious confit. Check occasionally and add 2 tablespoons of water if necessary.

3 Use a slotted spoon to put the carrots in a blender, then blitz to a fine purée, adding half the cooking liquor as you go to give you a light, shiny purée. Add the remaining butter and blitz once more to incorporate, then season with salt and pepper to taste.

4 Transfer the beef to a large plate, cover with kitchen foil and leave to rest in a warm place. Put the roasting tray over a medium heat and stir until the juices start to bubble. Add the red wine and deglaze the pan by stirring to remove any caramelized bits stuck to the bottom. Simmer until there is barely any liquid left. Add the stock, bring to the boil, stirring up any sediment, then turn the heat down to low and simmer for 8–10 minutes until reduced by half, shiny and thickened.

5 Remove the string from the beef, then cut it into slices. Spoon the sauce over the beef and serve with the carrot purée, putting any spare sauce into a bowl to serve at the table.

BRAISED OX CHEEKS WITH CRUSHED POTATOES

Up until a few years ago, ox cheeks were a forgotten cut of meat, but they're becoming very popular again and no wonder – they are so delicious. They can be a little tricky to prepare as you need to trim them carefully, removing all the sinew before cooking, but if you have a butcher, ask him to do this for you. Crushed new potatoes are perfect with this dish and I would recommend Vitelotte, Jersey Royal or Charlotte, or even Ratte – just don't forget a good glug of olive oil and the herbs.

SERVES 4
PREPARATION TIME 25 minutes, plus
    making the stock
COOKING TIME 5 hours

2 cloves
4 tbsp olive oil
2 garlic cloves
2 carrots, peeled and cut into
    1.5cm/⅝in chunks
2 shallots, cut into 2cm/¾in rings
1.25kg/2lb 12oz large ox cheeks,
    sinew and fat trimmed
6 tbsp sherry vinegar
300ml/10½fl oz/scant 1¼ cups
    red wine
300ml/10½fl oz/scant 1¼ cups
    Chicken Stock (see page 24)
200ml/7fl oz/scant 1 cup Beef
    Stock (see page 24)
¼ star anise
8 large new potatoes, such as
    Charlotte, Jersey Royals,
    Vitelotte or Ratte, scrubbed
1 tbsp chopped chives
sea salt and freshly ground black
    pepper

1 To blanch the cloves, bring a small saucepan of water to the boil, add the cloves, then return to a simmer for 1 minute. Drain, refresh in cold water and leave to one side.

2 Heat a large, flameproof casserole dish over a medium-high heat. Add 1 tablespoon of the oil and the garlic, carrots and shallots and cook for about 5 minutes until softened. Remove with a slotted spoon and leave to one side.

3 Add the beef to the casserole dish and cook for 15–20 minutes, turning the meat occasionally until browned all over. Add the sherry vinegar and deglaze the pan by stirring to remove any caramelized bits stuck to the bottom. When the vinegar has evaporated, add the red wine and cook for a further 5 minutes until reduced by half. Add both stocks and the star anise, return the cooked vegetables to the pan and bring the stock to a low simmer. Turn the heat down to low, partially cover with a lid and cook for 4½ hours, stirring every 30 minutes until the beef is very tender.

4 While the beef is cooking, prepare the potatoes. Put the potatoes in a saucepan, cover with water and bring to the boil over a medium-high heat. Turn the heat down to low and simmer for 30 minutes until very tender when pierced with the tip of a knife. Remove from the heat and leave to cool in the water.

5 Fifteen minutes before the beef has finished cooking, drain the potatoes, peel them carefully and return them to the pan. Drizzle with the remaining oil, season with salt and pepper and cover with a lid. Put the pan over a very low heat for 5–10 minutes until just heated through. Remove the lid and lightly crush the potatoes with the back of a fork until just broken up but not mashed, then add the chives and stir through. Serve the ox cheeks, carrots and sauce on top of the crushed potatoes.

VEGETABLE POT-AU-FEU WITH KOHLRABI

In winter especially, a pot-au-feu is often on my mind, as it is such a heart-warming dish. It's often cooked in a casserole, where everything goes into one pot. It usually includes meat, but this one is made only with vegetables. I've used an often-forgotten but delicious vegetable here, kohlrabi – a sort of turnip crossed with a cabbage which originated from Germany. I love it!

SERVES 6
PREPARATION TIME: 25 minutes
COOKING TIME: 1 hour 30 minutes

3 tbsp rapeseed (canola) oil
8 carrots, peeled and chopped
2 small leeks, chopped
2 onions, peeled but kept whole
1 kohlrabi, cut into small segments
1 small swede (rutabaga), peeled and diced
2 courgettes (zucchini), cut in half and chopped
3 litres/105fl oz/12¾ cups water
1 bay leaf
1 thyme sprig
1 parsley sprig
6 cloves
2 chervil sprigs, chopped
sea salt and freshly ground black pepper
Crôutons (see page 27), to serve

1 To make your vegetable stock, heat a large pan over a medium heat. Add the rapeseed (canola) oil and when hot, add all vegetable peelings and trimmings. Cook until golden brown but no longer, otherwise it will make the stock bitter. Add the water, the bay leaf, thyme and parsley, and simmer for 4–5 minutes. At this stage the stock should have a nice amber colour and good flavour. Place a large, heavy-based saucepan over a medium heat and strain the stock through a sieve (strainer) into the pan to remove the vegetable peelings. Keep the bay leaf.

2 Now add all the chopped vegetables, the reserved bay leaf and the cloves. Bring up to a simmer and cook for about 4–5 minutes, or until the vegetables have softened but still have a slight bite. Check the seasoning.

3 Serve hot in deep bowls and finish with some chopped chervil. Add some lovely sourdough crôutons to serve, if you like.

LEEK, PANCETTA & CHESTNUT MUSHROOM PIE

Creating a *pithivier* of mushroom, leek and pan-roasted pancetta is a delicious way to enclose these flavours. *Pithiviers*, or pies in the UK, are a great tradition. If you were to cross the UK, you would find a local pie speciality in every county, maybe every town, and it's the same in France. This one is lovely served warm with a chicory (Belgian endive) salad.

SERVES **6**
PREPARATION TIME: 40 minutes,
    plus 30 minutes chilling
COOKING TIME: 40 minutes

50g/1¾oz butter, plus extra to
    brush the pie dish
100g/3½oz pancetta,
    cut into cubes
2 tbsp olive oil
300g/10½oz chestnut (cremini)
    mushrooms, cut into cubes
400g/14oz leeks, chopped
300g/10½oz savoury pastry
    (see page 30)
plain (all-purpose) flour, for rolling
    out the pastry
1 large egg
2 egg yolks (1 for brushing the pie)
200ml/7fl oz/scant 1 cup crème
    fraîche
sea salt and freshly ground white
    pepper
chicory (Belgian endive) salad, to
    serve

1 Take a classic pie dish, non-stick if possible, and brush with melted butter. Set aside.

2 Put the pancetta into a small frying pan (skillet) over a medium heat and fry, stirring occasionally, until starting to crisp, then remove from the heat and place on some paper towel to drain off any excess fat.

3 Heat a saucepan over a medium heat. Add the oil and butter and when the butter starts to foam, throw in the mushrooms and sauté for a few minutes until soft and golden, then add the leeks and sauté, stirring occasionally, until softened but they still have that lovely, pale green colour. Both shouldn't be cooked through at this point. Remove from the heat and add the cooked pancetta. Keep in the refrigerator until needed.

4 Preheat the oven to 190°C/375°F/gas 5. Roll out the pastry on a lightly floured surface until 3–5mm/⅛in thick. Cut out a base for the pie, large enough to line the dish so that it overhangs by about 5cm/2in. Fill with the mushroom, leek and pancetta mixture. Place the pie in the refrigerator to chill for 30 minutes.

5 Put the egg, 1 of the egg yolks and crème fraîche into a large mixing bowl. Whisk well using an electric whisk and season to taste. Don't forget to go easy on the salt as pancetta can be a bit salty. Take the pie out of the refrigerator and spoon over the crème fraîche mixture. Roll out the remaining pastry and cut out a lid for the pie. Carefully cover the filling and trim off any overhang. Fold over the overhanging pastry from the base and, with your thumb and forefinger, pinch the edges to seal and crimp the pie. Cut a small hole in the middle. Brush all over with whisked egg yolk, twice if possible.

6 Place in the oven and cook for 10 minutes, then lower the oven to 170°C/325°F/gas 3 and bake for a further 45–50 minutes. Remove from the oven and leave to cool slightly before serving. Delicious with a crunchy chicory (Belgian endive) salad.

ASPARAGUS, PARSLEY & CHESTNUT MUSHROOM RISOTTO

SERVES 4

PREPARATION TIME: 25 minutes,
    plus 45 minutes for the stock
COOKING TIME: 35 minutes

1 litre/35fl oz/4¼ cups Vegetable
    Stock (see page 25)
1 small bunch of green asparagus,
    peeled and chopped but tips left
    whole
40g/1½oz butter
1 tbsp olive oil
1 large shallot or small onion, finely
    chopped
100g/3½oz chestnut (cremini)
    mushrooms, washed and diced
300g/10½oz risotto rice, such as
    Arborio or carnaroli
60ml/2fl oz/scant ¼ cup dry white
    wine
1 tbsp mascarpone cheese
1 tbsp crème fraîche
1½ tbsp finely chopped curly
    parsley
sea salt and freshly ground white
    pepper
pecorino cheese, to serve

When I was a guest chef on *Saturday Kitchen* together with a certain Italian gentlemen named Gennaro Contaldo, I remember he told me that in Italy there is no one special way of doing risotto, but so many ways. Every household, every village, every town and region has its own version. It's the same in France. At home, we like our risotto a little bit loose. This recipe is for a risotto which I particularly like; these ingredients go so well together – and the nuttiness coming from the mascarpone makes it extra special!

1 Pour the stock into a saucepan over a medium heat, bring to the boil, then reduce the heat and keep it at a simmer. Bring another saucepan of water to the boil, add a pinch of salt and throw in the asparagus tips. When water boils again, reduce the heat and simmer for 3–4 minutes, or until the tips are cooked but still firm, then refresh in cold water and set aside on some paper towel.

2 Melt the butter with the olive oil in a large, heavy-based saucepan over a medium heat. Add the shallots, mushrooms and the chopped asparagus spears, and sauté for 2–3 minutes until the shallots have softened and are just starting to colour. Add the rice and stir so that it's well coated in the butter and shallot mixture. Add the white wine and let it evaporate to remove the acidity. Add a ladleful of the stock and stir continuously until it is almost all absorbed, then repeat, adding the stock little by little, for about 18 minutes until the rice is cooked. It should be plump and still have some bite.

3 Now add the mascarpone and crème fraîche, folding them in gently. Check the seasoning, then add the asparagus tips and parsley, making sure you keep the rice warm. Serve immediately with a lovely pecorino ready to be grated over the top. A wild rocket (arugula) salad would be a bonus!

CRUSHED STRAWBERRIES & TARRAGON CRÈME FRAÎCHE

SERVES 4
PREPARATION TIME 20 minutes,
    plus 20 minutes macerating

800g/1lb 12oz/5⅓ cups
    strawberries, hulled and
    roughly chopped
115g/4oz/½ cup caster
    (superfine) sugar
juice of 1 small lemon
250g/9oz/1 cup crème fraîche
1 tbsp chopped tarragon leaves
300g/10½oz fresh brioche loaf,
    thickly sliced

This recipe is so French and holds great childhood memories for me. I must have picked strawberries in my garden hundreds of times, and every time with the same enthusiasm. I was always the first to answer when Mum said, "Who wants to go to pick some strawberries?" And I was often the last to come back as I was too busy eating them! We'd enjoy a big bowl with a slice of toasted brioche spread with lovely fresh farm butter – so good! But here is a new way to serve them with crème fraîche and freshly chopped tarragon.

1 Mix the strawberries with the sugar and lemon juice in a bowl, cover and leave to macerate in the refrigerator for 15–20 minutes.

2 Preheat the grill (broiler). Remove the strawberries from the fridge, add the crème fraîche and mix together, lightly crushing the fruit with the back of a fork. Add the tarragon and stir once more.

3 Toast the bread and serve with the tarragon cream strawberries.

CHAPTER 3
FROM MEADOW, STREAM & HEDGEROW

I love walking through meadows and along streams and hedgerows. In June, when I'm writing this, I can see so many flowers with such distinctive shapes, colours and scents. It is such a feast for the eyes and also a playground for so much wildlife: field mice, rabbits and the ever-so-beautiful and noble hare, proud and elegant, often found at the same spot overlooking his kingdom. In the distance a stream makes its way through the meadow with the delicate sound of running water, where herons and kingfishers can be found waiting patiently for the next catch of wild trout or other smaller fish; where, sometimes, crayfish hide and wild watercress and even water asparagus can be found.

SALMON MARINATED IN FENNEL & CORIANDER

SERVES 4
PREPARATION TIME 20 minutes, plus
24 hours curing

600g/1lb 5oz salmon fillet, skin on
2 tbsp sea salt, plus extra
    for seasoning
2 tbsp caster (superfine) sugar
1 tsp ground cumin
1 tsp ground coriander
2 small fennel bulbs, outer
    sections removed
finely grated zest of 1 and juice of
    ½ grapefruit
2 tbsp roughly chopped coriander
    (cilantro) leaves
1 tbsp olive oil
freshly ground black pepper

I have always loved marinated salmon and sea trout. It makes for a refreshing and delicate dish, which is unusual for your guests as very few people make this at home. It is very much up to you which herbs and fruit you use, as there are many ways to make this recipe, but coriander (cilantro) works well, chives and chervil too. Chervil is fairly difficult to find but as it is one of the tastiest herbs around, you might like to grow your own. You can also use other citrus fruits instead of the grapefruit. Orange, lemon, blood orange or kumquat all work well, but lime is my favourite. As long as you get the essential sugar-salt combination, you will have a great spring or early summer first course.

I Put the salmon, skin-side down, on a large piece of cling film (plastic wrap). Mix together the salt, sugar, cumin and ground coriander, sprinkle the mixture over the flesh side of the salmon, then finish with a little pepper. Using a mandolin, grate one of the fennel bulbs over the top of the mixture and press it down so it totally covers the fish. Wrap the whole lot in the cling film and put, flesh-side down, in a small baking sheet. Cover with another small tray and put a tin or similar weight on top, then put it into the refrigerator and leave to cure for 24 hours in total, following the instructions in step 2 during that time.

2 After the first 8–10 hours, remove the weight and turn the fish over, flesh-side up. Alternate between flesh-side up and down every 4–5 hours following this. You can go to bed, just turn it before you go to bed, then again when you get up!

3 The following day, remove the salmon from the refrigerator and carefully rinse it under cold running water to remove the excess cure, then pat dry on a clean dish towel. Slice as thinly as you can and put on a plate, spreading the slices attractively. Season with a little pepper, a tiny touch of sea salt, some of the grapefruit zest and juice and half the coriander (cilantro) leaves.

4 Finely slice the second fennel bulb on a mandolin or by hand, then toss it in a small bowl with the oil, grapefruit zest and the remaining grapefruit juice and coriander (cilantro) leaves. Season with a little pepper to taste, then serve with the salmon.

GOATS' CHEESE & DANDELION SALAD

SERVES 4
PREPARATION TIME 15 minutes,
plus making the croûtons
COOKING TIME 3 minutes

1 tbsp blanched hazelnuts
4 handfuls of dandelion leaves,
washed thoroughly
150g/5½oz soft goats' cheese log,
such as Golden Cross or Ste
Maure, rind removed, crumbled
1 small bunch of chives, cut into
5cm/2in lengths
1 tbsp chopped chervil leaves
2 small oranges
1 tbsp small Croûtons
(see page 27)

FOR THE DRESSING
1 tbsp clear honey
2–3 tbsp Chardonnay vinegar or
white wine vinegar
3 tbsp extra virgin olive oil
sea salt and freshly ground black
pepper

This is definitely a salad to try as it's both interesting and very different. We used to eat a more traditional version at my aunt's house and she would send us into the garden to collect the dandelion leaves – called *pissenlit* in French! We would bring back loads and then prepare them with my uncle. His version of this salad included lardons but my vegetarian alternative features a crumbly goats' cheese and tangy orange to go with the bitterness of the dandelion leaves. It's a lovely summer dish to serve with a glass of Viognier.

1 To toast the hazelnuts, put them in a small, dry frying pan (skillet) over a medium heat. Toast for 2–3 minutes, shaking the pan occasionally, until the nuts are lightly browned all over. Tip out onto a plate, leave to cool, then lightly crush.

2 Put the dandelion leaves on four large plates. Scatter the goats' cheese over the top, then the chives and chervil.

3 Peel the oranges, removing all the pith. Cut into segments, then cut each segment into 3 pieces, reserving the juice. Scatter the pieces over the salad, then finish with the toasted hazelnuts and croûtons.

4 To make the dressing, whisk together the honey, reserved orange juice, vinegar and oil in a small bowl until almost opaque, or you can blitz it with a hand-held blender. Season with salt and pepper to taste, then drizzle the dressing over the salad and serve immediately.

WILD ASPARAGUS, WILD GARLIC & POTATO SOUP

Wild asparagus can be found in the spring, between April and June. It is more common in Italy and the South of France – in fact, it can be bought over there at street markets. It is earthy, grassy and nutty, very much reminiscent of the surrounding terrain. It also has been harvested on the Greek Islands for centuries. This soup makes a great first course. If you can't find wild asparagus, use regular asparagus when in season, from the end of April until June.

SERVES 4
PREPARATION TIME 20 minutes, plus
    making the stock
COOKING TIME 35–40 minutes

30g/1oz butter
1 small shallot, chopped
200g/7oz wild asparagus (or
    regular if you can't get wild),
    peeled and chopped
1 large potato (about 120g/4oz),
    peeled and diced
800ml/28fl oz/scant 3½ cups
    Vegetable Stock (see page 25)
400g/14oz wild garlic leaves
4 tbsp crème fraîche
sea salt and freshly ground white
    pepper
crôutons (see page 27) or fried
    pancetta, to serve (optional)

1 Melt the butter in a saucepan over a low heat. Add the shallots and asparagus and sauté for 4–5 minutes, then add the diced potato and cook for 2 more minutes until just softened but not coloured, so keep the heat low.

2 Add the stock, then turn the heat up and simmer for 10–12 minutes, or until the potatoes have softened. Remove the pan from the heat, add the wild garlic and set aside for 4–5 minutes.

3 Transfer the mixture to a blender, season with a little salt and pepper, then blend until smooth, adding the crème fraîche at the end. Check the seasoning. To make sure you are happy with the texture, strain the soup through a sieve (strainer) into a clean saucepan and warm through gently, so as not to lose the fabulous, vibrant green colour. Serve with crôutons or fried pancetta, if you like.

WILD NETTLE, WILD WATERCRESS & POTATO SOUP

Wild nettle and watercress are full of vitamins A and C, iron and magnesium, so they're really good for us. The best time of year to collect them is April to May. Both are what we call superfoods. It's a shame wild nettle is so underused now; it was very popular in the past, and no wonder, as it's so full of goodness. Be sure to collect it when it's young and before it has flowered because it gives its goodness to the flowers rather than to us! Beware of their sting when picking them – but don't worry, this will go away when you blanch them.

SERVES 4
PREPARATION TIME 35 minutes
COOKING TIME 35–40 minutes

30g/1oz butter
2 shallots, chopped
300g/10½oz potatoes, peeled and diced
1 litre/35fl oz/4¼ cups Vegetable Stock (see page 25)
250g/9oz wild watercress, stalks removed and washed
200g/7oz wild nettle, stalks removed, washed and blanched
4 tbsp crème fraîche
sea salt and freshly ground white pepper
crusty bread, to serve

1 Melt the butter in a saucepan over a low heat. Add the shallots and cook, stirring occasionally, for 3–4 minutes. Add the potatoes and the vegetable stock, bring to a simmer over a medium heat and cook for about 12–15 minutes, or until the potatoes have softened.

2 Remove the pan from the heat, add the watercress, cover and set aside for 4–5 minutes. Transfer the mixture to a blender, lightly season, add the blanched nettles, then blend until smooth, adding the crème fraîche at the end. Check the seasoning again; both the wild nettle and watercress can take it.

3 Strain the soup through a sieve (strainer) into a clean saucepan and warm through gently, so as not to lose that wonderful, vibrant green colour. Serve with crusty bread and enjoy.

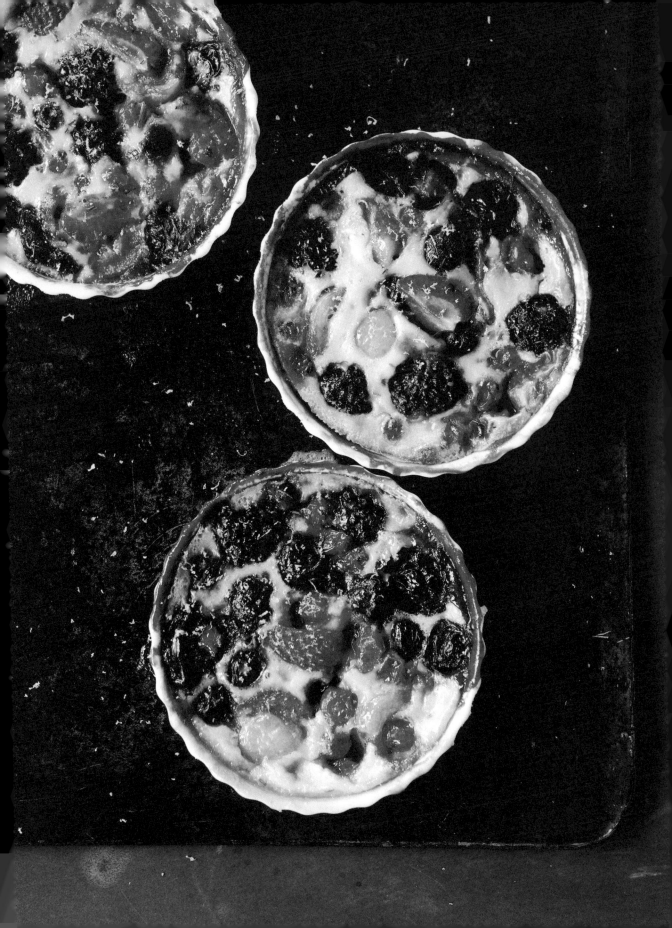

RED FRUIT CLAFOUTIS WITH FLAVOURED GREEK YOGURT

Imagine all the colours and flavours of these lovely summer berries in a rosemary-infused clafoutis. And the individual clafoutis are really just as good made with thyme or lavender flowers, but make sure the flowers are edible and untreated. Another great flavour combination is crushed black pepper and grated lime zest – enjoy experimenting!

SERVES 4
PREPARATION TIME 15 minutes, plus
    1 hour macerating
COOKING TIME 12 minutes

60g/2¼oz/heaped ⅓ cup
    blueberries
60g/2¼oz/heaped ⅓ cup
    blackberries
60g/2¼oz/½ cup redcurrants
60g/2¼oz/scant ⅓ cup cherries,
    pitted
60g/2¼oz/heaped ⅓ cup
    strawberries, hulled and
    quartered
80g/2¾oz/⅓ cup caster
    (superfine) sugar
½ tsp very finely chopped young
    rosemary leaves (from the tips)
4 tbsp Greek yogurt
50g/1¾oz unsalted butter, half
    softened and half melted
60g/2¼oz/½ cup plain
    (all-purpose) flour, sifted
a pinch of salt
1 egg
2 egg yolks
200ml/7fl oz/scant 1 cup full-fat
    milk

1 Wash the fruit, drain and put into a bowl. Add 2 tablespoons of the caster (superfine) sugar and the rosemary and turn to coat. Cover and leave to macerate at room temperature for 1 hour to release some of the juices from the fruit.

2 Preheat the oven to 180°C/350°F/gas 4. Strain the fruit and add half of the juices to the yogurt, reserving the other half. Mix well, then cover and chill until ready to serve.

3 Grease four large ramekins with the softened butter and sprinkle with 2 tablespoons of the caster (superfine) sugar, carefully turning the ramekins to make sure the sugar coats the insides, then tipping out any excess.

4 Sift the flour and salt into a mixing bowl. In a separate bowl, whisk together the egg, egg yolks and remaining sugar, then slowly add to the flour, mixing until incorporated and smooth. Gradually add the milk and the reserved fruit juices, stirring until the mixture has the consistency of a pancake batter, then add the melted butter and mix well until combined.

5 Divide the berries into the prepared ramekins and pour the batter over to just below the top. Bake for 10–12 minutes until set and golden brown. Serve with a dollop of the flavoured Greek yogurt, if you like, or you can serve it separately.

BALSAMIC & LIME RASPBERRIES WITH GOATS' MILK ICE CREAM

This was a bit of a discovery for me. I've been thinking about making a goats' milk ice cream for a while and I was really pleased with the results as it is easy to make and the lift from the lime zest is perfect. Buy raspberries in season for the best flavour and you need a very good, aged balsamic vinegar for the marinade – one that is slightly syrupy but not too acidic. It will specify the age on the label. The finished dessert is summer itself!

SERVES 4
PREPARATION TIME 20 minutes, plus at least 3½ hours freezing
COOKING TIME 5 minutes

1 tbsp fennel seeds
1 tbsp icing (confectioners') sugar

FOR THE GOATS' MILK ICE CREAM
300ml/10½fl oz/scant 1¼ cups goats' milk
100ml/3½fl oz/ scant ½ cup goats' cream
200g/7oz/heaped ¾ cup natural goats' milk yogurt
120g/4¼oz/scant 1 cup icing (confectioners') sugar
finely grated zest of ½ lime

FOR THE BALSAMIC AND LIME RASPBERRIES
200g/7oz/scant 1⅔ cups raspberries
3 tbsp good-quality balsamic vinegar
finely grated zest of ½ lime, plus extra for sprinkling
2 drops of lime juice

1 Line a medium-deep freezerproof tray with baking paper. Put all the ice cream ingredients in a bowl and whisk together until smooth. Pour into the prepared tray and freeze for at least 3 hours, or until hard. Remove and break into small chunks, put into a food processor and blend briefly to a smooth, firm purée – you don't want the mixture to defrost too much. Spoon into a small freezerproof container, smooth the top, cover and return to the freezer for 25–30 minutes until hard again.

2 Meanwhile, put the raspberries in a large bowl with 2 tablespoons of the balsamic vinegar, the lime zest and juice. Gently stir until combined, cover with cling film (plastic wrap) and put in the refrigerator.

3 Preheat the oven to 200°C/400°F/gas 6 and line a baking sheet with baking paper. Put the fennel seeds on the prepared baking sheet and dust with the icing (confectioners') sugar until lightly coated. Put in the oven for 4–5 minutes until light golden and caramelized. Return to the oven for a couple of minutes at a time if they are not ready. Remove and leave to cool, breaking up any seeds that may have stuck together.

4 Remove the raspberries from the refrigerator and, using a slotted spoon, spoon into serving bowls and put a small scoop of ice cream one on top of each bowl of raspberries. Drizzle any of the liquid from the raspberries and the remaining balsamic over the top and finish with a scattering of caramelized fennel seeds and a little extra lime zest.

APPLE, RASPBERRY & THYME PUFFS

SERVES 6
PREPARATION TIME 30 minutes,
    plus cooling
COOKING TIME 15 minutes

80g/2¾oz/⅓ cup caster
    (superfine) sugar
4 large Bramley apples or similar
    cooking apples, peeled, halved,
    cored and roughly chopped
a little flour, for dusting
750g/1lb 10oz ready rolled all-
    butter puff pastry, cut into
    12 x fluted 7.5cm/3in discs
1 egg
a pinch of salt
125g/4½oz/1 cup fresh raspberries
leaves from 1 thyme sprig

Depending on whether I had time to pop into the baker, I used to eat these *chaussons* – literally "slippers" – on the way to or from school, but we used to make them at home too. They are like apple turnovers – the same idea, but made in a slightly different way. The puff pastry gives them a beautifully warm, buttery crunch just before you reach the fruit, full of sweet acidity. There should be more fruit than pastry, so make sure the mix is not too runny or they may be tricky to close. And I can assure you that apple, raspberry and freshly picked thyme leaves are fabulous together!

1 Heat a large, non-stick frying pan (skillet) over a medium heat, add the sugar, 2 tablespoons of water and all the apples. Cover and cook gently for 8–10 minutes until the apples are cooked but not completely puréed. Remove the lid, then turn the heat up slightly so the liquid just starts to evaporate. Keep moving the apples around the pan with a spatula to help drive off the moisture and dry out the apples until you have a dry purée. Transfer to a bowl and leave to cool. (The purée must be dry and cold before you start to make your *chaussons*, otherwise the pastry will just melt and collapse.)

2 Preheat the oven to 180°C/350°F/gas 4 and line a baking sheet with baking paper. Dust a work surface with a very little flour, then lay a pastry disc on the dusted surface and roll with a rolling pin just once to the top and the bottom, so the disc is slightly oval. Repeat with the other discs. Lay all the discs out in front of you on the work surface with the oval shape top to bottom. Mix the egg and salt with 1 tablespoon of water in a small bowl to make an egg wash.

3 Put a spoonful of apple purée on the bottom one-third of the oval, 1.5cm/¾in from the sides. Put 4 raspberries on top of the purée and a little sprinkle of the thyme, then brush the egg wash around the bottom edge of the oval – nothing so far should have come above the halfway mark. Fold the top half of the pastry over to cover the filling, then gently press the edges together to seal. Brush the top of the pastry with the egg wash, taking care not to get any on the back of the folded pastry – this will run down and make the pastry stick to the tray. Using a spatula, carefully lift each one onto the prepared baking sheet. Use the back of a fork to make a criss-cross pattern on top.

4 Bake for 12 minutes until the pastry is golden brown. If not, return them to the oven for a further 2–3 minutes. Remove from the oven and serve warm with a cup of coffee or Earl Grey tea, ideally in front of the fire!

LEMON, WILD THYME & DANDELION FLOWER CAKE

These three wonderful ingredients transform this classic into something special. The scent of wild thyme, the acidity and fragrance of fresh lemon singing on your tongue and the sweet bitterness from the dandelion flower – they go so well together. This was another experiment during lockdown in spring 2020 and we all loved it. Prepare the tea, I'm on my way!

SERVES 6–8
PREPARATION TIME 30 minutes
COOKING TIME 45–55 minutes

60g/2¼oz unsalted butter, melted, plus extra for greasing
170g/6oz/1¼ cup plain (all-purpose) flour, plus extra for dusting
7 tbsp double (heavy) cream
1 small bunch of wild thyme
1 tsp baking powder
4 eggs
150g/5½oz/¾ cup caster (superfine) sugar
a pinch of salt
juice and zest of 1 lemon
1 handful of fresh dandelion flowers, sepal and bracts removed

FOR THE WILD THYME SYRUP
juice of 1 lime
juice of 1 lemon
2 wild thyme sprigs
4 tbsp caster (superfine) sugar

I Preheat the oven to 170°C/325°F/gas 3. Butter a 1kg/2lb 4oz loaf tin or use a silicone cake mould and dust with flour.

2 Put the cream in a small pan over a low heat and add the thyme. Heat gently until the cream is just starting to simmer, then remove from the heat and set the pan aside, covered with clingfilm (plastic wrap) for 15 minutes to allow the flavours to infuse.

3 Meanwhile, sift the flour and baking powder into a bowl. Crack the eggs into another large bowl and add the sugar and salt. Whisk using an electric whisk for a good 8–10 minutes until pale, thick and doubled in volume. Strain the thyme-infused cream, then fold into the egg and sugar mixture along with lemon juice and zest. Add the sifted flour and baking powder. Fold everything together gently. Finally, fold in the melted butter and half the dandelion flowers. Pour the mixture into the prepared tin or silicone cake mould. Bake for 35–40 minutes, or until a skewer inserted into the centre comes out clean. If not quite ready, bake for a further 5 minutes and check again. Remove from the oven and leave to cool.

3 Meanwhile, make the wild thyme syrup. Put the lime and lemon juice, wild thyme and sugar into a saucepan over a low heat. Once the sugar has dissolved, turn the heat up to medium and simmer until the syrup has reduced down to about 2 spoonfuls – just enough to drizzle on the cooled cake.

4 Sprinkle with the rest of the dandelion flowers. Slice and serve.

EARL GREY RICE PUDDING WITH BLACKBERRY MARMALADE

SERVES 4
PREPARATION TIME 5 minutes
COOKING TIME 40 minutes

FOR THE BLACKBERRY MARMALADE
250g/9oz/1⅔ cups blackberries
60g/2½oz/heaped ¼ cup caster
   (superfine) sugar

FOR THE RICE PUDDING
110g/3¾oz/½ cup Carnaroli
   risotto rice
500ml/17fl oz/2 cups full-fat milk
200ml/7fl oz/scant 1 cup
   whipping cream
4 Earl Grey teabags
2 tbsp caster (superfine) sugar

Most of my childhood memories are great – except for rice pudding. Sorry, Maman! She used to make it so often that I didn't want to eat it any more for quite a long time. This recipe somehow brings rice pudding to life. Why is the addition of blackberries, for me, ideal? Because not only do you need their acidity, but also their powerful flavour that is so specific to them. The marmalade is even better if you pick the blackberries yourself in late summer and make it from scratch. I use carnaroli rice as I think it is the perfect grain for the dish: strong enough and nutty enough too. Cook it very gently with all the other ingredients and it will taste delicious, but take note that I said "gently"; if you have the heat too high, the grain will explode and the mixture will burn. This is a very satisfying dish which can be magic!

1 Start by making the blackberry marmalade. Put the blackberries and sugar in a non-stick frying or sauté pan over a low heat and cook for 30–40 minutes, depending on how soft the berries are, stirring occasionally, until there is no juice left and the blackberries are fully cooked. You want the blackberries to release their juices as they cook so don't be tempted to increase the heat. Eventually, they will dehydrate and turn into a marmalade.

2 Meanwhile make the rice pudding. Put the rice, milk, cream and teabags in a saucepan. Stir once to make sure that all the rice is dispersed through the liquid, then bring to the boil over a medium heat. Turn the heat down to low and simmer for 18 minutes – you shouldn't need to stir, but just check a couple of times.

3 Remove the rice from the heat. There should be a little liquid left in the saucepan. Remove the teabags and squeeze them dry over the saucepan so the liquid goes into the rice, but be careful not to pierce the teabags. Only then do you add the sugar and fold it delicately into the cooked rice, adding a little more to taste. Keep turning the rice very gently for about 5 minutes to cool it down.

4 Serve the rice topped with a spoonful of the fresh blackberry marmalade.

RASPBERRY TART WITH CRÈME PÂTISSIÈRE & ROSEMARY

I have included a few recipes with raspberries in this chapter, and with herbs too, but I can assure you they are totally different. Here, for example, the touch of grated lime, the crème fraîche and the rosemary bring a unique balance to the dessert with its crunchy Breton *sablé* pastry.

SERVES 4
PREPARATION TIME 25 minutes,
    plus 20 minutes infusing
COOKING TIME 30 minutes

300g/10½oz/heaped 2⅓ cups
    raspberries
icing (confectioners') sugar,
    to decorate
grated zest of ½ lime
1 tsp chopped rosemary leaves
2 tbsp crème fraîche

FOR THE SABLÉ PASTRY
90g/3¼ oz/¾ cup plain (all-
    purpose) flour
1 tsp baking powder
70g/2½oz/heaped ½ cup icing
    (confectioners') sugar
60g/2¼oz unsalted butter, softened
a pinch of salt
2 egg yolks
grated zest of ½ lime

FOR THE CRÈME PÂTISSIÈRE
250ml/9fl oz/1 cup full-fat milk
½ vanilla pod, split lengthways
3 egg yolks
50g/1¾oz/scant ¼ cup caster
    (superfine) sugar
25g/1oz/scant ¼ cup cornflour
    (corn starch)
1 tbsp unsalted butter
juice of ½ lime

1 Preheat the oven to 170°C/325°C/gas 3. To make the *sablé* pastry, sift together the flour and baking powder in a bowl. Whisk together the sugar, butter, salt and egg yolks, using an electric whisk, until light and fluffy. Fold in the flour mixture and lime zest to make a soft dough. Flatten between two sheets of baking paper to about 1cm/½in thick, then transfer to a baking sheet, lifting off the top sheet of baking paper. Bake for 12–18 minutes until light golden. Remove from the oven and cut immediately into an 18cm/7in square while it is still soft and pliable, but then leave it to cool before lifting off the tray.

2 To make the crème pâtissière, put the milk in a saucepan over a low heat. Use a sharp knife to scrape the vanilla seeds into the milk, whisk the milk, then add the vanilla pod as well. Heat the milk until it is almost simmering, then remove from the heat, cover with cling film (plastic wrap) and leave to infuse for about 20 minutes. Remove the vanilla pod from the milk, rinse and dry on paper towel as you can use it again.

3 Meanwhile, whisk the egg yolks and sugar until light, thick and creamy. Gradually add the cornflour (corn starch), a spoonful at a time, whisking well after each addition to avoid any lumps forming. Slowly pour half the infused milk into the egg mixture, beating as you pour, then transfer the mixture back into the saucepan with the remaining milk. Put over a medium-low heat and stir continuously and quickly for about 10 minutes, or until the mixture begins to thicken. Remove from the heat, whisk in the butter and lime juice and continue to stir until the mixture has cooled down and is lovely and smooth, thick and slightly trembling.

4 Spread the crème pâtissière about 5mm/¼in thick over the pastry, leaving a small margin clear around the edge. Put the raspberries in lines over the top of the crème pâtissière to cover it completely. Dust with a shake of sifted icing (confectioners') sugar, and sprinkle with the lime zest and a little of the chopped rosemary. Mix the remaining rosemary with the crème fraîche and spoon into a piping bag, then pipe a small dot of crème fraîche on the top of every other raspberry all over the tart. Add a tiny piece of rosemary to each crème fraîche dot.

CHAPTER 4
FROM RIVER & SEA

Who doesn't like rivers and seas and all the sounds that come with them? Or the feel of the salty spray on your face when a sudden wind caresses the water? Or the gorgeous rush of the running river when it makes its way down a rocky terrain, creating cascades of beauty before calming at the final pool, which mirrors our own image? Or watching the fishermen waiting to catch what might perhaps be lunch or dinner, or laying a trap for lobster, crab or crayfish? What a beautiful sight it is, especially in the late evening when the sun reflects on the water and makes it glitter with silver.

PICKLED MACKEREL WITH WARM POTATO & RADISH SALAD

This colourful salad reminds me of the time I spent in Sweden as it is fairly typical of something you would eat for breakfast there. I was staying in the Grand Hotel in Lund and remember so well the breakfast table laden with smoked, marinated and pickled fish. It was amazing! My version features warm potatoes and fresh coriander (cilantro) with a French yogurt dressing. You could use some of the pickling liquid instead of the French dressing, if you like.

SERVES 4
PREPARATION TIME 20 minutes, plus 30 minutes cooling and 6 hours marinating
COOKING TIME 25 minutes

2 large pinches of coriander seeds
120ml/4fl oz/½ cup white balsamic vinegar
120ml/4fl oz/½ cup Chardonnay vinegar or white wine vinegar
4 tbsp light soft brown sugar
4 whole mackerel, about 250g/9oz each, heads removed, filleted and skin lightly scored
1 tbsp sea salt
1 small red onion, finely sliced
2 coriander (cilantro) sprigs, plus 2 tbsp chopped coriander leaves
1 garlic clove
300g/10½oz small new potatoes, such as Charlotte or Pink Fir Apple, scrubbed
3 tbsp French Dressing (see page 26)
2 tbsp Mayonnaise (see page 26)
1 tbsp Greek yogurt
finely grated zest and juice of 1 lime
8 large radishes, very thinly sliced
1 spring onion (scallion), thinly sliced diagonally
sea salt and freshly ground black pepper

1 Heat a frying pan (skillet) over a medium heat. Add the coriander seeds and lightly toast for 1 minute, shaking the pan occasionally, until they colour slightly and smell aromatic. Tip them onto a plate and lightly crush with the blade of a knife. Leave to one side.

2 Pour both vinegars into a small saucepan. Add the sugar and put over a medium heat to warm for 2–3 minutes, or just long enough for the sugar to dissolve, stirring occasionally. Remove from the heat, stir in the toasted coriander seeds and leave to cool.

3 Put the mackerel in a shallow, non-metallic dish, skin-side down, and sprinkle with the sea salt. Pour over the cold vinegar mixture and top with three-quarters of the red onion. Cover with cling film (plastic wrap) and leave to marinate in the refrigerator for about 6 hours until pickled, turning the fish halfway through.

4 Just before the mackerel is ready, put a saucepan of water, one-third full, on to simmer with a steamer insert on top. Put the remaining red onion, the coriander (cilantro) sprigs and garlic in the water. Put the potatoes in the steamer, cover and cook for 12–18 minutes until just tender. Turn the heat off and continue to steam the potatoes in the residual heat for a further 5 minutes.

5 While the potatoes are cooking, whisk together the French dressing, mayonnaise and Greek yogurt in a bowl, then stir in the lime juice and zest. Season with salt and pepper to taste. When the potatoes are cool enough to handle, cut into 5mm/¼in slices and put in a large serving bowl. Add the radishes and chopped coriander (cilantro), then drizzle the dressing over and toss gently without breaking up the potato slices. Scatter with the spring onion (scallion). Lift the mackerel out of the pickling liquor and put on serving plates. Scatter some of the red onion over the top and serve with the potato salad.

SCALLOPS WITH CAULIFLOWER PURÉE & HAZELNUT DRESSING

This noble shellfish is delicate and sweet, and simply needs sealing briefly in butter and olive oil before serving. Try to find scallops in the shell, but if you can't, you can use prepared or frozen scallops. The apple lends a fresh crispness to the dish and offers a contrast to the softness of the scallops and the cauliflower purée. Enjoy with a glass of Condrieu or Viognier.

SERVES 4
PREPARATION TIME 20 minutes
COOKING TIME 45 minutes

1 cauliflower, leaves and stem removed, cut into large florets
110g/3¾oz unsalted butter
2 tbsp olive oil
12 scallops, rinsed
5mm/¼in slice of crisp green eating apple, such as Granny Smith, unpeeled, cut into thin strips
sea salt and freshly ground black pepper

FOR THE HAZELNUT DRESSING
1 tsp hazelnut oil
2 tsp extra virgin olive oil
1 tsp white balsamic vinegar
½ tsp finely chopped celery leaves

1 Cut 2 of the large cauliflower florets into 12 mini florets, about 1cm/½in each, and leave to one side. Bring a large saucepan of salted water to the boil over a high heat, add the large cauliflower florets and cook for 7–8 minutes until very soft when pierced with a knife. Drain and pat dry with paper towel.

2 Heat a large sauté pan over a medium-low heat. Add 75g/2½oz of the butter, half the olive oil and the cooked cauliflower, then fry for 30 minutes, stirring occasionally, until the cauliflower is very soft (actually overcooked) and golden brown. Keep the heat medium-low and take care not to burn the butter or the cauliflower.

3 Meanwhile, make the hazelnut dressing. Whisk together the hazelnut oil, extra virgin olive oil and white balsamic vinegar in a bowl until just emulsified. Bring a small saucepan of salted water to the boil, add the small cauliflower florets and boil for 2 minutes until just tender. Drain and refresh under cold running water, then pat dry and add to the dressing.

4 Put the sautéed cauliflower in a blender with 2 tablespoons of hot water and blitz to a fine, smooth purée. Add a little extra hot water if the purée is too thick. Season with salt and pepper to taste, then pass the purée through a fine sieve (strainer), using a ladle to help you, into a small, clean saucepan. Cover with a lid and keep warm.

5 Remove the roes from the scallops, trim off any tough flesh and remove any veins, then season with salt and pepper. Heat half the remaining butter and oil in a non-stick frying pan (skillet) over a medium heat. When the butter is a hazelnut colour, add half the scallops and cook for 1½–2 minutes, depending on their size, until light golden. Turn the scallops over and cook for a further 1 minute, then set aside on paper towel and keep warm. Repeat with the remaining oil and butter to cook the remaining scallops.

6 Add the celery leaves to the dressing. Top the cauliflower purée with the scallops, then drizzle with the dressing. Scatter the florets over the top and finish with the apple strips to serve.

LANGOUSTINE OR PRAWN CEVICHE

SERVES 4
PREPARATION TIME 20 minutes,
   plus 3 hours marinating

20 medium to large raw, peeled
   langoustines or tiger prawns
   (jumbo shrimp), cleaned and
   intestinal thread removed
grated zest and juice of 1 lime
1 red chilli, deseeded and
   finely chopped
2 garlic cloves, crushed
2 tbsp Chardonnay vinegar
a pinch of sea salt
1 tsp chopped tarragon leaves
1 hard, green eating apple, such as
   Granny Smith
Mayonnaise (see page 26),
   flavoured with chilli, tarragon or
   garlic, to serve

What is ceviche? It is originally a Spanish word and is a speciality of Peru but now it is widely available in France. It is basically raw fish or shellfish marinated in plenty of citrus juice, fresh herbs, onion, shallots and other flavourings. If you use shellfish, make sure they are fresh or freshly frozen. Trust your fishmonger, as they will have the expertise you need. The best time for shellfish is from February to April when the quantity is plenty and the quality and flavour is the best. You will see that here I use garlic, but just enough to bring a little accent to the dish. Enjoy your ceviche served with mango or avocado, sweet potato and red onion salad with flat leaf parsley. I use Chardonnay vinegar in many recipes in preference to ordinary white wine vinegar as it imparts a better flavour.

1 Reserve 4 whole langoustines, then cut the rest into 1cm/½in chunks and put in a non-metallic bowl. Add the whole langoustines, then add the lime zest and juice, chilli, garlic, vinegar and a pinch of salt and gently fold everything together. Cover and leave to marinate in the refrigerator for 2–3 hours.

2 Just before you are ready to serve, core the apple, then cut it into thin slices from top to bottom, discarding the ends that are all skin. Stack the slices and cut through them to form thin matchsticks.

3 When ready to serve, remove the langoustines from the refrigerator, take out the whole langoustines, then add the tarragon and all but 1 tablespoon of the apple and fold together. Spoon the mixture into four glasses, then hang the whole langoustines on the edge of the glasses. Scatter the remaining apple over the tops and serve immediately with mayonnaise flavoured with your chosen spice or herb.

SCALLOP SOUFFLÉ WITH MUSHROOM & TARRAGON CREAM

SERVES 4
PREPARATION TIME 30 minutes, plus
  making the stock
COOKING TIME 12 minutes

100g/3½oz scallops, rinsed
1 large egg
185ml/6fl oz/¾ cup
  whipping cream
20g/¾oz unsalted butter
125g/4½oz button mushrooms,
  roughly chopped
1 tbsp roughly chopped
  tarragon leaves, plus 4 tiny
  tarragon sprigs
4 tbsp Vegetable Stock (see
  page 25)
sea salt and freshly ground white
  pepper

This is one of my favourite recipes to serve to friends. Although there's egg and cream, don't think for a minute that the soufflés will be heavy – on the contrary, they are fantastically light.

1 Remove the roes from the scallops, trim off any tough flesh and remove any veins. Put the scallops, egg and 4 tablespoons of the cream into a blender. Season with salt and white pepper and blend to a very fine, smooth, shiny purée. Pass the scallop mixture through a fine sieve (strainer) into a bowl. Whip 4 tablespoons of the remaining cream until soft peaks form, then whisk it into the purée. Spoon into a piping bag and put in the refrigerator.

2 Line a plate that will fit inside a large steamer basket with baking paper, then put four 5cm/2in diameter x 5cm/2in deep chef's rings on top, making sure that they do not touch each other. Cut four bands of baking paper 7.5cm/3in long x 5cm/2in deep and use to line the chef's rings. The paper needs to sit snugly inside the rings with the ends overlapping.

3 Remove the scallop mix from the refrigerator and snip the end to give a 1cm/½in opening. Pipe the filling into each ring until two-thirds full and about 1cm/½in below the rim, making sure that you hold onto the ring to stop it slipping. Cover the plate loosely with cling film (plastic wrap) so that no condensation can get in, yet the soufflés have space to rise. Put a large saucepan of water on to simmer, with a steamer insert on top. Put the plate of soufflés in the steamer, cover, then turn the heat down as low as possible and steam for 12 minutes until risen. Turn the heat off, remove the lid and leave the soufflés to rest for 2 minutes.

4 While the soufflés are cooking, make the mushroom cream. Heat a large frying pan (skillet) over a high heat. Add the butter and mushrooms and sauté for 3–4 minutes until they just turn golden brown. Add the chopped tarragon and toss to combine. Pour in the stock and the remaining cream and bring to a simmer, then season with salt and pepper to taste. Pour into a blender and blend to a fine, light, foamy purée.

5 Divide the mushroom cream into four soup plates. Remove the plate from the steamer and carefully take off the cling film (plastic wrap) then, using a small palette knife, transfer a soufflé to the centre of a plate of mushroom cream. Slide out the palette knife, holding the edge of the ring so that it doesn't move around. Lift the ring off and gently peel away the paper lining. Repeat with the remaining soufflés, then top each one with a tiny tarragon sprig to serve.

PAN-FRIED CHILLI SQUID WITH GARLIC MAYONNAISE

SERVES 4
PREPARATION TIME 25 minutes
COOKING TIME 6 minutes

4 squid, about 175g/6oz each
200g/7oz/2 cups panko
    breadcrumbs
1 tsp dried chilli flakes
3 eggs, beaten
2 red chillies, deseeded and
    finely chopped
100g/3½oz/heaped ¾ cup plain
    (all-purpose) flour
2 tbsp sunflower oil
80g/2¾oz unsalted butter
4 tbsp very finely chopped flat-leaf
    parsley leaves

FOR THE GARLIC MAYONNAISE
2 egg yolks
1 tbsp white wine vinegar
1 tbsp Dijon mustard
150ml/5fl oz/scant ⅔ cup
    sunflower oil
2 garlic cloves, crushed to a paste
grated zest of 1 lime
sea salt and freshly ground black
    pepper

Another dish which, like ceviche, demands that the produce be absolutely super fresh! This dish is very popular in the South of France and in the French Basque region. In the south it is called "supion", and in the Basque region it is called "chipiron". But it is in fact small calamari. I like it fried this way with the squid coated in spices breadcrumbs and deep fried until golden, then served with the perfect garlic mayonnaise. It's best to use Panko breadcrumbs, which are easily found in supermarkets. Funnily enough, Panko means breadcrumbs! They are processed to form flakes rather than fine crumbs, so create a crispier coating.

1 Start by preparing the squid. Wash them thoroughly, then pat dry, remove the tentacles and leave to one side, then remove and discard the beak. Cut the body in half lengthways, then rinse and pat dry again. Cut the body in half lengthways once more so you have 4 pieces for each squid, plus the tentacles. Pat dry with paper towel.

2 To make the garlic mayonnaise, put the egg yolks, vinegar and mustard in a medium bowl and whisk together. Whisking continuously, drizzle in the oil a little at a time until the mayonnaise is thick and creamy. Add the crushed garlic and lime zest and season with salt and pepper to taste. Cover and put in the refrigerator until ready to serve.

3 Put the breadcrumbs into a food processor with the dried chilli and blitz to a fine powder. Pour onto a plate. Break the eggs into a bowl and whisk with the chopped fresh chilli. Put the flour on a plate. Pass the squid through the flour, then drop into the chilli egg and finally into the chilli breadcrumbs, tossing to coat on all sides.

4 Heat a frying pan (skillet) over a medium-high heat. Add the oil and half the butter and when the butter is foaming, add half the squid and pan-fry for 2–3 minutes, turning once, until golden brown and crunchy. Drain on paper towel, then repeat with the remaining butter and squid.

5 Pile the squid on a large plate, scatter the parsley over the top and put it in the centre of the table with the garlic mayonnaise and let everyone help themselves.

BUTTERNUT SQUASH SOUP WITH MUSSELS & SAFFRON CREAM

This is such a lovely dish and there is so much flavour coming from the mussel bouillon and the saffron together with the nuttiness of the butternut squash. It's a very tasty and silky soup. For the perfect finish, you could also add some garlic crôutons.

SERVES 4
PREPARATION TIME 40 minutes
COOKING TIME 40 minutes

250g/9oz mussels
45g/1¾ oz butter
1 large onion, roughly chopped
2 parsley sprigs, plus a handful
    of chopped
a pinch of saffron threads
100ml/3½fl oz/scant ½ cup double
    (heavy) cream
2 tbsp olive oil
400g/14oz butternut squash,
    peeled and cut into small cubes
500ml/17fl oz/2 cups Vegetable
    Stock (see page 25)
juice of ½ lime
sea salt and freshly ground black
    pepper

1 Thoroughly scrub the mussels under cold running water and rinse well. (You may need to do this 2–3 times to remove the sand.) Discard any broken and floating ones when washed. Remove the beards by pulling them towards the large part of the shell. If any of the mussels are open, tap them hard against a work surface and if they don't close, discard them.

2 Melt half the butter in a saucepan over a medium heat. Throw in half of the onion, the parsley sprigs, saffron, cream and mussels. Cover with the lid and cook for 4 minutes, or until they start to open. Remove from the heat and set aside to cool.

3 Heat a large saucepan over a medium heat. Add the rest of the butter and the olive oil and when the butter starts to foam, add the butternut squash and the rest of the onion. Cook for 2–3 minutes until the onion has softened. Pour in the stock and simmer for 8–10 minutes, or until the butternut squash is tender enough to blend.

4 Take the pan with the mussels and strain the liquid through a sieve (strainer) into a clean saucepan. Remove the mussels from their shells and add three-quarters back in. Heat the pan gently over a medium heat to reduce the liquid by a quarter to increase flavour, but no more otherwise it will be too salty. Transfer the liquid and the butternut squash mixture to a blender, squeeze in some lime juice and blend until smooth (you might have to do this in two batches depending on the size of your blender). Check the seasoning; you shouldn't need salt as the mussel juice will be salty enough.

5 Serve hot with the reserved mussels on top and sprinkled with some chopped parsley.

PRAWN & PLAICE SOUP

This is almost a full meal on its own as so much goes into it. It is great for chilly late summer or autumn nights. You can substitute the plaice or monkfish with any fish that's available or in season; it's delicious with lemon sole or sea bream. Enjoy this with warm crôutons and a light mayonnaise with a hint of curry. Serve with a refreshing beer.

SERVES 6
PREPARATION TIME 50 minutes.
COOKING TIME 45 minutes

3 tbsp plain (all-purpose) flour
200ml/7fl oz/scant 1 cup single
    (pouring) cream
2 tbsp olive oil
20g/¾oz butter
1 large onion, finely chopped
100g/3½oz carrots, peeled and cut
    into small cubes
200g/7oz turnips, peeled and cut
    into small cubes
200g/7oz potatoes, peeled and cut
    into small cubes
1 tbsp curry powder
1 tbsp tomato purée
100ml/3½fl oz/scant ½ cup
    white wine
1.2 litres/40fl oz/4½ cups fish stock
    (see page 25)
4 tomatoes, deseeded and chopped
200g/7oz fresh raw prawns
    (shrimp), peeled, tail cut into
    3 pieces
200g/7oz plaice fillet or monkfish
    fillet, sliced into strips
2 tbsp finely chopped parsley
1 tbsp finely chopped chervil
sea salt and freshly ground white
    pepper
Garlic Crôutons (see page 27),
    to serve (optional)

1 Sift the flour into the cream, then whisk together, ensuring there are no lumps. Set aside.

2 Heat the olive oil and butter in a large, heavy-based saucepan over a medium heat. When the butter starts to foam, throw in the onion, carrots and turnips and cook until softened and golden. Add the potatoes, curry powder and tomato purée and mix gently. Pour in the white wine and evaporate by a third, then add fish stock and bring to the boil. Add the fresh tomatoes and the prawns (shrimp) and after a few minutes, when they are almost cooked, add the plaice or monkfish and simmer for few minutes more, until the fish is cooked but still firm.

3 Carefully add the flour and cream mixture, swirling it gently into the soup so that the fish fillets do not break. Check the seasoning and finish by adding the herbs. Serve hot. You could add garlic sourdough crôutons, if you like.

PAN-FRIED SKATE WINGS WITH CHILLI-LIME BUTTER

Skate wings are classically served with a Beurre Noisette (see page 30) and capers, but I think they go just as well with this chilli and lime butter. It's the same basic idea but the chilli brings a touch of heat and sunshine to the dish, which skate has the depth of flavour to take. Add, too, a splash of fresh lime and a little garlic and you have a cracking meal.

SERVES 4
PREPARATION TIME 10 minutes
COOKING TIME 5 minutes

4 skate wings, about 150g/5½oz
    each, cleaned and prepared
15g/½oz unsalted butter
1 tbsp olive oil
1 tbsp chopped flat-leaf
    parsley leaves
boiled new potatoes, to serve

FOR THE CHILLI-LIME BUTTER
250g/9oz unsalted butter, softened
1 red chilli, deseeded and finely
    chopped
1 garlic clove, crushed
finely grated zest of 1 lime
juice of ½ lime
leaves from 2 flat-leaf parsley
    sprigs, chopped
sea salt and freshly ground black
    pepper

1 To make the chilli-lime butter, put the butter, chilli, garlic, lime zest, lime juice and parsley in a non-metallic bowl and season with salt and pepper. Mix together with a wooden spoon, then put 4 heaped teaspoons to one side. (The rest of the chilli-lime butter can be frozen for future use. Wrap half the remaining butter in cling film (plastic wrap), roll it into a log shape and twist the ends. Repeat with the remaining butter. Wrap each log in a piece of foil and put in the freezer to firm up. You can then cut pieces off at your convenience for use on grilled (broiled), barbecued or pan-fried meats or fish.)

2 Briefly rinse the skate wings in ice-cold water, then pat dry with a clean dish towel (not paper as it will stick).

3 Heat a non-stick frying pan (skillet), large enough to hold the skate, over a medium heat. Add the unflavoured butter and the oil and heat until just melted. Add the skate wings and fry for 5 minutes, turning once, until just golden brown. As you turn the skate wings, add the reserved chilli-lime butter to the pan and spoon it over the fish. (Alternatively, cook the skate one or two at a time, using a little butter and oil for each one, and keep them warm in the oven at 140°F/275°F/gas 1 while you cook the remaining skate.)

4 Remove the skate wings from the pan and put on serving plates. Stir the parsley into the pan, then spoon the flavoured butter over the top of the skate wings. Serve with boiled new potatoes.

POACHED POLLOCK WITH LEMONGRASS & COCONUT MILK

In this recipe, I have poached the pollock in coconut milk with lemongrass to add an Asian accent, but not too much as I'm still influenced mainly by the cooking of my home country, France. This is a favourite of my wife, Claire – say no more, the girl knows! You can mix any leftover sauce into your mashed potatoes to go with this dish if you like.

SERVES 4
PREPARATION TIME 10 minutes
COOKING TIME 20 minutes

600ml/21fl oz/scant 2½ cups
   whipping cream
400ml/14fl oz/scant 1⅔ cups
   coconut milk
25g/1oz unsalted butter
1 tbsp olive oil
4 pollock fillets, skin on, about
   150g/5½oz each
4 garlic cloves, unpeeled,
   lightly crushed
1 lemongrass stalk, bruised
sea salt and freshly ground black
   pepper
Creamed Mashed Potatoes (see
   page 28), to serve

1 Put the cream and coconut milk in a wide, shallow sauté pan over a medium heat and bring to a simmer.

2 Meanwhile, heat the butter and oil in a large, non-stick frying pan (skillet) over a medium heat until the butter turns golden. Season the skin of the pollock with salt and pepper. Put in the frying pan, skin-side down, with the garlic and cook for 3–4 minutes until the skin is crisp and golden.

3 Turn the pollock over and put in the pan of simmering cream and coconut milk – the liquid needs to be just below the height of the fish so the skin doesn't soften. Add the garlic cloves and lemongrass to the liquid and simmer for 8 minutes, or until the fish is cooked. To check that the fish is ready, press lightly on the skin and you will see the flesh at the side of the fillet just start to flake away.

4 Lift the fish out of the pan, cover and keep it warm. Return the sauté pan to the heat and simmer for 5–8 minutes until the liquid has reduced by at least half and is thick enough to coat the back of a spoon. Add any juices from the resting fish, season with salt and pepper to taste, then pass the sauce through a fine sieve (strainer), using a ladle to help you. Spoon the sauce over the fish and serve with mashed potatoes.

CURRY-SPICED COD & MANGO PARCELS WITH COCONUT & CHERVIL SAUCE

I love cod, and I am always improvising new ways to cook it. My wife, Claire, always sneaks into the kitchen when I cook cod at home – it's the lovely smells wafting through the house that attracts her. Cooking it *en papillote* is one of my favourite methods – it's fun, fresh, fast and delicious. Here I am giving it a modern twist with Asian ingredients. Even if you like strong spices, stick to a mild curry powder or the cod will be overpowered and the balance of the dish will be lost.

SERVES 4
PREPARATION TIME 15 minutes
COOKING TIME 30 minutes

4 cod loins, about 150g/5½oz each, skin on
1 tsp light soft brown sugar
2 tbsp Chardonnay vinegar
1 small red onion, thinly sliced
1 firm mango, peeled, pitted and roughly chopped
2.5cm/1in piece of root ginger, peeled and grated
1 small red chilli, halved, deseeded and cut into julienne strips
1 tsp mild curry powder
20g/¾oz unsalted butter
1 tbsp olive oil
60ml/2fl oz/¼ cup Fish Stock (see page 25)
60ml/2fl oz/¼ cup coconut milk
100ml/3½fl oz/scant ½ cup whipping cream, lightly whipped
1 tbsp chopped chervil leaves
1 tsp lemon juice
sea salt and freshly ground black pepper

1 Preheat the oven to 200°C/400°F/gas 6 and cut four 46 x 25cm/ 18 x 10in rectangles of baking paper. The fish should have been pin boned but, if not, remove all small bones with a pair of fish tweezers.

2 Heat a small frying pan (skillet) until medium-hot, add the sugar and Chardonnay vinegar and cook for 1–2 minutes until the sugar has dissolved. Add the onion and sauté for 3–4 minutes, then reduce the heat to low, add the mango and ginger and cook for about 8 minutes until the mango has softened but is still holding its shape. Add the chilli, stir to combine, then remove from the heat and leave to cool.

3 Season the cod on both sides with curry powder, salt and pepper. Heat a non-stick frying pan (skillet) over a medium-high heat. Add the butter and oil and when the butter is foaming, add the cod, skin-side down, and sauté for 3–4 minutes until the skin is golden and crisp.

4 Put the baking paper rectangles on the work surface, then spoon the mango equally onto half of each sheet. Put the cod on top, skin-side up. Fold the paper over the filling and then fold along the edges to seal the liquid in securely. Put the parcels on a baking sheet and bake for 12 minutes. Remove from the oven and leave to rest for 2 minutes.

5 While the fish cooks, make the sauce. Heat a sauté pan over a medium heat. Add the stock and coconut milk and bring to the boil, then turn the heat down to low and simmer for 4–5 minutes until reduced by half.

6 Carefully open one side of each parcel and pour the juices into the sauce, then put the parcels on serving plates. Whisk the cream into the sauce, return it to the boil, then remove from the heat and season with salt and pepper to taste. Add the chervil and finish with the lemon juice. Serve the parcels *en papillote* at the table with the sauce served separately, or open the parcels, slide out the filling and spoon the sauce on top.

PANCETTA-WRAPPED MONKFISH WITH CARROT & MANDARIN PURÉE

I can't stress often enough that you will really taste the difference if you buy your fish fresh from your fishmonger. It is that simple with fish. Remember, too, how delicate the flesh is so don't overcook fish; monkfish is a meaty fish and therefore dries out quickly. The pancetta needs to be very thinly sliced and, if possible, a touch longer than normal so you can overlap the slices when wrapping the fish.

SERVES 4
PREPARATION TIME 20 minutes
COOKING TIME 1 hour 20 minutes

4 monkfish fillets, about 140g/5oz each, trimmed
20 thin slices of pancetta
200g/7oz carrots, peeled and thickly sliced
250ml/9fl oz/1 cup freshly squeezed mandarin juice
1 lemongrass stalk, bruised
grated zest of 1 lime
2 tbsp olive oil
25g/1oz unsalted butter
a few coriander (cilantro) leaves
sea salt and freshly ground black pepper

1 Season the monkfish with pepper, then wrap each fillet in the sliced pancetta until covered. Lay two sheets of cling film (plastic wrap) on top of each other, then put a monkfish fillet at one edge. Tightly wrap in the cling film to make a sausage shape. Twist and secure each end with a knot, pushing out any air. Repeat with each piece of monkfish. Put in the refrigerator while you prepare the carrots.

2 Put a large saucepan of water on to simmer, with a steamer insert on top. Put the carrots in the steamer, cover and cook for at least 1 hour until super soft.

3 While the carrots are steaming, put the mandarin juice in a small saucepan over a medium heat, add the lemongrass and half the lime zest and bring to a gentle boil. Turn the heat down to low and simmer for about 15 minutes until the liquid has reduced by two-thirds and is syrupy. Remove from the heat and keep warm.

4 Remove the carrots from the steamer and pat dry with a clean dish towel. Put them in a blender, then strain in the reduced mandarin juice, discarding the lemongrass, and blend to a smooth, soft purée. Season with salt and pepper, then leave to one side to keep warm.

5 Now put the monkfish in the steamer, cover and cook over a very low heat for 8–10 minutes. Remove from the steamer, then cut away and discard the cling film (plastic wrap). Put the monkfish onto a clean dish towel to absorb any of the liquid released while cooking.

6 Put half the oil in a sauté pan over a medium heat. Add the monkfish and cook for 3–4 minutes until crisp and golden brown on all sides. Remove from the pan and leave to rest on paper towel.

7 Gently reheat the purée until hot, then whisk in the butter and season with salt and pepper. Cut each piece of monkfish in half on the diagonal – if it's cooked properly then you will see a tiny rainbow on the flesh of the fish. Sprinkle the monkfish with the coriander (cilantro), the remaining lime zest and oil, then serve warm with the purée.

PLAICE WITH CELERIAC & PANCETTA GALETTE

This is my alternative to the classic *sole meunière* using plaice. The plaice must be in prime condition and I would recommend your fishmonger skin it for you as it is quite fiddly. Celeriac (celery root) is a beautiful root vegetable, which I personally love when it's roasted or, like here, grated with potatoes and mixed with pancetta to make a crisp and golden galette.

SERVES 4
PREPARATION TIME 15 minutes
COOKING TIME 30 minutes

50g/1¾oz pancetta lardons
200g/7oz floury potatoes, peeled and grated
200g/7oz celeriac (celery root), peeled and grated
1 tbsp chopped flat-leaf parsley leaves
120g/4¼oz unsalted butter
3 tbsp olive oil
3 tbsp plain (all-purpose) flour
2 plaice, skinned and left on the bone
finely grated zest and juice of 1 lime
sea salt and freshly ground black pepper

1 Preheat the oven to 160°C/315°F/gas 2½. To make the galette, bring a small pan of water to the boil. Add the pancetta and blanch for 1–2 minutes until just cooked. Drain and refresh in cold water, tip onto paper towel and pat dry. Mix the potatoes, celeriac (celery root) and pancetta in a bowl with half the parsley and season with pepper.

2 Heat a large, non-stick, ovenproof frying pan (skillet) over a medium heat. Add 20g/¾oz of the butter and 1 tablespoon of the oil and when the butter is foaming, add the potato mixture and lightly press it down with a spatula into an even layer. Fry for 5 minutes until golden brown, then put the pan in the oven for 3 minutes. Remove from the oven and put a large plate on top to cover the pan, carefully turn the pan upside-down to flip the galette over onto the plate, then slide it back into the pan.

3 Return the pan to a medium heat, add another 20g/¾oz of the butter and cook the galette for 3 minutes, then return the pan to the oven for a further 3 minutes. Slide the galette onto paper towel to drain for a few seconds, then wrap in kitchen foil to keep warm while you cook the fish.

4 Turn the oven up to 180°C/350°F/gas 4. Put the flour on a plate, season with salt and pepper, then dust the fish in the seasoned flour, patting to remove any excess. Heat 20g/¾oz of the butter and 1 tablespoon of the oil in the cleaned frying pan (skillet) over a high heat. When the butter is foaming, add the fish and cook for 6 minutes, then turn it over, add a further 20g/¾oz of the butter and, when melted, spoon it over the fish. Put the pan in the oven for 6 minutes until the fish is cooked. (Alternatively, if you have a smaller pan, cook the fish one at a time.)

5 Remove the fish from the oven, cover and leave to rest on a warm plate. Return the frying pan (skillet) to the hob, add the remaining butter and oil and stir in the remaining parsley and the lime zest and juice. Heat through briefly. Spoon the sauce over the fish and serve with segments of the galette.

PAN-FRIED COD LOIN WITH WHITE BEAN PURÉE & GARLIC CRISPS

This is another favourite of mine. When cod is really fresh (and line-caught if possible), you can see a small rainbow on the flesh. There's no better way to cook this lovely cod than to pan-fry it. Cooking the skin is not only tastier, it holds the flesh together. The white bean puree will bring so much nuttiness to this dish, which is a great companion. Garlic crisps bring the finishing touch of goodness.

SERVES 4
PREPARATION TIME 20 minutes, plus overnight soaking
COOKING TIME 40 minutes

8 garlic cloves, unpeeled
4 cod loins, skin on, about 150g/5½oz each, patted dry
40g/1½oz unsalted butter
2 tbsp olive oil

FOR THE WHITE BEAN PURÉE
150g/5½oz/¾ cup dried butter (lima) beans, soaked overnight, drained and rinsed
1 carrot, peeled
1 shallot
1 garlic clove
2 tbsp extra virgin olive oil
1 tbsp chopped flat-leaf parsley leaves
finely grated zest and juice of 1 lime

FOR THE GARLIC CRISPS
sunflower oil, for deep-frying
100ml/3½fl oz/scant ½ cup full-fat milk
4 large garlic cloves, thinly sliced
3 tbsp plain (all-purpose) flour
sea salt and freshly ground black pepper

1 To make the white bean purée, put the soaked butter (lima) beans in a saucepan, cover with cold water and bring to the boil over a high heat, skimming off any foam that rises to the surface. Add the carrot, shallot and garlic, turn the heat down to a simmer, partially cover and cook for 40 minutes until tender.

2 While the beans are cooking, make the garlic crisps. Heat enough sunflower oil to deep-fry the garlic to 160°C/315°F, or until a cube of bread browns in 45 seconds. Bring the milk to a gentle boil in a small saucepan, add the sliced garlic and blanch for 2–3 minutes until softened slightly but not breaking up. Remove and pat dry with paper towel, discarding the milk. Lightly dust the garlic in the flour, then drop a few slices at a time into the hot oil and fry for 2–3 minutes until golden brown. Drain on paper towel. Season and set aside.

3 Blanch the 8 garlic cloves in a small saucepan of boiling water for 4–8 minutes until softened, then drain, refresh in cold water and pat dry with paper towel.

4 Season the skin of the cod with salt and pepper. Heat a lidded, non-stick frying pan (skillet) over a high heat. Add the butter and olive oil and when the butter is foaming, add the cod, skin-side down, and cook for 3–5 minutes until the skin is crisp and golden. Turn the heat down to medium-low, add the blanched garlic cloves, partially cover with a lid and cook for 3–4 minutes. Remove the lid, turn the fish over and cook for a further 2–3 minutes until just cooked through.

5 Meanwhile, strain the beans, reserving 3–4 tablespoons of the cooking liquor, then discard the carrot, shallot and garlic. Put the beans in a blender with 3 tablespoons of the reserved cooking liquor and blend to a smooth purée. Add the extra virgin olive oil and blend once more. Add the remaining cooking liquid if the purée is too thick. Season with salt and pepper to taste, then stir in the parsley, half the lime zest and all the lime juice. Serve the cod on a bed of the bean purée with the buttery garlic sauce spooned over the top. Sprinkle with the garlic chips and the remaining lime zest before serving.

NORWEGIAN FJORD TROUT, NEW SEASON PEAS, MINT BEURRE BLANC

SERVES 4
PREPARATION TIME 45 minutes
COOKING TIME 35 minutes

1.4kg/3lb peas in their pods
100ml/3½fl oz/scant ½ cup
    Chardonnay vinegar (white)
20g/¾oz/⅛ cup golden caster
    (superfine) sugar
75g/2½oz banana shallots,
    thinly sliced
olive oil, for drizzling
4 Norwegian Fjord trout fillets,
    about 140g/5oz each, skin on
1 punnet of pea shoots

MINT BEURRE BLANC
250g/9oz unsalted butter
75g/2½oz banana shallots, finely
    chopped
1 mint sprig
100ml/3½fl oz/scant ½ cup
    good white wine
sea salt and freshly ground black
    pepper

This is a lovely spring recipe. When it's pea season, you will really notice the freshness of the peas, kept slightly crunchy here and only partially crushed. However, the real star of this dish is the Fjord trout, still pink in the middle, and the final touch will be the mint in the beurre blanc. What a delightful, tasty dish!

1 Shell the peas, reserving 4 of the best pods for plating. Blanch the peas very quickly, then refresh in ice and set aside.

2 Put the Chardonnay vinegar and sugar into a small pan over a low-medium heat and warm gently until the sugar dissolves.

3 Put the shallots in segment into a shallow dish and pour over the vinegar mixture so that it covers the shallots. Set aside to pickle while finishing the recipe. They will be ready when you need them at the end.

4 Make a classic beurre blanc (see page 141), but this time infused with fresh mint; just a couple of mint leaves, as you want freshness but you don't want it too strong. Set aside in a warm place – the sauce will split if the temperature changes too quickly.

5 Preheat the oven to 160°C/325°F/gas 3. Place a sheet of greaseproof paper in a large, non-stick frying pan (skillet) over a medium heat, and drizzle over a little olive oil. When warm, but not smoking hot, place the trout in the pan, skin-side down. Cook for 4–5 minutes until the fish turns a lovely colour and the skin is almost crispy but not burnt. Ensure the trout isn't overcooked; it needs to stay nice and pink in the middle.

6 To serve, warm up the peas, crush half of them with a fork and divide between the plates. Position the trout fillets on top and scatter a few whole peas around. Finish with a pea pod, drizzle with mint beurre blanc and top with a few pea shoots. Finally, spoon some pickled shallots on top. They will bring a lovely, refreshing contrast to the dish, some crunch and sweet acidity.

HALIBUT WITH JERUSALEM ARTICHOKES, & A LIGHT CURRY SAUCE

The halibut season is from April to August, and it's generally caught in the Atlantic and the North Sea. In the north of France (especially around Dunkirk) it's really popular slightly smoked. What a great fish! It's not used enough at home as the price can be a bit steep, but I do recommend trying it when it's in season, as it's absolutely delicious, especially when simply pan-fried with a light curry sauce.

SERVES 4
PREPARATION TIME 45 minutes
COOKING TIME 35 minutes

4 halibut fillets, about 150g/5½ oz
  each
2 tbsp olive oil
50g/1¾ oz butter
400g/14oz Jerusalem artichokes,
  peeled and sliced
1 shallot, finely chopped
200g/7oz chestnut (cremini)
  mushrooms, sliced
150ml/5fl oz/⅔ cup double (heavy)
  cream
100ml/3½fl oz/scant ½ cup
  Fish Stock (see page 25)
2 pinches of curry powder
1 small handful of chervil or chives,
  chopped
zest of 1 lime
sea salt and freshly ground black
  pepper
steamed rice, to serve

1 Pat dry the fish fillets on some paper towel and season. Heat half the oil and butter in a frying pan (skillet) over a medium heat. When the butter starts to foam, add the Jerusalem artichokes and cook for about 4–5 minutes until they're nice and golden. Add the shallot and mushrooms and sauté for another 3–4 minutes, or until they're also a lovely golden colour. Remove from the pan and keep warm.

2 Heat the rest of the butter and oil in the same pan over a medium heat. When the butter starts to foam, add the halibut fillets and cook for 2–3 minutes on one side. Turn them over and cook for a further 2–3 minutes. Remove from the pan and keep warm on a plate covered with kitchen foil.

3 Whip half the cream, using an electric whisk. Using the same pan again, over a medium heat, pour in the fish stock, add the unwhipped cream and the curry powder and cook gently until half reduced. Add the whipped cream and the herbs and simmer for 2–3 minutes, or until it's thick enough to coat the back of a spoon.

4 Drizzle the sauce over the fish and the vegetables and grate over some lime zest. Serve with steamed rice.

NORWEGIAN SEA TROUT SHARING PLATTER WITH CHILLI, GARLIC & WILTED SPINACH

SERVES 4
PREPARATION TIME 10 minutes
COOKING TIME 10 minutes

4 Norwegian sea trout fillets, about
    140g/5oz each, skin on, halved
2 garlic cloves, chopped
1 red chilli, deseeded and roughly
    chopped
olive oil
85g/3oz butter
1 bunch of parsley, chopped
a dash of Chicken Stock
    (see page 24)
2 limes
200g/7oz baby spinach,
    washed and dried
2 tbsp olive oil

If you love sharing platters, this one is perfect for dinner parties or a family supper. It really could not be easier to prepare and looks great in the middle of the table outdoors. Chilli and garlic add a gentle kick to the sea trout. I just recommend that you keep the trout slightly pink to appreciate its lovely nuttiness.

1 Marinate the trout fillets in the garlic, chilli and a splash of olive oil, then set aside, covered in the refrigerator, for 30 minutes to allow the flavours to develop.

2 Heat a large frying pan (skillet) over a medium heat. Add the butter and 1 tablespoon of oil and, once the butter has melted, pan-fry the fillets for 2–3 minutes on each side, basting the fish in the butter as it cooks. Add the parsley, chicken stock and lime juice to taste.

3 Heat a saucepan over a medium-high heat. Add the olive oil and when warm, but not smoking, throw in the spinach. Mix with a wooden spoon for barely 2 minutes, until half cooked, then remove and place on some paper towel. The spinach leaves should still be whole but wilted.

4 Serve the trout fillets on a large sharing platter with the wilted spinach and slices of lime, then drizzle with the sauce from the frying pan (skillet).

DANIEL'S TIP This is a very simple dish but the trick to cooking the fish to perfection is being extra careful not to overcook it, or it will lose its goodness and delicate flavours.

WINE SUGGESTION **Weingut Egon Müller, Riesling QBA, Scharzhof, Mosel, Germany, 2014 (Top Selection)** A superb wine with a hint of residual sugar to appease the heat sensation of the chilli. This Riesling however retains a great freshness with ripe lemon and quince notes. The palate is slightly oily with a chalky minerality.

RISOTTO WITH CRAB & SAMPHIRE

There are two types of samphire: the marsh samphire and the rock samphire, both of which are sea vegetables and grow along the coasts of Northern Europe. Some of the best samphire is to be found in the UK on the Norfolk coast from June to September. It's funny to think that it used to be called "the poor man's asparagus", because it's so delicious. Make sure you get some good-quality crab meat from your fishmonger rather than using canned, as they are a world apart when it comes to flavour.

SERVES 4
PREPARATION TIME 20 minutes, plus 45 minutes for the stock
COOKING TIME 35 minutes

1.2 litres/40fl oz Fish Stock (see page 25)
2 tbsp olive oil
1 large shallot or small onion, very finely chopped
300g/10½oz risotto rice, carnaroli if possible
50ml/2fl oz white wine
50g/1¾oz brown crab meat
1 tbsp mascarpone
1 tbsp crème fraiche
100g/3½oz white crab meat
1½ tbsp finely chopped chives
100g/3½oz samphire, picked and briefly blanched
grated pecorino cheese, to serve

1 Pour the stock into a pan over a medium heat, bring to the boil, then reduce the heat to low and keep it at a simmer.

2 Heat a large, heavy-based pan over a medium-low heat. Add the olive oil and the shallot or onion and sauté for 2–3 minutes, or until softened. Add the rice and stir so that it's well coated in the oil and shallot mixture, then add the wine and let it evaporate to remove the acidity. Always use a good wine, one which you will drink with your risotto; never use a bad wine for cooking! Add the brown crab meat and stir. Add a ladleful of the stock and stir continuously until it is almost all absorbed, then repeat, adding the stock little by little for about 18–20 minutes until the rice is cooked. It should be plump and still have some bite. I like my risotto to be a little loose, not too dry, although this is personal.

3 Now it is time to add the mascarpone and the crème fraîche. Fold in gently so you don't damage the rice and it should become shiny and loose. Fold in the white crab meat, chives and samphire and serve while hot. Have some grated pecorino ready to sprinkle over your risotto. Delicious!

MUSSEL, GINGER & LEMONGRASS GRATIN

Moules marinière is the classic way to cook mussels and a very good way at that, but mussels in a gratin with a creamy, aromatic sauce flavoured with lemongrass, ginger and fresh coriander (cilantro) is rather delicious, too. Mussels are very good value and easy to cook; just make sure that they are very fresh and throw away any with broken shells before cooking and those that don't open once cooked. Don't forget a fresh baguette or homemade chips (french fries) to dip into the sauce – it wouldn't be the same without them!

SERVES 4
PREPARATION TIME 20 minutes, plus making the stock
COOKING TIME 20 minutes

3kg/6lb 8oz mussels, rinsed
40g/1½oz unsalted butter, softened
2 tbsp olive oil
1 large shallot, roughly chopped
2 lemongrass stalks, bruised
50g/1¾oz piece of root ginger, peeled and roughly chopped
250ml/9fl oz/1 cup not too acidic or dry white wine, perhaps an Alsace or Riesling
2 handfuls of coriander (cilantro) leaves, chopped
200ml/7fl oz/scant 1 cup Fish Stock (see page 25)
400ml/14fl oz/scant 1⅔ cups whipping cream
50g/1¾oz pecorino cheese, grated
sea salt and freshly ground black pepper

1 Thoroughly scrub the mussels under cold running water and rinse well. Remove the beards by pulling them toward the large part of the shell. If any of the mussels are open, tap them hard against a work surface and if they don't close, discard them.

2 Generously butter four flameproof 18cm/7in gratin dishes. Heat a large, deep saucepan over a medium heat. Add the oil, shallot, lemongrass and ginger and fry for 2–3 minutes until just softened but not coloured. Turn the heat up to high, add the wine and cook until reduced by one-third, allowing the alcohol to evaporate. Add the mussels and half the coriander (cilantro) leaves, cover with a lid and cook for about 5 minutes at the very most, shaking the pan occasionally, until the mussels have opened. Discard any that remain closed. Remove from the heat and scoop all the mussels into a colander using a slotted spoon. Leave to cool slightly before shelling them. Discard the shells.

3 Spoon the shelled mussels into the prepared gratin dishes and put on a grill (broiler) tray. Strain the juices from the pan and bowl through a fine sieve (strainer) into a measuring jug. Reserve 200ml/7fl oz/scant 1 cup of the liquid.

4 Preheat the grill (broiler) to high. Pour the mussel liquid into a sauté pan and add the stock and cream. Put over a low heat and bring almost to the boil, then simmer for about 5 minutes until reduced by half and thickened enough to coat the back of a wooden spoon. Season with pepper to taste and a little salt, if necessary.

5 Ladle the cream sauce over the mussels in the gratin dishes. Sprinkle the remaining coriander (cilantro) on top, then finish with a sprinkling of cheese, making sure the cheese covers the coriander so that it doesn't discolour. Put under the hot grill (broiler) for a minute or so until bubbling and golden brown. Serve hot.

PAN-ROASTED LANGOUSTINES WITH CORIANDER

What makes this dish is the quality and freshness of the langoustines – make sure they are absolutely fresh and you will have a super simple, yet very tasty dish. The shellfish come in a fragrant butter sauce, flavoured with aromatic coriander (cilantro), garlic and fresh lime juice. This is great served with buttery pilau rice flavoured with fresh ginger or just a simple salad.

SERVES 4
PREPARATION TIME 10 minutes
COOKING TIME 8 minutes

16 whole langoustines, shell on
1 tsp olive oil
150g/5½oz unsalted butter
2 garlic cloves, finely chopped
1 handful of coriander (cilantro)
    leaves, roughly chopped
1 lime, cut into wedges
Thai-Style Pilau Rice (see page 29),
    to serve

1 Preheat the grill (broiler) to high. To prepare the langoustines, cut them in half lengthways, then put cut-side down on paper towel to absorb any water. This is particularly important if the langoustines have been frozen.

2 Heat a large, non-stick frying pan (skillet) over a high heat until searing hot. Add the oil and one-third of the butter and when the butter is foaming, put half the langoustines, flesh-side down, in the pan. Cook for about 2 minutes, then flip them over, transfer to a roasting tray and repeat with the remaining langoustines.

3 Melt the last of the butter in the frying pan (skillet) until foaming. Stir in the garlic and coriander (cilantro), then spoon straight away over the langoustines. Put under the grill (broiler) for 2 minutes, then squeeze the lime juice over the top and serve with pilau rice.

LEMONGRASS-SKEWERED PRAWNS WITH SAUCE VIÈRGE

Another shellfish recipe which means very fresh produce is needed for it! It's always best to buy from sustainable fishing sources; if you can't, frozen is also a very good option, as generally prawns (shrimp) are frozen at sea only a few hours after the catch. Using lemongrass as a skewer imparts its superb fragrance to the prawns. So do choose fresh green stalks, as it will make a huge difference. I suggest you cook plenty of them as everyone will be asking for more! The sauce vièrge finishes the dish beautifully.

SERVES 4
PREPARATION TIME 15 minutes
COOKING TIME 25 minutes

48 large raw peeled tiger prawns
   (jumbo shrimp)
12 lemongrass stalks
2.5cm/1in piece of root ginger,
   peeled and grated
80g/2¾oz unsalted butter
125ml/4fl oz/½ cup olive oil
sea salt and freshly ground black
   pepper
Thai-Style Pilau Rice (see page 29),
   to serve

FOR THE SAUCE VIÈRGE
125ml/4fl oz/½ cup extra virgin
   olive oil
1 tomato, peeled, deseeded
   and diced
1 tsp lightly crushed
   coriander seeds
grated zest and juice of 1 lemon
2 tbsp chopped coriander
   (cilantro) leaves

1 Preheat the oven to 140°C/275°F/gas 1 and line a baking sheet with kitchen foil. Make a small hole through the centre of each prawn (shrimp) with a sharp knife, then thread 4 prawns onto each lemongrass stalk as a skewer. Sprinkle with the ginger, then season with salt and pepper.

2 Heat a large, non-stick frying pan (skillet) over a medium-high heat. Add 20g/¾oz of the butter and 2 tablespoons of the olive oil and when the butter is foaming, add 3 skewers and fry for 2–3 minutes on each side until just cooked through and golden. You will be able to see the prawns (shrimp) change colour to pink as they cook. Transfer to the prepared tray and put it in the oven, but leave the oven door open – you just want to keep them warm, not for them to cook any more. Repeat with the remaining skewers, butter and olive oil.

3 While the last batch is cooking, make the *sauce vièrge*. Put the extra virgin olive oil, the tomato, coriander seeds, lemon zest and juice in a small saucepan over a low heat and season with salt and pepper. Warm through very gently for 2 minutes, stirring occasionally – you don't want the oil to actually get hot. Remove from the heat, add the coriander (cilantro) leaves, then stir to combine.

4 Simply serve the skewers with the sauce drizzled over the top, with an Asian-style steamed rice of your choice.

CHAPTER 5
FROM ORCHARD
& GARDEN

There are so many memories for me in this chapter as, when I was young, I passed a lot of time in the orchard eating fruit – or stealing it from the farm next door and being chased by the farmer when he caught me eating cherries from his tree! So much fun!

The garden too has a special place in my mind as we often helped Mum with the heavy task of turning the ground and planting – then waiting – before finally picking the vegetables or herbs when they were ready. All of us sitting around the table and preparing what was going to be lunch or dinner. It was a special time and I often think of those precious moments.

PROVENÇALE SALAD WITH COURGETTE FLOWERS TEMPURA

SERVES 4
PREPARATION TIME 25 minutes,
plus marinating and chilling
COOKING TIME 25 minutes

1 courgette (zucchini), cut
    lengthways into long, thin strips
2 tbsp olive oil
a pinch of edible lavender flowers
1 tbsp white balsamic vinegar
2 tbsp extra virgin olive oil
juice of ½ lemon
6 purple baby artichokes
2 thick slices of pancetta, about
    40g/1½ oz, cut into lardons
1 handful of rocket (arugula) leaves
1 handful of baby red chard leaves
½ white onion, finely sliced
6 yellow cherry tomatoes, halved
2 tbsp black olives, pitted and
    roughly chopped
sea salt and ground black pepper

FOR THE TEMPURA
sunflower oil, for deep-frying
2 eggs
250ml/9fl oz/1 cup cold sparkling
    or still water
2 tbsp cornflour (corn starch)
160g/5¾oz/1¼ cups plain
    (all-purpose) flour
a pinch of salt
1 tsp lemon juice
8 courgette (zucchini) flowers with
    the small courgettes attached

I Mix the courgette (zucchini) with ½ teaspoon of the olive oil and half the lavender flowers, then season with salt and pepper. Cover with cling film (plastic wrap) and leave to marinate in the refrigerator for about 30 minutes. Whisk together the balsamic vinegar and extra virgin olive oil in a bowl until just combined, then season with a little salt and pepper. Leave to one side.

2 While the courgettes (zucchini) are marinating, prepare the artichokes. Fill a large bowl with water and stir in the lemon juice. Remove and discard the outer leaves from the first artichoke and cut off the top. Trim and peel the stalk, then cut the artichoke into quarters lengthways. Cut out and discard the choke (the 'furry' centre) and put the artichoke in the lemon water to stop it discolouring. Repeat with the other artichokes, then drain and pat dry.

3 Heat a large frying pan (skillet) over a medium heat. Add 1 tablespoon of the olive oil and the artichokes and cook for about 8–10 minutes, turning occasionally, until just tender. Transfer to a plate and leave to one side. Add the remaining olive oil and the lardons to the frying pan and fry for 3 minutes until golden brown and crisp. Drain on paper towel and leave to one side. Bottled artichokes don't need cooking.

4 Heat a ridged griddle pan over a high heat until very hot. Add the courgette (zucchini) slices and griddle for 10 seconds on each side until just coloured in places. Transfer to a plate and leave to one side.

5 To make the tempura, pour in enough sunflower oil to fill a deep-fat fryer or deep, wide saucepan by two-thirds. Heat to 170°C/325°F, or until a cube of bread browns in 40 seconds. While the oil is heating, prepare the batter. Beat together the eggs and water in a large bowl until foaming. Sift the cornflour (corn starch) and flour over the top and gently mix with a pair of chopsticks until just combined. It doesn't matter if the batter is slightly lumpy as it's important not to over-whisk it. Stir in the salt, lemon juice and a handful of ice cubes, cover with cling film (plastic wrap) and leave to rest in the refrigerator for 5 minutes. Dip the courgette (zucchini) flowers and courgettes, one at a time, into the batter, then lower them straight into the hot oil. Deep-fry for 2 minutes, then flip over and fry for a further 2 minutes until the batter is crisp but not coloured. Drain on paper towel and season with a pinch of salt.

6 Top the rocket (arugula) and chard with the artichokes, courgettes (zucchini), onion, tomatoes and olives. Drizzle the dressing over the salad and add the lardons. Toss to combine, then put the courgette flowers on top and serve immediately while the batter is still crisp.

RADISH, CHICORY & MARINATED PEAR SALAD

This is the perfect salad for autumn and the best season for buying pears. In France, there are lots of different varieties of pear, so there is a wide selection to choose from. I'm a fan of the Pascatan, but I guess it's best to choose your own favourite. Using two colours of chicory (Belgian endive) makes the salad particularly attractive, but you can just use yellow chicory if you like. You can serve the salad as a meal on its own, or it goes very well with a charcuterie board, or even a chicken liver terrine.

SERVES 4
PREPARATION TIME 15 minutes, plus 2 hours marinating
COOKING TIME 10 minutes

25g/1oz unsalted butter
2 large slightly under-ripe pears, peeled, cored and each cut into 8 wedges
1 tbsp light soft brown sugar
4 tbsp white balsamic vinegar
1 shallot, halved lengthways and thinly sliced
2 tsp Dijon mustard
80ml/2½fl oz/⅓ cup light olive oil, plus 1 tbsp for the croûtons
50g/1¾oz stale sourdough bread, torn into bite-sized pieces
1 tbsp olive oil
12 small radishes, finely sliced
2 large yellow chicory (Belgian endive), outer leaves discarded and leaves separated, cut into 3 diagonally
2 large red chicory (Belgian endive), outer leaves discarded and leaves separated, quartered lengthways
4 spring onions (scallions), green part only, roughly chopped
50g/1¾oz/½ cup walnuts, toasted and lightly crushed

1 Melt the butter in a non-stick frying pan (skillet) over a medium heat. Add the pears and cook for 3–4 minutes, turning once, until just tender and light golden. Sprinkle with the sugar, then turn the pears to coat them in the sugary butter. Transfer the pears to a dish, spoon over the balsamic vinegar and shallot and stir together. Cover and leave to marinate at room temperature for 2 hours.

2 Pour off the marinade from the pears and put 2 tablespoons in a small bowl, discarding the rest. Whisk the mustard into the marinade, then slowly add the light olive oil, whisking until it thickens and becomes glossy. Leave to one side.

3 Preheat the grill (broiler) to high. Scatter the bread in the grill pan, then drizzle with the olive oil and mix until combined. Grill (broil) for 2–3 minutes, turning halfway, until golden and crisp. Tip the bread and any crumbs into a bowl, carefully wipe the pan clean and put the pears in the pan. Grill for about 1–2 minutes until just warmed through.

4 Toss the warm pears gently with the radishes, chicory (Belgian endive) and spring onions (scallions). Scatter the croûtons and walnuts over the top, drizzle with the dressing and serve while the pears are still warm.

TOMATO CONFIT, CHILLI & LEMON THYME TARTS

This classic tart represents, for me, all that I love about the Mediterranean, such as the climate, the colours, the heat, the scents and the goodness of the fresh local and seasonal ingredients. My new additions of tomato confit, chilli and lemon thyme give a freshness and great depth of flavour. You could also top the tarts with a few rocket (arugula) leaves.

SERVES 4
PREPARATION TIME 20 minutes
COOKING TIME 2 hours 20 minutes

8 large vine-ripened plum
    tomatoes, cut into 1cm/½in
    round slices, ends discarded
4 tbsp olive oil
leaves from 6 lemon thyme sprigs
375g/13oz ready-rolled puff pastry
6 vine-ripened tomatoes
1 garlic clove, unpeeled,
    lightly crushed
1 white onion, finely diced
2 long red chillies, deseeded and
    finely diced
3 tbsp extra virgin olive oil, plus
    extra for drizzling
sea salt and freshly ground black
    pepper
Chicory and Radish Salad (see
    page 26), to serve

1 Preheat the oven to 150°C/300°F/gas 2 and line a baking sheet with baking paper. Put the sliced plum tomatoes on the prepared tray, drizzle with half the olive oil, scatter over one-third of the lemon thyme and season with salt. Bake for 2 hours, turning once, until dried and wrinkly. If they don't look quite ready, return the tomatoes to the oven for a further 30 minutes, then check once more. Leave to one side on the baking sheet.

2 Turn the oven up to 180°C/350°F/gas 4. Cut the pastry into 4 discs, each about 10cm/4in in diameter, then prick all over with a fork. Put the pastry discs on a flat baking sheet and put a second baking sheet on top. Put the pastry, sandwiched between the baking sheets, in the oven for 10–12 minutes, or until golden brown and cooked through. Carefully lift off the top baking sheet and leave the pastry to cool.

3 Meanwhile, with a sharp knife, cut a small cross on the bottom of each of the remaining tomatoes, then put in a heatproof bowl and cover with boiling water. Leave for 30 seconds, then lift them out with a slotted spoon and put in a bowl of iced water. Lift the tomatoes out, then peel off and discard the skins. Cut the tomatoes into quarters, remove and discard the seeds, then roughly chop the flesh.

4 Heat a sauté pan over a medium heat. Add the remaining olive oil and the chopped tomatoes and cook for a few minutes to release the tomato juices. Add the garlic, onion and chillies, turn the heat down to medium-low and cook for 20–30 minutes until thickened and very soft. Stir once in a while to make sure that the tomato mixture doesn't catch or stick to the bottom of the pan. Season with salt and pepper to taste, then add another one-third of the lemon thyme and the extra virgin olive oil.

5 To assemble the tarts, divide the chopped tomato mixture between the pastry discs and spread it over the tops. Lay the slices of tomato confit on top, overlapping them slightly. Drizzle with a little extra virgin olive oil and scatter over the remaining lemon thyme. Return to the oven for a further 5–8 minutes to warm through. Serve the tarts warm with a chicory (Belgian endive) and radish salad.

GLAZED CHICORY & THYME TART

Chicory (Belgian endive) is a very versatile vegetable and while it is perfect uncooked in a salad, it also tastes delicious cooked in a tart. Here, it is combined with orange juice, a drop of honey and fresh thyme, which lift the chicory to new heights. The orange zest and walnuts sprinkled over the top to finish the dish beautifully.

SERVES 4
PREPARATION TIME 25 minutes,
  plus 30 minutes chilling and 20
  minutes cooling
COOKING TIME 1 hour

75g/2½oz unsalted butter, plus
  extra for greasing
250g/9oz ready-made puff pastry
plain (all-purpose) flour,
  for dusting
6 heads of chicory (Belgian
  endive), trimmed and halved
  lengthways
finely grated zest and juice of
  1 orange
2 tbsp clear honey
¼ tsp thyme leaves
25g/1oz/¼ cup walnuts, chopped
2 tbsp chopped celery leaves
¼ eating apple, peeled, cored
  and diced
sea salt and freshly ground black
  pepper

1 Lightly grease a 20cm/8in loose-bottomed tart tin. Roll out the pastry on a lightly floured work surface until 25cm/10in diameter x 3mm/⅛in thick and use to line the base and the sides of the tart tin, pressing it into the edges without overstretching the dough. Trim any excess pastry, prick the base with a fork and chill for 30 minutes to prevent the pastry shrinking during baking.

2 Meanwhile, make the filling. Heat a large sauté pan over a medium heat. Add 50g/1¾oz of the butter and the chicory (Belgian endive), cut-side down, and cook for 4–5 minutes until slightly coloured. Take care not to let the butter burn. Pour enough water into the pan to fill by 1cm/½in, then add the remaining butter. Pour in the orange juice, season with salt and pepper and stir to combine. Cover the chicory with a *cartouche* (see page 232), turn the heat down to very low and simmer for 35–40 minutes until very tender and caramelized. Check occasionally to make sure that it is not burning and add more water, if necessary.

3 While the chicory (Belgian endive) is cooking, preheat the oven to 170°C/325°F/gas 3. Line the pastry case with baking paper and cover with baking beans. Bake for 12 minutes, then remove the paper and baking beans and bake for a further 3–5 minutes until the pastry is cooked and just golden. Remove from the oven and leave to cool in the tin on a wire rack. Turn the oven up to 200°C/400°F/gas 6.

4 Lift the chicory (Belgian endive) out of the pan onto a clean dish towel to dry and leave to cool. Add the honey and thyme to the pan and warm through, gently stirring, until you have a light syrup. Remove from the heat.

5 When the chicory (Belgian endive) has cooled, lay it tightly together in the pastry case, then brush generously with the orange-honey syrup. Bake for 10–12 minutes until warmed through. Remove the tart from the oven and the tin. Scatter the walnuts, orange zest, celery leaves and apple over the top and serve warm.

SOUS-VIDE LITTLE GEMS WITH EWES' CHEESE

SERVES 4
PREPARATION TIME 15 minutes,
    plus making the croûtons
COOKING TIME 20 minutes

4 baby Little Gem lettuces, outer
    leaves removed and quartered
    lengthways
125ml/4fl oz/½ cup olive oil
120g/4¼oz ewes' cheese, such as
    Ossau Iraty, crumbled
1 tbsp small Croûtons (see
    page 27)
sea salt and freshly ground black
    pepper

With this dish, I'm trying to encourage you to cook more salad vegetables as it is a much-neglected style of cooking. My home-style "vacuum-packed" Little Gem lettuces are topped with a slightly crumbly ewes' cheese, crunchy croûtons and a drizzle of olive oil and are just delicious. Enjoy this recipe as a vegetable dish with sourdough bread or as an accompaniment to roast pork. If you have a small vacuum-pack machine, follow the instructions in the method using vacuum bags (see page 16) instead of cling film (plastic wrap). Alternatively, you can use small freezer bags with a seal, making sure that the air is squeezed out before you close them. You can also cook the parcels in a microwave for just 40 seconds on full power.

1 Put four 20cm/8in square sheets of cling film (plastic wrap) on a work surface. Top each sheet with a quartered Little Gem, putting the pieces in a pile in the centre. Drizzle 1 tablespoon of the oil over each pile, then season with a little salt and pepper. Tightly wrap the Little Gem in the cling film to make 4 small parcels, pressing out any air.

2 Put a saucepan of water on to simmer, with a steamer insert on top. Put the parcels in the steamer, cover and cook for 12–14 minutes until they are just tender.

3 Remove the parcels from the steamer and unwrap over a small saucepan to catch any juices. Pat dry with paper towel and put in a grill (broiler) pan, putting the contents of each parcel closely together so you have four separate portions. Scatter the ewes' cheese over the lettuce, then season with more salt and pepper and leave to one side.

4 Preheat the grill (broiler) to high. Put the pan of reserved cooking juices over a medium-high heat and cook until reduced by half, then whisk in the remaining oil. Drizzle the sauce over the Little Gems and put under the grill for 2–3 minutes until the cheese is golden brown and a little puffed up. Sprinkle with the croûtons and serve hot.

RAGOÛT OF SUMMER VEGETABLES WITH VANILLA BEURRE BLANC

This is a perfect summer dish as it's colourful, light and fresh. The vegetables only need a minimal amount of cooking before they are coated in a light butter sauce, scented with fresh vanilla seeds and thyme. One small point – don't over do the vanilla or you will disturb the delicately balanced flavour of the dish. It's delicious served on its own or with roasted meats.

SERVES 4
PREPARATION TIME 20 minutes, plus
    making the stock
COOKING TIME 40 minutes

100g/3½oz podded broad
    (fava) beans, grey outer
    casing removed
200g/7oz peas, podded
100g/3½oz green beans, halved
100g/3½oz baby carrots, scrubbed
100g/3½oz baby leeks, trimmed
    and each cut into 3 pieces
100g/3½oz baby turnips, peeled
    and quartered
1 bunch of asparagus tips
1 baby cauliflower, cut into florets
leaves from 1 thyme sprig
sea salt and freshly ground black
    pepper

FOR THE VANILLA BEURRE BLANC
500ml/17fl oz/2 cups Vegetable
    Stock (see page 25)
200g/7oz unsalted butter, softened,
    cut into cubes
1 shallot, finely chopped
finely grated zest and juice of
    ½ lime
1 vanilla pod, split in half
    lengthways and seeds scraped
    out (you can keep the pod for
    vanilla sugar)

1 Pour the stock for the vanilla *beurre blanc* into a small sauté pan and cook over a medium-high heat for 15 minutes until reduced to 150ml/5fl oz/scant ⅔ cup. Leave to one side.

2 Meanwhile, bring a saucepan of salted water to the boil over a high heat and cook the vegetables, one type at a time, for 2–5 minutes each until just tender. Lift out with a slotted spoon, refresh in iced water, then drain once more, tip carefully into a bowl and leave to one side. Put a lid on the pan of water and reserve for reheating the vegetables just before serving.

3 To make the *beurre blanc*, melt 20g/¾oz of the butter in a small pan over a medium heat and fry the shallot for 2 minutes until just softened. Stir in the lime juice, then add the reduced stock and the vanilla seeds. Bring to a simmer and cook for 5–8 minutes until there is about 110ml/4fl oz/scant ½ cup of buttery stock.

4 Turn the heat down to very low and gradually whisk in the remaining softened butter, a few cubes at a time. Keep whisking until the butter has been incorporated before adding the next batch. This will stop the sauce splitting by keeping it at a constant temperature. As you are whisking, you should see a foam of tiny bubbles form on top of the mixture and when all the butter has been added, the sauce should be pale in colour and light in consistency, similar to a very thin custard, and should just coat the back of the spoon. This will take 10–12 minutes. At this point, season with salt and pepper to taste and add the lime zest. Cover with a lid and leave to one side in a warm place.

5 Return the saucepan of water to the boil over a high heat and add the vegetables. Cook for a minute or so until heated through, then drain on paper towel. Serve the vegetables with the vanilla *beurre blanc* spooned over the top and sprinkled with the thyme.

CRUSHED PEA & MINT TORTELLINI WITH PEA SHOOTS

Not only is the pea one of Britain and France's favourite vegetables, but it's also my wife and my son's too – although, botanically speaking, a pea is actually a fruit! The salad is optional but I like it with this dish.

SERVES 4
PREPARATION TIME 40 minutes, plus 60 minutes resting
COOKING TIME 15 minutes

FOR THE PASTA
300g/10½oz/2¾ cups pasta flour
1 egg
1 egg yolk
1 tbsp olive oil

FOR THE TORTELLINI
50g/1¾oz unsalted butter
300g/10½oz/scant 2 cups fresh podded peas or frozen, defrosted (if there are no really fresh ones around)
1 tbsp chopped mint leaves
semolina flour, for dusting
100g/3½oz soft goats' cheese log, such as Ste Maure, rind removed
sea salt and freshly ground black pepper

FOR THE PEA SHOOT SALAD
75g/2½oz pea shoots
1 tbsp olive oil
1 tbsp pumpkin seeds

1 Blitz the pasta ingredients in a food processor until small granules form, then tip onto a work surface and form a firm dough. Wrap in cling film (plastic wrap) and put in the refrigerator for 30–60 minutes.

2 To make the filling, pour 3½ tablespoons of water into a saucepan over a medium heat, add the butter, season with salt and pepper and bring to the boil. Add the peas and cook for 4–8 minutes for fresh or 2–3 minutes for frozen, or until just tender. Taste one and it should be sweet but with the merest hint of a crunch. Using a slotted spoon, lift the peas out of the water and put 200g/7oz/1⅓ cups in a bowl. Crush them lightly with a fork, season with salt and pepper to taste, then fold in the mint. The mixture should be really moist. Cover with cling film (plastic wrap) and leave to one side.

3 To make a pea coulis, put the remaining peas in a food processor and blitz until very smooth, then add a little of the cooking liquor and blitz until thick enough to coat the back of a spoon. Pass through a fine sieve (strainer) into flameproof pasta bowls, cover and set aside.

4 Lightly dust a work surface and a baking sheet with semolina flour. Roll out the pasta to 1cm/½in thick, then cut into 2 rectangles big enough to fit through your pasta machine. Roll through the machine, decreasing the thickness gauge each time until it reaches the thinnest setting possible, dusting with semolina flour to prevent it sticking. Cut out 20 x 7.5cm/3in discs of pasta. Put a teaspoon of crushed peas onto each disc, just below the centre. Brush the edges of the pasta lightly with water, then fold the top half over the filling and press the edges lightly to seal. Pick up the pasta crescent and twist the edges together, forming a lip on the outside edge, and put the tortellini on the prepared baking sheet.

5 To make the salad, toss the pea shoots, oil and pumpkin seeds in a small bowl, then season with salt and pepper to taste.

6 Bring a large pan of salted water to the boil over a high heat, add the tortellini and cook for 4–5 minutes until the pasta floats to the top of the pan. Drain the tortellini, then spoon on top of the coulis on serving plates. Crumble the cheese over the top and top with a little of the salad and a twist of black pepper to serve. Alternatively, you can grill (broil) it for a few moments until light gold.

SPRING VEGETABLES WITH WATERCRESS DRESSING

I am not a vegetarian, but I do eat a lot of vegetarian dishes, especially in the spring and summer when I really like the colours, taste and freshness of them. The only downside is I am often left wanting more, so I like to make generous portions. That's what you'll find with these spring vegetables complemented with a modern watercress dressing and some perfectly poached quail's eggs.

SERVES 4
PREPARATION TIME 20 minutes, plus making the dressing
COOKING TIME 50 minutes

2 bunches of watercress, main stems discarded
250ml/9fl oz/1 cup French Dressing (see page 26)
120g/4¼oz Chantenay carrots, scrubbed
100g/3½oz baby leeks, trimmed
100g/3½oz baby turnips, trimmed
100g/3½oz baby courgettes (zucchini)
100g/3½oz baby corn
2 small bunches of fine asparagus, trimmed and cut in half
200g/7oz fine green beans, cut in half
100g/3½oz baby new potatoes, scrubbed
1 bunch of spring onions (scallions), white part only, green part kept for another dish
175g/6oz baby chargrilled artichokes, drained
16 quail's eggs
2 tsp white wine vinegar
sea salt and freshly ground black pepper

1 Put 2 small handfuls of watercress leaves to one side. Bring a small saucepan of salted water to the boil, add the remaining watercress and blanch for 30 seconds. Drain and refresh in iced water, then drain briefly so that there's still water on the leaves. Put into a spice grinder or small blender and blitz to a fine purée. Pass through a fine sieve (strainer), pressing down into the sieve to release as much juice as possible; there should be about 6 tablespoons of juice. Whisk the juice into the French dressing, season with salt and pepper and leave to one side.

2 Bring a large saucepan of salted water to the boil, add the carrots and blanch for 2–5 minutes until just tender. Use a slotted spoon to lift them out of the pan, then drain and refresh in iced water, drain once more and tip carefully into a bowl. One at a time, blanch all the other vegetables except the artichokes in the same way and put them in the bowl. Keep the saucepan of water for reheating when you are ready to serve.

3 Bring another small saucepan of salted water to the boil, add the vinegar and then crack the eggs into the water and return it to just above a simmer – you want the water to be bubbling so that the eggs don't stick to the bottom of the pan. Simmer for 2 minutes, then lift out the eggs and refresh in a bowl of iced water. Drain on paper towel, then season with salt and pepper.

4 Return the saucepan of vegetable water to the boil, add all the vegetables, including the artichokes, and cook for 2 minutes until hot. Lift out of the pan using a slotted spoon and put onto paper towel to drain. Add the quail's eggs to the pan of water and heat through for 15-20 seconds until hot, then drain and pat dry.

5 Drizzle the vegetables with the watercress dressing, and top with the quail's eggs, then serve with a scattering of watercress leaves.

LEMONGRASS & SAFFRON-SCENTED CAULIFLOWER GRATIN

SERVES **6**
PREPARATION TIME **30 minutes**
COOKING TIME **30 minutes**

2 cauliflowers
1.2 litres/40fl oz/4½ cups
   semi-skimmed milk
a pinch of saffron threads
2 lemongrass stalks, bruised
70g/2½oz butter
70g/2½oz/½ cup plain
   (all-purpose) flour
100g/3½oz pecorino cheese, grated
sea salt and freshly ground white
   pepper

I have yet to find someone who doesn't like cauliflower gratin! During lockdown I made it with saffron and lemongrass. It was a bit of an experiment but the flavours go so well together. Be careful not to overpower the dish with saffron; it must be there but not "in your face", so to speak. This is a great vegetarian dish by itself, or delicious with roast pork.

1 Preheat the oven to 200°C/400°F/gas 6.

2 Cut each of the cauliflowers into large florets, then wash under running water for 1 minute. Place in a saucepan over a medium heat, add 200ml/7fl oz/scant 1 cup of the milk and cover with water. Add some salt and cook for about 8 minutes until softened but still slightly firm. The milk in the water will help the cauliflower to stay really white. Remove from the heat and set aside.

3 Meanwhile, pour the rest of the milk into a separate pan over a medium-low heat. Add the saffron and the bruised lemongrass and as soon as it starts to simmer, turn off the heat and leave to infuse.

4 Now make a classic béchamel sauce. Melt the butter in a heavy-based saucepan over a medium heat. When it starts to foam, sift in the flour, mix well with a wooden spoon and cook for a couple of minutes. Slowly pour in the infused milk to avoid lumps, stirring continuously. Cook for a further 3 minutes until lovely and silky, then season. It will have a beautiful saffron colour and a scent of lemongrass.

5 Remove the cauliflower florets from their liquid and pat dry slightly with paper towel. They should still be firm. Place in an ovenproof dish, pour over the béchamel sauce and cover with the grated pecorino. Cook in the oven for 15 minutes.

COCOA-INFUSED PAIN PERDU WITH ROASTED PEACHES

My mum often made *pain perdu* for me when I was growing up. It was seen as a sin to throw bread away, so any leftover bread was sliced and dipped into egg and milk and fried in butter. In this new version, the cocoa transforms this classic dish to create a stylish, modern dessert with the added elegance of roasted peaches. You can also adapt this dish and serve it with pears, apricots or plums instead of peaches, if you like, or even make it with coconut milk instead of cow's milk.

SERVES 4
PREPARATION TIME **10 minutes**
COOKING TIME **25 minutes**

75g/2½oz unsalted butter
2 large, firm peaches, quartered and stones removed
3 tbsp maple syrup
20g/¾oz/scant ¼ cup good-quality dark cocoa powder
200ml/7fl oz/scant 1 cup full-fat milk, slightly warmed
2 eggs, lightly beaten
2 tbsp caster (superfine) sugar
4 x 2.5cm/1in slices of *pain de campagne* or country-style bread
20g/¾oz/scant ¼ cup flaked almonds, toasted
3 tbsp crème fraîche
1 tsp chopped rosemary leaves

1 Preheat the oven to 180°C/350°F/gas 4. Heat an ovenproof sauté pan over a medium heat. Add half the butter and sauté the peaches for 2–3 minutes, turning once, until golden on both sides. Add 2 tablespoons of the maple syrup, turn to coat the peaches in the syrup, then transfer to the oven and roast for 5–8 minutes until just soft. Remove and leave to one side on a plate, but leave the oven on.

2 Mix half the cocoa powder with the warm milk, eggs and sugar in a wide, shallow bowl, stirring until the sugar dissolves. Leave to cool slightly, if necessary. Add 2 slices of the bread and soak both sides. Put the bread on a clean dish towel to drain slightly, then repeat with the remaining slices of bread.

3 Heat a large, non-stick frying pan (skillet) over a medium heat. Add the remaining butter and maple syrup and, when melted, swirl the pan until combined. Put the egg-soaked bread in the pan and cook for 1–2 minutes on each side until just golden and slightly crisp, taking care they do not burn. You may need to do this in batches.

4 Put the *pain perdu* in a shallow baking sheet and top with the roasted peaches, a sprinkling of toasted almonds and a dusting of the remaining cocoa powder. Heat through in the oven for 2–3 minutes.

5 Meanwhile, mix together the crème fraîche and rosemary. Serve the *pain perdu* and peaches with the rosemary crème fraîche.

PINEAPPLE, CHILLI & LEMONGRASS TARTE TATIN

One of the sweetest fruits – and a particular favourite of mine – is the pineapple. This exotic fruit tastes wonderful cooked in a tarte tatin in place of the traditional apples and, of course, it needs less added sugar. The confident aroma and lusciousness of the pineapple pairs remarkably well with stronger spices and flavourings, and in this recipe I have contrasted it with fragrant lemongrass and a hint of chilli. You may be surprised by how successfully these two spices marry with the fruit – and with the buttery flavour of the pastry – to make a truly superb dessert. If you like, you can serve it with a scoop of coconut ice cream or sorbet.

SERVES 4
PREPARATION TIME 20 minutes, plus 30 minutes chilling and at least 5 minutes resting
COOKING TIME 1 hour

220g/7¾oz ready-made puff pastry, defrosted if frozen
plain (all-purpose) flour, for dusting
80g/2¾oz/⅓ cup caster (superfine) sugar
1.2kg/2lb 10oz pineapple, peeled, cored and cut into large wedges
40g/1½oz unsalted butter
1 red chilli, deseeded and finely chopped, plus ½ red chilli in strips, to serve (optional)
½ lemongrass stalk, bruised and halved lengthways

1 Roll out the pastry on a lightly floured work surface, then cut out a circle slightly larger than a 20cm/8in tatin pan or flameproof baking dish. Roll the pastry over the rolling pin and transfer to a baking sheet, cover with cling film (plastic wrap) and chill in the refrigerator for 30 minutes to prevent the pastry shrinking during baking.

2 Preheat the oven to 190°C/375°F/gas 5. Melt the sugar gently in the tatin pan over a medium heat until golden brown. Add the pineapple and cook for 6–8 minutes, or until lightly golden. Remove the pan from the heat. Using a slotted spoon, transfer the pineapple to a plate and leave to rest for 5–8 minutes to release the juice.

3 Stir the butter into the sugar in the pan. Sprinkle one-third of the chopped chilli over the pan. Put the pineapple wedges tightly around the edge of the pan in a circle, then make smaller circles of tightly fitting pineapple within this circle until the base is covered and all the pineapple is used. Put the lemongrass on top of the pineapple, add the strips of chilli, if you like, and bake for 30 minutes.

4 Remove from the oven and sprinkle another one-third of the chilli over the pineapple. Put the pastry on top, pushing the edges into the pan. Return the pan to the oven and bake for a further 20 minutes, or until the pastry is golden brown and crisp.

5 Remove the tart from the oven and leave to cool for a few minutes. Put an upside-down plate, slightly larger than the pan, on top of the tart and, holding both the plate and pan, turn the pan over to transfer the tart to the plate. Sprinkle with the remaining chilli, if you like. Serve warm, removing the lemongrass and chilli strips before cutting into portions.

PINEAPPLE BEIGNETS WITH MANGO CARPACCIO

In my view, pineapple is made for a *beignet* or fritter, as its fresh, slightly sharp taste has just the right amount of acidity to cut through the batter coating. The slices of sweet mango go well with the acidity of the pineapple, too, while the piquancy of the pink peppercorns add that unusual finishing touch.

SERVES 4
PREPARATION TIME 20 minutes,
    plus 20 minutes cooling
COOKING TIME 25 minutes

FOR THE MANGO CARPACCIO
1 large semi-ripe mango, peeled, pitted and thinly sliced
50g/1¾oz/scant ¼ cup caster (superfine) sugar
2 pinches of dried pink peppercorns

FOR THE PINEAPPLE BEIGNETS
1 small pineapple, peeled, cored, quartered lengthways and cut into small chunks about 1.5cm/⅔in thick
125g/4½oz/1 cup plain (all-purpose) flour
2 eggs, separated
a pinch of salt
125ml/4fl oz/½ cup beer, preferably bitter, or good dry cider
2 tbsp sunflower oil, plus extra for deep-frying
2 tbsp caster (superfine) sugar, plus extra for dusting

1 To make the carpaccio, put the mango in a deep-sided roasting tin. Put the sugar and 150ml/5fl oz/scant ⅔ cup of water into a small saucepan and bring to the boil over a medium heat, swirling the pan occasionally, until the sugar dissolves. Pour it over the mango and scatter with the peppercorns. Cover with cling film and leave to infuse and cool.

2 Strain the mango over the small pan. Put the mango on serving plates and leave to one side. Return the peppercorns to the pan with the syrup and bring to the boil, then boil for 5 minutes until the syrup is thick enough to coat the back of a spoon. Remove from the heat and leave to cool once more.

3 To make the *beignets*, line a baking sheet with a clean dish towel and spread the pineapple out on the tray in a single layer. Cover with another dish towel and press down firmly to remove any liquid. Leave to dry, covered, while you prepare the batter. Mix together the flour, egg yolks, salt, beer and oil to make a thick, smooth paste. Whisk together the egg whites and sugar in a separate bowl, using an electric whisk, until soft peaks form. Gently fold them into the beer batter.

4 Meanwhile, pour enough oil to deep-fry the *beignets* into a deep-fat fryer or a deep, wide saucepan and heat to 170°C/325°F, or until a cube of bread browns in 40 seconds.

5 Thread a piece of pineapple onto a long skewer and dip briefly into the batter until completely coated. Using a fork, carefully push the pineapple off the skewer into the hot oil. Repeat with the rest of the pineapple, frying about 6 pieces at a time. When the *beignets* start to float to the surface, carefully turn them over and continue to fry for about 4–5 minutes until golden and crisp. Remove with a slotted spoon, drain on paper towel, then dust immediately with sugar. Put the *beignets* on top of the mango carpaccio, then spoon over a little of the cooled syrup to serve.

LEMON & CHILLI CAKE WITH CHILLI GLAZE

I'm not a pastry chef as such, but when I have the time I love to experiment. The strength of chilli can be deadly! But then the much-needed lemon brings balance and freshness. I just knew the combination would work. Lemon is a classic flavouring for cake but the chilli is the icing on it (so to speak!). Make sure that you soak the cake while it is still warm so that it can absorb the syrup. This makes a fabulous desert but you could also enjoy a slice with a cup of Earl Grey tea in the afternoon!

SERVES 6–8
PREPARATION TIME 25 minutes, plus 5 minutes infusing and 30 minutes cooling
COOKING TIME 40 minutes

110g/3¾oz/scant 1 cup plain (all-purpose) or superfine cake flour
½ tsp baking powder
finely grated zest and juice of 2 small lemons
200g/7oz/heaped ¾ cup caster (superfine) sugar
4 eggs
60g/2¼oz/¼ cup crème fraîche
3 red chillies, deseeded and finely chopped

1 Preheat the oven to 160°C/315°F/gas 2½. Line the base and sides of a 1kg/2lb 4oz loaf tin, preferably non-stick, with baking paper. Sift together the flour and baking powder into a bowl.

2 Whisk together half the lemon juice, 125g/4½oz/heaped ½ cup of the sugar and the eggs in a large bowl, using an electric whisk, for about 10 minutes until pale, thick and doubled in volume. Whisk in the crème fraîche, then gently fold in the sifted flour mixture. Fold in 2½ of the chillies and all the lemon zest until combined.

3 Pour into the prepared loaf tin, smooth the top and bake for 15 minutes, then open the oven door. Carefully pull the shelf out slightly with the loaf tin on it and mark the cake with a knife lengthways down the centre. (This will help the cake open up and give it a light texture.) Slide it back into the oven and bake for a further 20 minutes.

4 While the cake finishes baking, make the syrup. Put the remaining lemon juice, 2 tablespoons of the sugar and 2 tablespoons of water in a saucepan and heat over a high heat for 2 minutes until the sugar dissolves and the liquid turns syrupy. There should be about 3–4 tablespoons of liquid. Remove from the heat and leave to one side.

5 Check to see if the cake is cooked by inserting a skewer into the deepest part and if it comes out clean, then it is ready. If not, return the cake to the oven, bake for a further 5 minutes and check again. Leave the cake to cool for 5 minutes, then turn out onto a wire rack placed over a baking sheet. Peel away the baking paper and put the cake top-side up. Immediately spoon the lemon syrup evenly over the top of the cake, then leave on the rack to cool completely.

6 Put the remaining sugar in a saucepan with 3½ tablespoons of water and heat over a medium heat for 5 minutes, or until it forms a thick, shiny syrup. Remove from the heat and add the remaining chilli, then leave to infuse for 5 minutes. When the cake is completely cool, brush the top with the chilli syrup to give a nice, shiny coating.

ORANGE & TARRAGON GÂTEAU WITH CANDIED ORANGE

Who thought a beautiful juicy orange would partner a bold herb like tarragon? Make sure you wait for the perfect season, as tarragon will be at its best from the end of April until August. It is a shame the oranges are not in season at the same time but, thankfully, you can still find some great ones. When I had the idea of using them together, it took a while to get the right balance, but finally I got the measure right for this gateau. It is really all in the quantity, as you cannot be heavy-handed with tarragon. The end result is magic!

SERVES 4–6
PREPARATION TIME 30 minutes, plus 30 minutes cooling
COOKING TIME 30 minutes

50g/1¾oz unsalted butter, melted
90g/3¼oz/scant 1 cup ground almonds
40g/1½oz/⅓ cup plain (all-purpose) flour
½ tsp baking powder
4 egg whites, about 100ml/3½fl oz/scant ½ cup
40g/1½oz/scant ¼ cup caster (superfine) sugar
finely grated zest and juice of 1 small orange
2 tbsp roughly chopped tarragon leaves, plus leaves from 1 tarragon sprig, to decorate

FOR THE CANDIED ORANGE
100g/3½oz/scant ½ cup caster (superfine) sugar
1 large unwaxed orange, cut crossways into 5mm/¼in thick slices, discarding the end slices

1 Preheat the oven to 160°C/315°F/gas 2½. Lightly grease a loose-based 18cm/7in cake tin with about 1 tablespoon of the melted butter and line the base with baking paper. Sift the ground almonds, flour and baking powder into a bowl and leave to one side.

2 Whisk together the egg whites and sugar in a large bowl, using an electric whisk, until soft peaks form. Mix together the orange juice and remaining melted butter, then gently fold into the whisked egg whites. Gradually fold in the almond mixture, orange zest and chopped tarragon, a spoonful at a time, until incorporated.

3 Pour the mixture into the prepared cake tin and level the top, then bake for 18–20 minutes until risen and golden. Check the cake is cooked by inserting a skewer into the deepest part. If it comes out clean, then it is ready. If not, bake for a further 2–3 minutes. Remove from the oven and leave to cool for 5 minutes before turning out onto a wire rack, bottom-side up, removing the paper and leaving to cool.

4 Meanwhile, make the candied orange. Line a baking sheet with baking paper. Pour 150ml/5fl oz/scant ⅔ cup of water into a saucepan and stir in the sugar. Heat over a high heat until the sugar dissolves and the liquid becomes slightly syrupy. At the same time, put the orange slices in a small saucepan and just cover with water. Bring to the boil over a high heat, then discard the water. Repeat this again with fresh water. Drain the oranges again, add them to the pan containing the syrup and bring to a simmer. Cook for a further 5 minutes until they are tender but still hold their shape. Lift the orange slices out of the syrup and leave to cool on the baking sheet.

5 Return the syrup to a low heat and simmer for 8–10 minutes until thick enough to coat the back of a spoon. Leave to cool. Once cooled, cut each slice in half. Lay the orange slices, slightly overlapping, around the edge of the cake. Brush the warm syrup over the top of the oranges, then sprinkle the remaining tarragon over the top.

ORANGE-BLOSSOM STRAWBERRIES WITH LIME SHORTBREAD

SERVES 4
PREPARATION TIME 25 minutes, plus
   20 minutes macerating
COOKING TIME 20 minutes

500g/1lb 2oz/3⅓ cups
   strawberries, hulled and
   quartered
4 tsp sherry vinegar
100g/3½oz/scant ½ cup caster
   (superfine) sugar
juice of 2 oranges
4 tsp orange blossom extract

FOR THE LIME SHORTBREAD
finely grated zest of 1 lime
175g/6oz unsalted butter, softened
75g/2½oz/scant ⅓ cup caster
   (superfine) sugar, plus extra for
   sprinkling
200g/7oz/scant 1⅔ cups plain flour

When I was younger, we used to grow strawberries, and our favourite dessert was freshly picked ripe strawberries folded into whipping cream, just a touch, sprinkled with caster (superfine) sugar and chilled for an hour or so. We would then crush them with a fork before eating them. When I go home in the summer, I still love to eat them like this. Another family favourite is this stylish strawberry dessert, which I often call Strawberry Soup, although it isn't really a soup. I just call it that because the strawberries are served with lots of wonderful fresh fruit juice, scented with orange blossom. You could use the orange zest to make candied orange (see page 152) and sprinkle it over the top of the soup before serving.

I Preheat the oven to 160°C/315°F/gas 2½. To make the lime shortbread, beat together the lime zest, butter and sugar in a large bowl, using an electric mixer, until light and fluffy, then fold in the flour to make a soft dough. Press out between two sheets of baking paper until about 1cm/½in thick. Transfer to a baking sheet and lift off the top sheet of paper. Mark a pattern on the top with a fork, if you like. Bake for 12–18 minutes until just light golden and slightly firm to the touch.

2 Cut the shortbread straight away into whatever shape you fancy and sprinkle with sugar. You must cut the shortbread as soon as it comes out of the oven, while still soft and pliable. Put the baking sheet on a wire rack and leave the shortbread to cool and crisp up.

3 While the shortbread is baking, put the strawberries into a bowl and add the sherry vinegar. Reserve 2 tablespoons of the sugar, then sprinkle the remainder over the strawberries. Toss them together, cover with cling film (plastic wrap) and put in the refrigerator to macerate for 15–20 minutes only.

4 Pour the orange juice into a bowl and add the orange blossom extract. Take the strawberries out of the refrigerator and turn them in the macerating liquid. Using a slotted spoon, divide the strawberries into four large *coupé* glasses, leaving the residual juice in the bowl. Add the orange juice to the strawberry juice, mix well, then spoon over the strawberries and serve with the lime shortbread.

SPICED AUTUMN FRUITS WITH PAN-FRIED BRIOCHE

I've chosen my favourite fruits for this recipe – including yellow peaches, which I love – but be adventurous as it's a great way of using up any surplus stone fruits or apples or pears you may have. You can also use vanilla instead of star anise, or even black pepper to substitute for the cinnamon, but use them with care to avoid overpowering the fruit. I like to use Drambuie but you can use whisky instead, if you like.

SERVES 4
PREPARATION TIME 15 minutes
COOKING TIME 10 minutes

4 Victoria plums, halved and stones removed
4 greengages, halved and stones removed
1 yellow peach, quartered and stone removed
1 nectarine, quartered and stone removed
2 figs, quartered
75g/2½oz/heaped ⅓ cup light soft brown sugar
2 small cinnamon sticks
2 star anise
generous 4 tbsp Drambuie
juice of ½ lime
2 large eggs
4 slices of brioche loaf, about 1.5cm/⅝in thick
50g/1¾oz unsalted butter
Real Vanilla Ice Cream (see page 31), to serve

1 Heat a large, non-stick frying pan (skillet) over a medium-high heat. Add the fruit in a single layer, cut-side down, and cook for 1 minute. Sprinkle one-third of the sugar over the top, add the cinnamon and star anise, then continue to cook for 3–4 minutes until the fruits start to release their juices and soften slightly; they should still keep their shape.

2 Pour the Drambuie into the pan and immediately set it alight (it should burn for a few seconds), then turn the heat down to low so some of the Drambuie remains in the pan and cook for a further 1–2 minutes, taking care not to let the fruit soften too much. Stir in the lime juice and remove from the heat. Cover the pan to keep the fruit warm while you cook the brioche.

3 Beat the eggs with the remaining sugar in a large, shallow bowl until thick and creamy. Dip each side of the brioche briefly into the egg mixture until just coated, then leave to one side.

4 Heat a second large, non-stick frying pan (skillet) over a medium-high heat. Add the butter and when foaming, add the brioche and cook for a few minutes on each side until just golden brown and slightly crisp. Serve with the fruits and juice spooned over the top and with vanilla ice cream.

DECONSTRUCTED POACHED RHUBARB & PISTACHIO CRUMBLE

This is a very different type of crumble from the one your grandmother used to make, as the rhubarb is gently poached in a lemongrass-infused syrup and then elegantly layered in a glass with a lemon and lime cream and topped with a crispy pistachio crumble. It makes a deliciously elegant and modern twist on an old favourite.

SERVES 4

PREPARATION TIME 20 minutes, plus at least 3 hours chilling

COOKING TIME 50 minutes

400g/14oz rhubarb, peeled, peelings reserved, cut into 2.5cm/1in long pieces
100g/3½oz/scant ½ cup caster (superfine) sugar
1 lemongrass stalk, split and bruised

FOR THE LEMON AND LIME CREAM
185ml/6fl oz/¾ cup double (heavy) cream
2 tbsp caster (superfine) sugar
2 tbsp lemon juice
finely grated zest of ½ lemon
finely grated zest of ½ lime

FOR THE PISTACHIO CRUMBLE
100g/3½oz/heaped ¾ cup icing (confectioners') sugar
100g/3oz/heaped ¾ cup plain (all-purpose) flour
a pinch of salt
75g/2½oz/¾ cup ground almonds
40g/1½oz/scant ⅓ cup shelled pistachios, roughly chopped
100g/3½oz unsalted butter, softened

1 To make the lemon and lime cream, put the cream and sugar in a small saucepan over a high heat and bring to the boil. Put the lemon juice and both zests in a small jug and as soon as the cream comes to the boil, pour it into the jug and mix quickly to combine. Pour the hot cream mixture into four small sundae glasses, leave to cool, then chill in the refrigerator for at least 3 hours.

2 Put the rhubarb, rhubarb peelings, sugar and lemongrass in a sauté pan and just cover with water. Heat over a low heat until simmering, then cook for 15–20 minutes until the rhubarb is just tender but keeps its shape. Strain through a fine sieve (strainer) into the cleaned pan, then return the syrup to the heat and cook until it has reduced by half and is thick and syrupy. Meanwhile, discard the rhubarb peelings and the lemongrass and put the rhubarb in a shallow non-metallic dish. Pour the reduced syrup over the top of the rhubarb and leave to cool while you make the crumble.

3 Preheat the oven to 160°C/315°F/gas 2½. Put all the crumble ingredients in a large mixing bowl and rub gently with your fingertips to make a coarse crumb mixture. Tip onto a baking sheet in an even layer and bake for 20–25 minutes until golden brown. Turn the crumble mixture, bringing the edges into the centre and spreading it out into an even layer again every 6–8 minutes to make sure it cooks evenly. Remove from the oven and leave to cool completely until crunchy.

4 Take the cream-filled glasses out of the refrigerator and top with the rhubarb. Drizzle with the syrup and finish with the crumble, gently sprinkling it over the top. Serve immediately while the crumble is still crunchy.

HONEY PARFAIT WITH POACHED RHUBARB

SERVES 4
PREPARATION TIME 20 minutes,
  plus at least 8 hours freezing
COOKING TIME 10 minutes

5 egg yolks
1 vanilla pod, split in half
  lengthways and seeds
  scraped out
300g/10½ oz clear honey, such
  as lavender, thyme, chestnut
  or acacia
160ml/5¼fl oz/⅔ cup
  whipping cream
4 rhubarb sticks, chopped into
  large pieces
a few edible lavender flowers,
  to serve

There are so many types of honey to choose from, so do experiment to find the ones you like the best. I find the subtle flavours of flower honeys delicious, and they perfectly complement the flavour of delicate pink rhubarb.

1 Line a 500g/1lb 2oz loaf tin or terrine with cling film (plastic wrap), leaving a generous overhang. Put the egg yolks in a mixing bowl and add the vanilla seeds, reserving the pod for another recipe. Put 50g/1¾oz of the honey in a saucepan over a low heat and heat gently until melted. Then scrape into the egg yolks and whisk for about 10 minutes, using an electric whisk, until the mixture has cooled and forms a light ribbon when the beaters are lifted out of the bowl.

2 Whip the cream, then fold it into the cold egg and honey mixture. Pour into the prepared loaf tin, cover with the overhanging cling film (plastic wrap) and put in the freezer for at least 8 hours until firm.

3 To poach the rhubarb, pour 500ml/17fl oz/2 cups of water and the remaining honey into a saucepan and bring to the boil over a high heat. Turn the heat down to low and simmer for 3–4 minutes until it forms a very light syrup. Add the rhubarb and poach gently for about 5 minutes until just soft. Using a slotted spoon, scoop out the rhubarb and put on a plate to cool. At the same time, leave the syrup to cool. When both have cooled, return the rhubarb to the syrup, then sprinkle with the lavender flowers and serve with a slice of the honey parfait.

STRAWBERRY JELLY PURÉE WITH ELDERFLOWER YOGURT & SESAME NOUGATINE

I recommend that you wait for the strawberry season before making this dish – the quality of the fruit will make a massive difference to the taste of the jelly. I also use a lovely elderflower cordial, which is not as sweet as some cordials. To finish the dessert, I use black and white sesame seeds made into a lovely transparent, glass-like type of nougatine, which is very crunchy, but absolutely delicious!

SERVES 4
PREPARATION TIME 35 minutes,
    plus at least 30 minutes chilling
    and cooling
COOKING TIME 25 minutes

FOR THE STRAWBERRY JELLY PURÉE
2 leaves of gelatine, about 3g/¹⁄₁₆oz
    total weight
500g /1lb 2oz/3⅓ cups
    strawberries, hulled
1 tbsp caster (superfine) sugar
2 tbsp white balsamic vinegar

FOR THE ELDERFLOWER YOGURT
300g/10½oz/scant 1¼ cups
    Greek yogurt
150g/5½oz cream cheese
3 tbsp elderflower cordial
1 tbsp icing (confectioners')
    sugar, sifted

FOR THE SESAME NOUGATINE
50g/1¾oz/⅓ cup black sesame
    seeds
50g/1¾oz/⅓ cup white
    sesame seeds
2 tbsp liquid glucose
90g/3¼oz/heaped ⅓ cup
    caster (superfine) sugar
70g/2½oz unsalted butter

1 To make the jelly, put the gelatine in a medium bowl with enough cold water to cover, then leave to soften for 5 minutes. Drain and return the gelatine to the bowl. Heat a large, non-stick frying pan (skillet) over a high heat, add 280g/10oz/scant 2 cups of the strawberries and the sugar and cook for 2 minutes, tossing to coat the strawberries in the sugar. Remove from the heat, cover and leave for 3 minutes.

2 Transfer the strawberries and any juices in the pan to a blender and blend to a purée, then pass through a fine sieve (strainer), using a ladle to help you, directly onto the soaked gelatine and whisk briskly until it dissolves. Put the bowl directly in a larger bowl of iced water to cool rapidly. When the jelly starts to set, divide it equally into four whisky tumblers. Put them in the refrigerator to set for at least another 30 minutes. Meanwhile, cut 120g/4¼oz of the remaining strawberries into a fine dice, put in a bowl with the vinegar and leave to macerate for 20 minutes.

3 Put all the elderflower yogurt ingredients in a separate bowl and mix well to combine, then leave in the refrigerator until needed.

4 When the jelly has set, spoon the yogurt into the four glasses. Using a slotted spoon, add the macerated strawberries on top, then leave in the refrigerator to set while you make the nougatine.

5 Preheat the oven to 180°C/350°F/gas 4 and line a baking sheet with baking paper. Put all the nougatine ingredients in a non-stick frying pan (skillet). Add 1 tablespoon of water and stir to combine, then heat over a medium heat for 3 minutes, or until the butter melts and the sugar dissolves. Turn the heat up and cook for 4–5 minutes until it just starts to turn golden. Pour onto the prepared tray and spread out with a wet spatula. Bake for 12 minutes until golden brown – it shouldn't be as dark as caramel. Remove from the oven and leave to cool on the tray until crisp. Break the nougatine into large pieces. Remove the glasses from the refrigerator and balance a piece of nougatine on the top of each dessert, then put the rest in a bowl to share.

PAN-FRIED PLUMS & ALMOND BISCOTTI WITH AMARETTO CREAM

Pan-fried plums are always tasty, with their touch of acidity and lovely, delicate texture, so I thought a biscuit (cookie) would be good with them – and a biscotti seemed just the right choice. It's unusual, perhaps not often baked at home, and the almonds give it a good nutty crunch. For a change, try serving the dish with some silky Greek-style yogurt with a sprinkling of cinnamon.

SERVES 4
PREPARATION TIME 30 minutes
COOKING TIME 40 minutes

FOR THE ALMOND BISCOTTI
100g/3½oz unsalted butter, softened
75g/2½oz/scant ⅓ cup caster
    (superfine) sugar
3 eggs
seeds from ½ vanilla pod
250g/9oz/2 cups plain (all-
    purpose) flour, plus extra
    for dusting
grated zest of ½ lemon
a pinch of ground star anise
20g/¾oz/scant ¼ cup
    ground almonds
½ tsp baking powder
4 tbsp whole blanched
    almonds, toasted
a pinch of salt

FOR THE PLUMS
100g/3½oz/scant ½ cup caster
    (superfine) sugar
10 plums, halved, stoned, then each
    cut into 8 segments
1 tbsp amaretto

FOR THE AMARETTO CREAM
30g/1oz/¼ cup icing
    (confectioners') sugar
1 egg
125g/4½oz mascarpone
125ml/4fl oz/½ cup double
    (heavy) cream
2 tbsp amaretto

1 Preheat the oven to 180°C/350°F/gas 4 and line a baking sheet with baking paper. To make the biscotti, whisk together the butter and sugar, using an electric whisk, until very pale and fluffy. Add 2 of the eggs, one at a time, beating in between each addition, then add all the vanilla seeds and all the remaining biscotti ingredients except the remaining egg and the salt. Continue to mix on a slow speed until the mixture just comes together. Scoop the dough out onto a lightly floured work surface and form into a log about 20 x 7.5cm/ 8 x 3in. Using the palms of your hands, roll the log until it is 2.5cm/1in thick, then put on the baking sheet – it should just fit.

2 Whisk the remaining egg with the salt and 1 tablespoon of water. Brush over the top of the loaf, then bake for 8 minutes. Turn the tray around front to back, turn the oven down to 150°C/300°F/gas 2 and cook for a further 20–25 minutes until pale golden.

3 To cook the plums, put a frying pan (skillet) over a low heat, add the sugar and cook gently for a few minutes until it turns to a light golden caramel. Add the plums a few pieces at a time, mix them into the caramel and cook for 5 minutes until they are soft, then drizzle over the amaretto and stir gently. Leave to cool to room temperature.

4 To make the amaretto cream, whisk the icing (confectioners') sugar and egg in a large bowl until very light and pale. Mix the mascarpone and cream in a separate bowl, then whisk in the amaretto. Fold the mixtures together, then whisk until just holding soft peaks.

5 Remove the biscotti from the oven, transfer to a chopping board and cut off both ends of the loaf, then cut the rest into 1cm/½in slices and lay them on the baking sheet. Return to the oven and bake for a further 5–8 minutes until they are just dry and light golden. Crumble the ends of the biscotti into 5mm/¼in pieces in a small bowl.

6 Sprinkle half the plums with the crumble and half the amaretto cream, then spoon more plums on top and finish with the rest of the cream. Balance a biscotti on top and serve the rest separately.

CARAMELIZED APRICOTS WITH PISTACHIO NUTS & PEACH SAUCE

SERVES 4
PREPARATION TIME 10 minutes
COOKING TIME 25 minutes

100g/3½oz/scant ½ cup caster
   (superfine) sugar
2 large ripe peaches, stone
   removed and roughly chopped
juice of 1 lemon
1 tbsp chopped pistachio nuts
2 tbsp clear honey
8 large, firm apricots, halved and
   stone removed
20g/¾oz unsalted butter
Pain de Gênes (see page 216),
   to serve

If there is a season I wait for with impatience, it is spring. Why? One of the reasons is the start of the apricot season; I love this fruit so much. When they are very fresh and ripe, they smell like fresh girolles – sweet, with a hint of dry leaf scent and a touch of flower blossom – gorgeous! So imagine what they are like when pan-fried and then served with crushed pistachio nuts and a lemony peach syrup. You know what, I think I should stop talking about them now – let's just make and enjoy them! By the way, fruit will always cook better when it has either been brought back to room temperature before cooking or has been stored at room temperature. Never cook fruit straight from the refrigerator as the shock of the heat will quite often make the fruit split or stick to the pan.

1 Heat a non-stick frying pan (skillet) over a medium heat, add the sugar and 300ml/10½fl oz/scant 1¼ cups of water and heat until the sugar has dissolved and the liquid has just started to simmer. Add the peaches and lemon juice, return to a simmer and poach for 8–10 minutes until very soft and almost puréed, but still holding a little shape. Strain through a sieve (strainer), catching the syrup in a clean bowl, and leave to one side so that the juices can drip into the syrup.

2 Put the pan that you've just used for the peaches back over a medium heat, add the pistachios and cook gently for a few minutes until golden and slightly sticky. Drain on a clean dish towel, fold the dish towel over and gently crush the nuts using a rolling pin so they are just partially crushed.

3 Put the same frying pan (skillet) back onto the heat again. Add the honey and when it is just foaming, add the apricots, cut-side down, and instantly start gently swirling the pan around so that the apricots don't stick or burn. Add the butter and when foaming, turn the apricots over and cook for a few minutes until they are nicely caramelized. Add about 100ml/3½fl oz/scant ½ cup of the syrupy peach juices and cook for a further 3–4 minutes until the apricots are lovely and tender but are still holding their shape.

4 Spoon the apricots over the peaches and drizzle with the last of the peach syrup. Sprinkle with the crushed pistachio pieces and serve with *pain de gênes*.

CHERRY AND ALMOND CREAM TARTS

Kirsch was originally made from Morello cherries, grown in the Black Forest in Germany, although it is now made from many types of cherry. Where I come from in eastern France, kirsch is a speciality of a town called Fougerolles. It is a clear fruit brandy made with a double-distillation of whole cherries – hence the slight taste of bitter almond. That hint of bitterness is just what we are looking for in this tart, for which we are using almonds, cherries, of course, and a lovely sabayon made with this beautiful *eaux de vie*.

SERVES 8
PREPARATION TIME 40 minutes,
   plus 50 minutes chilling
COOKING TIME 20 minutes

FOR THE SWEET PASTRY
grated zest of ½ blood orange
90g/3¼oz unsalted butter,
   softened, plus extra for greasing
a pinch of salt
70g/2½oz/heaped ½ cup icing
   (confectioners') sugar
25g/1oz/¼ cup ground almonds
1 egg
175g/6oz/heaped 1⅓ cups plain
   (all-purpose) flour

FOR THE ALMOND CREAM
100g/3½oz unsalted butter,
   softened
75g/2½oz/heaped ½ cup icing
   (confectioners') sugar
75g/2½oz/¾ cup ground almonds
3 eggs
1 tbsp kirsch

FOR THE TOPPING
225g/8oz cherries, pitted and
   halved or quartered, depending
   on the size
50g/1¾oz/⅓ cup flaked almonds

Real Vanilla Ice Cream (see page
   31), to serve

1 To make the pastry, beat the orange zest, butter, salt, sugar, ground almonds and egg in a bowl until light and fluffy. Sift in the flour and fold through and as soon as the dough is formed, stop! You don't want to work this pastry at all. Wrap in cling film (plastic wrap) and put in the refrigerator for 20 minutes.

2 Grease eight 9 x 4cm/3½ x 1½in loose-bottomed individual tart tins with a little butter if they are not non-stick. Roll the pastry between two sheets of baking paper until 3mm/⅛in thick, then cut out 8 discs, each about 18cm/7in in diameter. One at a time, roll each pastry disc over the rolling pin and lift over a tart tin. With one hand, lift the pastry edge and with the other, gently tuck the pastry into the bottom and sides of the tin so that it fits tightly. Don't overstretch it or it'll break, just press gently to push out any bubbles. Trim off any excess pastry by rolling the pin over the top edge of the tin. Prick the bases with a fork and chill for 30 minutes to prevent the pastry shrinking during baking.

3 Preheat the oven to 160°C/315°F/gas 2½. To make the almond cream, whisk together the butter, sugar and ground almonds in a large bowl, using an electric whisk, or in a food mixer, until light and fluffy. Add the eggs one at a time so that the mixture doesn't split. Add the kirsch, then mix for about 8–10 minutes until very light and smooth. Spoon the mixture into the pastry cases, taking care to leave a good 1cm/½in clear from the top of the pastry. Cover the mixture with the cherry pieces (if you feel like it, you can arrange them perfectly, but random is fine!) and sprinkle some flaked almonds on top. Sit the tins on a baking sheet.

4 Bake for 20 minutes until a skewer inserted through the deepest part comes out clean. If not, return it to the oven for a further 3–5 minutes and check again. Serve warm with a lovely vanilla ice cream.

ORANGE, CARDAMOM & THYME SALAD

I love to make this refreshing salad with blood oranges when they are in season. Oranges combine so well with so many desserts, especially those with chocolate, as the soft, sweet acidity cuts through that rich texture. Try this with my Chocolate, Chilli and Lemongrass Tart (see page 224). The hint of thyme adds an elegant and unexpected touch that will surprise your guests.

SERVES 4
PREPARATION TIME 15 minutes, plus 30 minutes macerating and 30 minutes cooling

2 small blood oranges or
    ordinary oranges
2 cardamom pods, lightly crushed
2 tbsp caster (superfine) sugar
½ tsp freshly picked thyme leaves

I Finely pare the orange zest, then peel and segment the oranges over a bowl to catch the juices. Put the cardamom into the juice and leave for 30 minutes. Pat the orange segments dry on a clean dish towel.

2 Put the zest in a saucepan, cover with cold water and bring to the boil over a medium heat. Remove from the heat, drain, refresh under cold water, drain, then repeat the process. Return the zest to the pan, add the sugar and 3 tablespoons of water and stir to dissolve. Bring to the boil and cook for 5 minutes until the zest is transparent, then leave to cool.

3 Strain the flavoured juice into a small pan over a medium heat and cook for a few minutes until reduced by half and syrupy. Stir in the zest and syrup, then leave to cool. Toss with the orange segments in a bowl, then add the thyme leaves to serve.

CARAMELIZED PEAR & ROSEMARY CAKE

I love the flavour of just-ripe autumn pears, roasted in a red wine syrup with flaked almonds, in a *tatin*, with chocolate and vanilla ice cream or simply on their own when they're juicy. But you will never enjoy them more than when they are caramelized, then folded into a cake mix with a hint of scented rosemary. Of course, you could replace that with spices but somehow that did not feel right. I wanted some freshness to spread through the cake while it was cooking so I added the rosemary only after the pears were caramelized and cooling to allow the scent to infuse the cake.

SERVES 6–8
PREPARATION TIME 25 minutes
COOKING TIME 30 minutes

FOR THE PEARS
100g/3½oz/scant ½ cup caster (superfine) sugar
50g/1¾oz unsalted butter
2 pears at room temperature, peeled, halved, cored and roughly chopped
leaves from 1 rosemary sprig, finely chopped

FOR THE CAKE
100g/3½oz unsalted butter, plus extra for greasing
a little flour, for dusting
60g/2¼oz/½ cup icing (confectioners') sugar
3 eggs
110g/3¾oz/scant 1 cup plain (all-purpose) flour
1 tsp baking powder

1 Preheat the oven to 160°C/315°F/gas 2½ and butter and flour a 1kg/2lb 4oz loaf tin or use a silicone mould. To cook the pears, put a large frying pan (skillet) over a low heat, add the sugar and cook gently for a few minutes until it turns to a light golden caramel. Add the butter and when foaming, add the pears. (Once more, it is essential that the pears are at room temperature, otherwise the caramel will block – it will form lumps of hardened caramel and then it's a matter of starting again!) Cook the pears for about 10 minutes until they are soft and caramelized. Remove from the heat, add the rosemary and toss to combine, then lay the pears on a clean dish towel to cool and dry out slightly – you want the dish towel to absorb any juices.

2 To make the cake, the butter mixture needs to be really light in colour and in texture so whisk the icing (confectioners') sugar and butter, using an electric whisk, until almost white in colour and very light and fluffy. Only then, add the eggs, one at a time, beating well between each addition. Sift the flour and baking powder together into a bowl, then sift two-thirds into the mixture. Add the pears to the reserved flour and toss to coat thoroughly, then fold the dusted pears gently into the cake mix.

3 Spoon the mixture into the prepared tin and bake for 25 minutes until a skewer inserted into the centre comes out clean. If not, return the cake to the oven for a further 5 minutes and check again.

4 Transfer the cake to a wire rack and leave to cool for as long as you can wait, then cut a slice and serve with a cup of tea. And if I were you, I'd sneak a slice quickly before everyone else smells it and wants some too.

CARAMELIZED MELON WITH ROSEMARY FLOWER & GRAPEFRUIT JUICE

When I hear "caramelized" in relation to fruit, I can almost taste it already, whether it's pineapple, apple, peach or apricot. In this recipe I've used melon. You will need a just-ripe, tasty fruit, so you can appreciate the full flavour and sweetness of it contrasting with the bitterness of the grapefruit. And finally the delicate scent from the rosemary flower. A delightful trio! Serve warm with a lovely slice of cake.

SERVES 4
PREPARATION TIME 45 minutes
COOKING TIME 25 minutes

2 small, just-ripe charentais melons, peeled, cored and cut into large slices
100g/3½ oz brown soft sugar
100ml/3½fl oz/scant ½ cup pink grapefruit juice
1 tbsp cardamom pods, crushed
2 rosemary sprigs
30g/1oz unsalted butter
1½ tbsp sweet white wine
1 small handful of rosemary flowers
freshly ground black pepper

1 Line up all the melon slices on a baking sheet and sprinkle with the sugar. Set aside. Infuse the grapefruit juice with the cardamom and rosemary sprigs for about 30 minutes to get a good flavour.

2 Melt the butter in a large frying pan (skillet) over a medium heat. When the butter starts to foam, add the melon slices and cook for 1 minute on each side. Add the sweet white wine and let half of it evaporate. Remove the melon from the pan and arrange on a serving plate. Pour the pink grapefruit juice into the pan. Turn the heat down and simmer until a shiny syrup starts to form and caramelize to a lovely golden brown. Coat the melon slices with the syrup and sprinkle with rosemary flowers and black pepper to serve.

CHAPTER 6
FROM BARN & FARMYARD

This is the noisy part of the farm, as there is often such
a mix of animals, from ducks to geese to chickens to
roosters, and even sometimes pigs. This is the way it was
at Aunty Suzanne's smallholding next to La Ferme des
Grands Bois, where you really could have written a play
about all the characters – especially the early mornings
when you were likely to be woken up by the rooster
telling you to get up and start the day, or the geese when
a stranger was walking past. A joyful cacophony of sound!
What a lovely time I had.

CHICKEN & LEMONGRASS BROTH

My mother never let anything go to waste. She always made use of everything, so if we had a roast chicken she would keep the carcass and use it as the base of a beautiful clear soup, then add extras such as vegetables, herbs and lentils. I have always enjoyed making broths at home, and here I've added a new twist with fragrant lemongrass and lime zest. To make a more substantial soup, you could add a handful of cooked rice or lentils to the broth and heat through thoroughly before ladling it over the chicken.

SERVES 4
PREPARATION TIME 30 minutes
COOKING TIME 2 hours

FOR THE BROTH BASE
1 tbsp olive oil
1 small chicken, about 1kg/
    2lb 4oz total weight
2 carrots, peeled and
    roughly chopped
1 lemongrass stalk, bruised
3 thyme sprigs
1 small bunch of coriander
    (cilantro), leaves picked and
    stalks reserved

FOR THE CHICKEN AND
    LEMONGRASS BROTH
2 large carrots, peeled and
    quartered lengthways
3 lemongrass stalks: 2 bruised,
    1 peeled
2 thyme sprigs
finely grated zest of 1 lime
2 tbsp extra virgin olive oil
sea salt and freshly ground
    black pepper

1 To make the broth base, heat a large, flameproof casserole dish or frying pan (skillet) over a medium heat. Add the olive oil and chicken and seal for 3–4 minutes on each side until just starting to turn a light golden brown. Add the carrots, lemongrass stalk, thyme and half the coriander (cilantro) stalks and cook for a further 5 minutes until the chicken is browned all over and the vegetables just coloured.

2 Transfer the browned chicken and vegetables to a large, deep saucepan, cover with about 2l/70fl oz/8 cups of cold water and bring to the boil over a high heat, skimming off any foam that rises to the surface, as this helps to keep the soup clear. Add the quartered carrots, the bruised lemongrass, the thyme and the remaining coriander (cilantro) stalks. Return to a simmer, then turn the heat down to very low, cover with a lid and simmer for 1¼–1½ hours until the chicken is very tender and starts to fall apart.

3 Carefully remove the chicken from the pan and leave to one side to cool slightly. Strain the vegetable broth into a clean pan, reserving the solids, and return the broth to a low heat. Simmer for about 10–15 minutes, uncovered, until the broth has reduced by one-third and is full of flavour.

4 Meanwhile, carefully lift the quartered carrots out of the strainer, discarding the rest of the solids. Finely chop the carrots and put in soup bowls. When the chicken is cool enough to handle, remove and discard the skin, then pull the chicken meat off the bones and tear it into small pieces. Add the chicken and a pinch of salt and pepper to the soup bowls, then scatter over the coriander (cilantro) leaves. Sprinkle the lime zest over and drizzle with the extra virgin olive oil.

5 Remove the tough outer leaves, top and root from the remaining lemongrass stalk, then slice very thinly and add to the bowls. By now, the broth should be ready, so simply add a couple of ladlefuls to each bowl before serving.

SMOKED DUCK & LENTILS WITH LAVENDER

You can hot-smoke your duck at home or use a cold-smoked, air-dried duck, sliced and served as a salad with the hot lentils. Either way, corn-fed, free-range birds will give the best results. I enjoy both and usually decide depending on the weather, but these flavour combinations always works well.

SERVES 4
PREPARATION TIME 20 minutes
COOKING TIME 35 minutes

FOR THE CRYSTALLIZED ORANGE
1 large orange, washed
    and scrubbed
2 tbsp caster (superfine) sugar

FOR THE SMOKED DUCK
100g/3½oz/½ cup basmati rice
3 tbsp green tea
1 tsp caster (superfine) sugar
2 small lavender sprigs
1 tbsp rapeseed (canola) oil
2 duck breasts, about 200g/
    7oz each
1 tbsp clear honey
a few chervil leaves

FOR THE LENTILS
200g/7oz/1 cup Puy lentils, picked
    over and rinsed
1 onion, finely chopped
2 cloves
1 bouquet garni, made with 1 thyme
    sprig and 1 parsley sprig, tied
    together with kitchen string
50g/1¾oz unsalted butter
sea salt and freshly ground black
    pepper

1 To crystallize the orange zest, pare the zest from the orange into fine strips using a peeler or small, sharp knife, cutting away the pith. Put the zest in a small saucepan, cover with cold water and bring to the boil over a medium heat. Remove from the heat, drain, refresh under cold water, then drain again. Repeat this blanching process.

2 Return the zest to the pan over a low heat and add the sugar and 3 tablespoons of water, stirring until dissolved. Raise the heat to medium and bring to the boil, then turn the heat down to low and simmer for 4–5 minutes, or until the zest becomes transparent. Remove from the heat and leave the strips to cool in the syrup.

3 Put a large piece of kitchen foil, shiny-side down, in the bottom of a wok or steamer. Add the rice, tea, sugar and 1 lavender sprig, and drizzle with the rapeseed (canola) oil. Cover with a wire rack or steamer insert and lid, and put over a medium heat for 5 minutes, or until the mixture starts to smoke. Quickly put the duck breasts inside, cover with kitchen foil to help seal the duck, then put the lid on, turn the heat to low and smoke for 5 minutes.

4 Meanwhile, put the lentils in a small saucepan and cover with cold water. Bring to the boil, then skim off any foam that rises to the surface. Add the onion, cloves and bouquet garni, turn the heat down to low and simmer for 5–7 minutes until only just tender. Season with salt and pepper to taste, then strain, discarding the flavourings.

5 When the duck is almost ready, heat a non-stick frying pan (skillet) over a medium heat. Turn off the heat under the smoker and lift out the duck. Put the duck, skin-side down, in the frying pan and cook for 4–5 minutes. Flip the duck over, brush the skin with the honey and sprinkle over a little of the remaining lavender, then cook for 5 minutes. Lift out, cover with foil and leave to rest.

6 Heat a non-stick frying pan (skillet) until hot, add the butter and lentils and stir-fry for a few minutes until hot. Cut the duck into chunks and serve on top of the lentils, sprinkled with the orange zest strips with a little of the syrup, the chervil leaves and a pinch more lavender.

CORIANDER & STAR ANISE PORK RILLETTES

In my first book, the *French Brasserie Cookbook,* I included a recipe for a classic duck rillettes, but in this book I wanted to bring a different and more modern character to this popular dish by replacing the herbs with spices such as star anise. It brings an exotic yet delicate scent that goes perfectly with the pork. Use the whole spice rather than ground as the latter just doesn't have the same depth of flavour.

SERVES 4
PREPARATION TIME 10 minutes,
    plus 6–12 hours marinating
    and at least 24 hours chilling
COOKING TIME 4 hours

1.2kg/2lb 10oz pork shoulder, diced
60g/2¼oz/¼ cup sea salt
2 tsp coriander seeds
2 star anise
1.5kg/3lb 5oz goose fat
leaves from 2 coriander
    (cilantro) sprigs
freshly ground black pepper
toast or warm crusty bread,
    to serve

1 Put the pork, salt, half the coriander seeds and 1 star anise in a large bowl and season with pepper. Turn everything until combined, then cover with cling film (plastic wrap) and leave to marinate in the refrigerator for 6–12 hours. The longer you leave the pork to marinate, the better the flavour will be.

2 After the pork has marinated, preheat the oven to 140°C/275°F/ gas 1. Rinse the marinade off the pork, reserving the star anise, and pat dry with paper towel.

3 Melt the goose fat in a large, flameproof casserole dish over a low heat. Add the pork and turn until well coated, then transfer the casserole dish to the oven and cook, uncovered, for 4 hours until the meat falls apart when prodded with a fork. Strain the pork through a fine sieve (strainer), reserving the fat, and put in a bowl. Shred the pork using two forks, then add about 125ml/4fl oz/½ cup of the cooking fat to moisten.

4 Transfer the shredded pork to a sealable jar or small earthenware dish and press down lightly. Pour enough of the cooking fat over the top to cover the pork and seal it, then add the reserved star anise and scatter with the remaining coriander seeds and coriander (cilantro) leaves. (If there is any remaining goose fat, it can be put in a jar and kept for other uses, such as roasting potatoes.) Cover with a lid or baking paper and chill for at least 24 hours before serving to allow the flavours to mingle. Serve with warm crusty bread.

EGGS EN COCOTTE WITH DRIED MUSHROOMS & ROSEMARY CROÛTES

I've used duck's eggs to give a rich and interesting flavour to the *cocottes,* but do watch the timing so the yolks remain soft and runny. The dried mushrooms add an intense burst of flavour to the finished dish. They can be prepared up to a week in advance and kept in an airtight container.

SERVES 4
PREPARATION TIME 30 minutes,
    plus 1 hour infusing
COOKING TIME 25 minutes,
    plus 2½ hours drying

FOR THE DRIED MUSHROOMS
200g/7oz button mushrooms,
    thinly sliced
2 egg whites, lightly beaten
1 tsp crushed sea salt, plus
    extra to season

FOR THE ROSMARY CROÛTES
3 tbsp olive oil
leaves from 1 rosemary sprig
8 slices of day-old baguette,
    about 3mm/⅛in thick each

FOR THE EGGS
200g/7oz mixed wild mushrooms,
    roughly chopped
1 tsp olive oil
½ small shallot, finely diced
½ garlic clove, finely diced
5 thyme sprigs, leaves picked from
    1 sprig
40g/1½oz unsalted butter, softened
4 duck's eggs or large hen's eggs
300ml/10½fl oz/scant 1¼ cups
    chilled whipping cream (it must
    be straight from the refrigerator)
freshly ground black pepper

1 To dry the mushrooms, preheat the oven to 70°C/150°F/gas ¼, not on a fan setting, and line a baking sheet with baking paper. Put the mushrooms on the prepared tray in a single layer, brush lightly with the egg whites, sprinkle with the salt and bake for 2½ hours until dry and crisp. Remove from the oven and leave to cool. Blitz 2 small handfuls to a powder in a mini food processor, then leave to one side.

2 To make the rosemary croûtes, put the oil and rosemary leaves in a saucepan and warm through. Take off the heat and leave to infuse for 1 hour. Strain through a sieve (strainer) and discard the rosemary.

3 Turn the oven up to 140°C/275°F/gas 1 and line a baking sheet with baking paper. Put the bread slices on the prepared tray and brush both sides with the rosemary oil. Cover with a second sheet of baking paper and a slightly smaller baking sheet, which fits inside the large one. This will help the bread stay flat and cook evenly. Bake for 8–10 minutes until light golden, then leave to cool between the trays.

4 Meanwhile, bring a saucepan of water to the boil, add the chopped wild mushrooms and return to the boil. Drain well, then tip the mushrooms onto paper towel and pat dry. Heat a large frying pan (skillet) over a medium heat. Add the oil, shallot and garlic and cook for 2 minutes until softened but not coloured. Turn the heat up to high, add the mushrooms and sauté for a further 2 minutes until just softened. Season with salt and pepper to taste, then add the thyme leaves, cover with a lid and leave to one side.

5 When the croûtes are ready, turn the oven up to 180°C/350°F/gas 4 and brush the insides of four 150ml/5fl oz/scant ⅔ cup ramekins with the softened butter. Spoon the mushrooms into the ramekins and crack an egg into each one. Pour the cream over to just cover, season with salt and pepper and top each one with a thyme sprig. Put the ramekins in the roasting tray, pour in enough hot water to come halfway up the sides and bake for 10–12 minutes until the tops are just set. Turn off the heat and leave in the oven for a further 2–3 minutes but make sure the yolks remain runny. Sprinkle with the dried mushrooms and serve with the rosemary croûtes for dipping into the egg.

GOATS' CHEESE, SUMMER VEGETABLE & HERB QUICHE

This quiche says summer to me – the warmth and sun of the Mediterranean – with its colourful mix of artichokes, red chard and aromatic lemon thyme. Not forgetting the crumbly goats' cheese, which, when cooked slowly, adds an almost almondy flavour to the quiche. Try it with the Reduced Balsamic Vinegar as it gives the tart an added depth of flavour. Enjoy the quiche with a red chard salad and pickled shallots.

SERVES 4
PREPARATION TIME 20 minutes, plus making the pastry and vinegar and 30 minutes chilling
COOKING TIME 1 hour

15g/½oz unsalted butter, plus extra for greasing
250g/9oz Savoury Short Pastry (see page 30)
plain (all-purpose) flour, for dusting
200ml/7fl oz/scant 1 cup double (heavy) cream
100g/3½oz soft goats' cheese log, such as Golden Cross or Ste Maure, rind removed, crumbled
2 lemon thyme sprigs
2 tbsp olive oil
1 onion, finely chopped
75g/2½oz drained bottled artichokes, thinly sliced
75g/2½oz carrot, peeled and finely diced
50g/1¾oz red chard leaves
25g/1oz watercress leaves
2 eggs, lightly beaten
¼ tsp freshly grated nutmeg
1 tbsp Reduced Balsamic Vinegar (see page 27)
sea salt and freshly ground black pepper

1 Lightly grease a 20cm/8in loose-bottomed tart tin. Roll out the pastry on a lightly floured work surface until 25cm/10in diameter x 3mm/⅛in thick and use to line the base and the sides of the tart tin, pressing it into the edges without overstretching the dough. Trim any excess pastry, prick the base with a fork and chill for 30 minutes to prevent the pastry shrinking during baking.

2 Meanwhile, make the filling. Pour the cream into a saucepan, add two-thirds of the goats' cheese and the lemon thyme and warm over a low heat for 3–5 minutes, whisking until smooth and silky. Remove from the heat and leave to cool while you make the rest of the filling.

3 Heat a non-stick frying pan (skillet) over a medium heat. Add the butter, oil and onion and fry for 5 minutes, stirring occasionally, until softened but not browned. Add the artichokes and carrot, mix well and cook for 5 minutes until softened, then add the red chard and watercress and cook for a further 2 minutes until wilted. Tip out onto paper towel and press dry.

4 Add the eggs and nutmeg to the cooled cream mixture, season with salt and pepper, then whisk to combine.

5 Preheat the oven to 170°C/325°F/gas 3. Line the pastry case with baking paper and cover with baking beans. Put the tart tin on a baking sheet and bake for 12 minutes, then remove the paper and baking beans and turn the oven up to 180°C/350°F/gas 4. Brush the base of the pastry case with the reduced balsamic vinegar. Spoon the vegetable mixture over the base of the pastry case and sprinkle with the remaining goats' cheese. Pour in the egg mixture and bake for 35 minutes, or until firm to the touch. Serve warm or at room temperature.

LIME-LEAF POACHED CHICKEN

I love the fragrance of kaffir lime leaves. In fact, it reminds me of my time in the army in the South of France. In the village I was based, when walking past orange trees, lemons and limes, you did not need to be right next to them to appreciate their fragrance. Just as the light breeze and the heat together brought that beautiful blossom smell right to me, so, here in this recipe, the lime leaf gently lifts the bouillon by adding a delicate scent and freshness to the chicken. It works so well.

SERVES 4
PREPARATION TIME 10 minutes, plus making the stock
COOKING TIME 30 minutes

4 chicken breasts, skin on, about 175g/6oz each
1 tbsp olive oil
1 thick slice of fresh horseradish
6 kaffir lime leaves
1.2l/40fl oz/4¾ cups Chicken Stock (see page 24)
300g/10½oz potatoes, peeled and cut into 1cm/½in dice
400g/14oz pointed or sweetheart cabbage, finely sliced
1 small handful of coriander (cilantro) leaves, roughly chopped
sea salt

1 Put the chicken breasts in a large saucepan and just cover with lukewarm water. Put over a medium-low heat for about 5 minutes and gently bring to a simmer. Lift the chicken out of the water and drain on paper towel, then, when cool enough to handle, carefully remove the skin from each breast and reserve. Cover the chicken breasts with cling film (plastic wrap) and leave to one side. Discard the poaching water.

2 Preheat the oven to 190°C/375°F/gas 5 and line a baking sheet with baking paper. Put the skin, flesh-side down, on the prepared tray and brush with the oil. Cover with a second sheet of baking paper and a slightly smaller baking sheet, which fits inside the large tray. This will help to keep the skin flat and let it cook evenly. Roast for 10–12 minutes until golden brown and nearly crisp. If it's not ready, return it to the oven for a further 5 minutes, then check again. Leave the skin to cool between the baking sheets so that it crisps up further.

3 Meanwhile, to make the bouillon, put the horseradish, kaffir lime leaves and stock in the sauté pan and bring almost to the boil over a high heat. Turn the heat down to medium and simmer for 10–12 minutes until reduced by one-third, skimming off any foam that rises to the surface.

4 Add the poached chicken breasts and potatoes to the simmering bouillon and cook for 8 minutes, then add the cabbage and simmer for a further 2 minutes until the chicken is cooked through and the cabbage just wilted. Season with salt to taste, then scatter over the coriander (cilantro) leaves.

5 Remove the chicken, lime leaves and horseradish from the bouillon. Leave the chicken to one side and discard the flavourings. Ladle the bouillon and vegetables into shallow soup bowls. Slice the chicken breasts and put them on top, then break the crisp chicken skin into pieces and scatter over before serving.

ALMOND MILK CHICKEN SCENTED WITH LEMONGRASS, GARLIC & THYME

SERVES 4
PREPARATION TIME 30 minutes, plus
   12 hours marinating
COOKING TIME 1 hour

1 chicken, prepared and cut into
   8 pieces
1 tbsp ground turmeric
1 litre/35fl oz/4¼ cups almond milk
4 lemongrass stalks
500ml/17fl oz/2 cups Chicken
   Stock (see page 24)
2 tbsp olive oil
1 small onion, roughly chopped
2 parsley sprigs
sea salt and freshly ground black
   pepper
Thai-Style Pilau Rice (see page 29),
   to serve

The almond milk here helps to tenderize the chicken. It's best to marinate it overnight so the flavours really infuse the meat and we get that lovely scent of garlic, thyme and lemongrass. Accompanied by Thai rice, this is an absolute delight.

1 Place the pieces of chicken in a large, shallow Pyrex dish, then season with the turmeric and some black pepper. Pour in the almond milk, cover the dish and leave it overnight in the refrigerator.

2 The following day, bruise the lemongrass stalks to release their flavour. Pour the stock into a saucepan over a medium heat and add the lemongrass. Bring to the boil, then reduce the heat to low and keep it at a simmer so the stock starts to infuse. When the liquid has reduced by half, remove from the heat and set aside to further infuse.

3 Place the chicken on some paper towel and pat dry. Heat a large, heavy-based saucepan over a medium heat. Add the oil and the chicken pieces. Cook until they're a nice golden colour all over, then throw in the onion and sauté for 2–3 minutes until softened. Deglaze the pan with 200ml (7fl oz/scant 1 cup) of the milk marinade, bring to a simmer and cook, covered, for 20 minutes until the chicken just starts to become tender. Add the chicken stock and simmer for a further 20 minutes over a medium-low heat, or until the chicken is cooked through. Check the seasoning, then serve with Thai-Style Pilau Rice.

MARINATED CHICKEN WITH GINGER, LEMON & GARLIC

At home we love these flavours with the chicken, it's so delicious. Loads of garlic, a touch of ginger, slices of caremelized lemon and fresh basil. (You could also add a touch of chilli but those three ingredients together will be plenty.) A great feast to share with friends on a spring day outdoors – or in if it's raining! I made this a few times during lockdown and it works very well indeed. It's great comfort food!

SERVES 4
PREPARATION TIME overnight
  marinating
COOKING TIME 45 minutes

4 small lemons, sliced
1 head of garlic, unpeeled, each
  clove slightly crushed
1 bulb of fresh ginger, thinly sliced
2 basil sprigs
4 small poussin chickens or 1 large
  (1.6kg/3 lb 8 oz), prepared by
  your butcher
4 tbsp olive oil
sea salt and freshly ground black
  pepper
grilled (broiled) vegetables and
  roasted new potatoes, to serve

1 Take a large shallow dish and scatter in half of the garnish – the lemon slices, garlic, ginger and basil. Place the prepared poussins or chicken on top and press down. Add the rest of the garnish on top, drizzle with 2 tablespoons of olive oil, cover with cling film (plastic wrap), press down once more and place in the refrigerator overnight.

2 The following day take it out of the refrigerator 1 hour before cooking so it gets to room temperature. Preheat the oven to 180°C/350°F/gas 4. Remove the cling film (plastic wrap) and transfer the chicken or poussin and garnish to a roasting pan. Remove the basil. Drizzle with the rest of the olive oil and season with salt and pepper. Place in the oven for a good 45 minutes for the poussin or 1 hour plus for the chicken until the skin is crispy but not burnt. Make sure you turn it halfway through the cooking process. Baste it every 15 minutes to help the crispiness. Serve with some grilled (broiled) vegetables and roasted new potatoes.

STUFFED CHICKEN BREASTS WITH CABBAGE & CHESTNUTS

SERVES 4

PREPARATION TIME 20 minutes, plus
   making the stock

COOKING TIME 35 minutes

120g/4¼oz unsalted butter
4 tbsp olive oil
165g/5¾oz button mushrooms,
   thinly sliced
4 chicken breasts, skin on
1 large Savoy cabbage, shredded
12 cooked whole chestnuts
4 tbsp Chicken Stock (see page 24)
4 tbsp whipping cream
1 tbsp chopped tarragon leaves
sea salt and freshly ground black
   pepper

1 Heat a large, non-stick frying pan (skillet) over a high heat. Add 30g/1oz of the butter and 1 tablespoon of the oil and when the butter is foaming, add the mushrooms and sauté for 4–5 minutes until they have released all their juices and are just golden. Remove and tip onto paper towel to dry. Wipe the frying pan, then return it to a medium heat, add another 30g/1oz of the butter and 1 tablespoon of the oil and when the butter is foaming, add the chicken breasts, skin-side down. Cook one side only over a medium heat for 5 minutes until the skin is golden, then remove them from the pan and put, skin-side up, on a board.

2 Cut the chicken breasts horizontally through the middle and three-quarters of the way through so that you can open them out like a book. Spread half the mushrooms over the bottom half of each breast, season with salt and pepper, then fold the top half back over to make a chicken-mushroom sandwich. Tightly wrap each chicken breast in cling film (plastic wrap) to make a sausage shape. Twist and secure each end with a knot, pushing out any air.

3 Put a large saucepan of water on to simmer, with a steamer insert on top, and bring another saucepan of salted water to the boil. Put the chicken parcels in the steamer, cover and cook for 12 minutes until cooked through. Remove and leave to rest on a plate for 6 minutes.

4 While the chicken is cooking, blanch the cabbage in the boiling salted water for about 3–4 minutes until only just tender, then drain well and pat dry. While the chicken is resting, heat a further 30g/1oz of the butter and 1 tablespoon of the oil in the frying pan (skillet) over a medium heat and when the butter is foaming, add the blanched cabbage. Cook for 2–3 minutes, then add the remaining cooked mushrooms and the chestnuts and toss for a further 2–3 minutes until heated through. Transfer to a warm bowl, cover and leave to one side.

5 Once the chicken has rested, remove the cling film (plastic wrap) and pour any cooking juices into a small pan over a medium-high heat. Add the stock and cook for 2–3 minutes until reduced by half. Whip the cream until soft peaks form, add it to the pan and let it melt into the sauce, without stirring. As soon as the sauce starts to simmer, remove it from the heat. Season with salt and pepper to taste, then stir in the tarragon.

6 Meanwhile, heat the frying pan (skillet) over a medium-high heat. Add the remaining butter and oil and fry the chicken, skin-side down, for about 3 minutes until crisp and golden. Quarter the chicken rolls and serve on top of the braised cabbage with the sauce spooned over.

CHICKEN & CUCUMBER EN PAPILLOTE WITH TOASTED ALMONDS

SERVES 4
PREPARATION TIME **20 minutes**
COOKING TIME **30 minutes**

4 chicken breasts, about
   165g/5¾oz each, skin on
20g/¾oz unsalted butter
2 tbsp sunflower oil
1 cucumber, peeled, halved
   lengthways and deseeded
2 tbsp olive oil
1 tsp smoked sweet (mild) paprika
185ml/6fl oz/¾ cup
   whipping cream
1 tbsp chopped flat-leaf
   parsley leaves
2 tbsp flaked almonds, toasted
sea salt and freshly ground black
   pepper

1 Season the skin of the chicken with salt and pepper. Heat a large frying pan (skillet) over a medium-high heat. Add the butter and sunflower oil and when the butter is foaming, add the chicken, skin-side down, and cook for about 5 minutes until the skin is golden and crisp. Remove from the pan and leave to one side.

2 To prepare the cucumber, cut each piece in half crossways about the same length as the chicken breasts, then slice into julienne strips, about 3mm/⅛in thick. Wipe the frying pan (skillet) clean, then heat over a medium-high heat. Add the olive oil and cucumber, season with salt and pepper and sauté for 4–5 minutes, tossing continuously, until the cucumber is translucent but still retaining its crunch. Add the paprika and stir to coat the cucumber, then drain on paper towel.

3 Preheat the oven to 180°C/350°F/gas 4. Lay four large sheets of baking paper, about 30cm/12in square, on a work surface. Put one-quarter of the cucumber on one of the sheets, positioning it lengthways in the centre. Put the chicken lengthways on top and fold in the sides and the bottom end of the paper so the top is still open. Pour 3 tablespoons of the cream into the top, then fold the paper over and tightly fold the top to seal and make a parcel. Repeat to make 4 parcels in total.

4 Put the parcels in a roasting tray and roast for 8–10 minutes. Remove from the oven and leave for 2 minutes until cool enough to handle. Turn the oven off and leave the door ajar (this will keep the chicken warm without cooking it.) Carefully open one end of each parcel and pour the juices into a small sauté pan. Close the parcels again and return the chicken to the oven. Put the sauté pan over a medium heat and bring to the boil, then turn the heat down to low and simmer, uncovered, for about 5 minutes until reduced by half.

5 Meanwhile, whip the remaining cream until soft peaks form. Remove the pan from the heat and whisk the cream into the reduced chicken juices. Return to the heat and bring to a simmer, then immediately remove from the heat. Stir in the parsley and season with salt and pepper to taste. Slide the parcels carefully onto plates and open the tops. Spoon any sauce over the chicken and sprinkle with the toasted almonds before serving.

SMOKED CHICKEN, COURGETTE, GARLIC & ROSEMARY CASSEROLE

A steamer works perfectly as a smoker so, if you have one, do give this recipe a try. You put the smoking mix in the bottom and the chicken in the top, but do keep it on a low heat – you don't want your smoke alarm to go off, so take it easy and don't get too excited! The green tea will bring a lovely flavour to the chicken, which will infuse into the courgettes (zucchini).

SERVES 4
PREPARATION TIME 10 minutes, plus
   making the stock
COOKING TIME 50 minutes

100g/3½oz/½ cup basmati rice
2 tbsp green tea
2 tsp caster (superfine) sugar
4 chicken legs, with thighs and
   drumsticks separated
20g/¾oz unsalted butter
2 tbsp sunflower oil
2 tbsp olive oil
400g/14oz courgettes (zucchini),
   cut in half lengthways, then cut
   into 2.5cm/1in pieces
12 garlic cloves, unpeeled
4 tbsp sherry vinegar
500ml/17fl oz/2 cups Chicken
   Stock (see page 24)
1 rosemary sprig
1 tsp chopped rosemary leaves
sea salt and freshly ground black
   pepper

1 Put a large piece of kitchen foil, shiny-side down, in the bottom of a steamer, then put the rice, tea and sugar on the foil, cover with a steamer insert and lid and put over a medium heat for about 5 minutes until the mixture starts smoking. Quickly lift the lid and put all the chicken inside. Put the lid back on, turn the heat down to low and smoke for 5 minutes. Lift out the chicken and put on a plate to rest, wrapping the smoking ingredients in the foil and discarding them as quickly as you can.

2 Season the chicken with salt and pepper. Put a flameproof casserole dish over a medium-high heat. Add the butter and sunflower oil and when the butter is foaming, add the chicken, skin-side down, and cook for 6–8 minutes until golden brown all over, turning occasionally. Remove from the pan and put in a bowl, cover with cling film (plastic wrap) and leave to rest.

3 Discard the oil from the casserole dish and wipe the excess away with paper towel, taking care not to disturb the sediment. Return the dish to a medium-low heat, add the olive oil, courgettes (zucchini) and garlic and cook for 4–5 minutes until coloured and just tender.

4 Move the courgettes (zucchini) to the sides of the pan and put the chicken pieces in the centre to reheat. Turn the heat up to medium and when you can actually hear the food starting to cook, add the sherry vinegar straight away; it should evaporate immediately. Quickly pour the stock over the top and throw in the rosemary sprig. When the stock comes to a simmer, gently wriggle the pan around a little so that nothing is stuck to the bottom, then put the lid on top without closing it completely – you just want a little gap so that condensation doesn't create too much liquid, but not too large so that the liquid evaporates. Cook for 15 minutes.

5 Remove the lid and discard the rosemary. Turn the heat to high and cook for a further 5 minutes, stirring to remove any caramelized bits stuck to the bottom, until the sauce is shiny and just thick enough to coat the back of the spoon. Add the chopped rosemary leaves and season with salt and pepper to taste, then serve hot.

POACHED CHICKEN WITH LEMON ZEST & BLACK OLIVES

Here I have modernized a classic *poulet au pot,* bringing in some Mediterranean flavours with olives and lemon. You would normally serve the bouillon first as a soup, then the garnish – the vegetables – with the chicken as a main course. But I have taken some of the liquid and reduced it to a sauce, then added olives, thyme and lemon zest – it makes it very refreshing. Try both and see which one you prefer; that would make a really interesting comparison.

SERVES 4
PREPARATION TIME 30 minutes
COOKING TIME 1½ hours

1.5kg/3lb 5oz chicken
4 carrots, peeled
4 small turnips
4 small new potatoes, such as
    Charlotte, scrubbed
4 baby leeks
1 thyme sprig
150ml/5fl oz/scant ⅔ cup
    whipping cream
1 large handful of pitted black
    olives
grated zest and juice of 1 lemon
1 tbsp thyme leaves
1 tbsp extra virgin olive oil

1 Tie the legs of the chicken together by the top of the cavity with a piece of kitchen string. Put the chicken in a large, flameproof casserole dish, cover with cold water and bring to the boil over a high heat. When it starts to simmer, skim off any foam that rises to the surface; this helps to keep the soup nice and clear.

2 Add the carrots and cook over a very low heat for 15 minutes, just keeping the water simmering. Add the turnips and cook for 15 minutes, then the potatoes and cook for 15 minutes, and finally the leeks and thyme sprig and cook for a further 15 minutes. It will have simmered for 1 hour in total and the chicken should be cooked through, so the juices run clear when the thickest part is pierced with the tip of a sharp knife, and the vegetables all perfectly tender.

3 Remove from the heat and ladle out 300ml/10½fl oz/scant 1¼ cups of the cooking liquor straight into a sauté pan. Put over a low heat, add 100ml/3½fl oz/scant ½ cup of the cream, bring to a simmer and simmer for 10–12 minutes until reduced by half.

4 Whip the remaining cream in a small bowl, then add it to the sauce, return to a simmer, then remove from the heat. The sauce should just be thick enough to coat the back of a spoon. Add the olives, lemon zest and a squeeze of lemon juice, then taste before adding any more lemon juice; it should just be slightly lemony, but not acidic. Add the thyme leaves and stir through.

5 Lift the chicken and potatoes out of the bouillon – you can use the bouillon and remaining vegetables for a soup. Discard the string, cut the chicken into 4 pieces and put straight onto a serving plate. Crush the potatoes with a little extra virgin olive oil and serve alongside, then spoon the sauce over the top.

WARM SOY-GLAZED QUAIL SALAD

Quail is very tasty and delicate – and yet, it is also very much underrated. In France, it is very popular on restaurant menus, but also at home. The best birds come from the region of Anjou in the Pays de Loire, just next to Brittany. In this recipe I use Asian flavours, as they complement the quail very nicely.

SERVES 4
PREPARATION TIME 30 minutes,
　plus making the croûtons
COOKING TIME 40 minutes

4 quails, about 140g/5oz each,
　gutted and cleaned
250g/9oz duck or goose fat
4 quail's eggs
12 baby courgettes (zucchini),
　sliced into thin ribbons using a
　vegetable peeler
leaves from 1 thyme sprig
2 tbsp olive oil
1 tbsp clear honey
2 tbsp rice wine vinegar
1 tbsp soy sauce
½ tsp Szechuan peppercorns,
　toasted and crushed
　(see page 212)
2 small or 1 large head of chicory
　(Belgian endive), sliced
　crossways
1 handful of Croûtons (see page 27)
1 handful of flat-leaf parsley
　leaves, chopped
sea salt and freshly ground black
　pepper

1 Prepare the quails by removing the legs and breasts from each one (or ask your butcher to do this for you). Wrap each leg tightly in cling film (plastic wrap) and then kitchen foil. (Leave the breasts to one side, covered.) Spoon the duck fat into a saucepan over a low heat until melted and starting to shimmer. Add the foil-wrapped legs and return the fat to a shimmer. Cook for 20–25 minutes until cooked tender. Remove from the heat and leave to one side in the fat.

2 Meanwhile, bring a small saucepan of water to the boil, add the quail's eggs and cook for 2 minutes, then drain and refresh in iced water – the yolks should still be slightly runny. Peel and set aside.

3 Put the courgette (zucchini) ribbons in a bowl with the thyme and oil, season with salt and turn until coated. Heat a ridged griddle pan over a high heat until very hot, then griddle the courgettes in batches for 1–2 minutes, turning once, until charred in places. Keep warm.

4 Unwrap the quail legs and brush with half the honey. Heat a large frying pan (skillet) over a high heat. Add 1–2 tablespoons of the duck fat from the pan, then add the quail legs, skin-side down, and cook for 2–3 minutes until the skin is crisp and golden brown. Transfer to a plate, cover with foil and leave to rest while you cook the breasts.

5 Season the quail breasts, then put them in the frying pan (skillet), skin-side down, and cook over a high heat for 2–3 minutes until the skin starts to crisp. Turn the breasts over and cook for about a further 2 minutes until cooked through but still nicely moist. Transfer to the plate with the legs. Pour the rice wine vinegar and soy sauce into the pan and deglaze by stirring to remove any caramelized bits. Stir in the Szechuan peppercorns and remaining honey and heat briefly. Before the honey starts to colour, add the quail legs and turn to coat them in the honey glaze, then remove and add the breasts to the pan, skin-side down only, and glaze until they are a lovely golden colour.

6 Cut the quail breasts in half diagonally, then put on top of the chicory (Belgian endive) and the courgette (zucchini) ribbons with the legs. Halve the quail's eggs and put on top, then sprinkle with the croûtons and parsley. Drizzle with any glaze left in the pan and serve.

PAN-ROASTED DUCK BREAST WITH SPICED PEACHES

SERVES 4
PREPARATION TIME 15 minutes, plus
    making the stock
COOKING TIME 40 minutes

100g/3½oz/scant ½ cup caster
    (superfine) sugar
2.5cm/1in piece of cinnamon stick,
    broken
4 unripe peaches
4 duck breasts, preferably wild
2 pinches of roasted, crushed
    Szechuan peppercorns (see
    page 212)
4 tbsp sunflower oil
50g/1¾oz unsalted butter
1 shallot, chopped
4 tbsp sherry vinegar
125ml/4fl oz/½ cup Chicken Stock
    (see page 24)
sea salt and freshly ground black
    pepper

Wild duck goes well with lots of fruits and spices. I like to use peaches, and you should still be able to find them in autumn when duck comes into season. If you buy your duck from a butcher, ask for a female bird as they tend to be more tender.

1 Put the sugar in a large sauté pan and add the cinnamon stick and 750ml/26fl oz/3 cups of water over a medium heat. Cook until the sugar dissolves, stirring occasionally, and the syrup comes to a simmer. Add the peaches and poach for 10 minutes. Using a slotted spoon, lift the peaches out of the syrup, leave to cool slightly, then remove the skins. Transfer the poaching syrup and cinnamon to a bowl and leave to one side. Halve the peaches, remove the stones, then cut each half into 4 long slices.

2 Preheat the oven to 180°C/350°F/gas 4. Season both sides of the duck, then sprinkle the Szechuan pepper over the skin. Heat an ovenproof frying pan (skillet) over a medium heat. Add the oil and when it starts to shimmer, add the duck, skin-side down. Cook for 4–5 minutes until golden brown, then turn the duck over and put the pan in the oven for 4–5 minutes. Remove from the oven and put the duck in a small baking sheet; cover and leave to rest for 5 minutes. Reserve the fat and turn the oven up to maximum.

3 Meanwhile, put the cleaned sauté pan over a medium heat, add half the butter and the peaches and cook for 5 minutes, turning occasionally, until lightly brown. Remove and leave to one side on a plate. Add the cinnamon and 125ml/4fl oz/½ cup of the reserved poaching syrup to the pan. Cook over a medium heat for 3–4 minutes until the syrup just starts to turn a caramel colour, then return the peaches, toss to coat in syrup, then remove from the heat. Cover the pan with foil and leave to one side.

4 Discard all but 1 tablespoon of the fat in the duck pan and return it to a medium heat. Add the shallot and cook for 5 minutes until softened, then pour in the sherry vinegar and deglaze the pan by stirring to remove any caramelized bits stuck to the bottom. Add the stock, bring to the boil, then simmer, stirring, for about 5 minutes until reduced by half. Add the remaining butter and swirl the pan to combine and make a shiny sauce. Add the juices from the rested duck, cover and leave to one side.

5 Reheat the duck in the hot oven for 2 minutes. If the peaches have cooled, warm them through. Cut the duck in half lengthways, Pour the peach juices into the sauce and bring it quickly to the boil. Serve the duck surrounded by the peaches, with the sauce spooned over.

FARMED RABBIT CASSEROLE WITH MUSTARD & PARSLEY

Rabbit and parsley, what a combination! I love this recipe because it reminds me of how we used to feed the rabbits with parsley at my aunty Suzanne's smallholding, for the last three to six weeks before eating. This dish is truly delightful with a touch of mustard and new-season steamed carrots.

SERVES **6**
PREPARATION TIME **25 minutes**
COOKING TIME **1 hour 20 minutes**

1 large farmed rabbit, about
    1.6kg/3lb 8oz, cut into pieces
    (ask your butcher to prepare it
    for you)
4 tbsp Dijon mustard
30g/1oz butter
2 tbsp sunflower oil
1 large onion, roughly chopped
100g/3½oz pancetta, diced
1 tbsp plain (all-purpose) flour
200ml/7fl oz/scant 1 cup
    white wine
250ml/9fl oz/1 cup Chicken Stock
    (see page 24)
2 garlic cloves, chopped
1 bunch of flat-leaf parsley,
    chopped
sea salt and freshly ground black
    pepper
tagliatelle, to serve

1 Using a pastry brush, coat the rabbit pieces with the mustard. Heat a large, heavy-based saucepan over a medium heat. Add the butter and the oil and when the butter starts to foam, place the coated rabbit pieces in the pan. Cook gently for few minutes, or until they start to colour, then turn and cook for another few minutes.

2 Throw in the onion and pancetta and cook for a few minutes, or until golden. Sift in the flour and stir everything with a wooden spoon. Pour in the wine to deglaze the pan, letting it evaporate to remove the acidity. Add the stock, the garlic and half the parsley. Cover the pan with a lid, leaving a small gap, and bring to a simmer. Cook for about 1 hour, then check; it should be cooked through but not quite falling off the bone.

3 Remove the parsley stalks and check the seasoning. You should have a lovely silky sauce but not to reduce. Throw in the reserved chopped parsley and serve warm with some tagliatelle.

PORK SHOULDER WITH CHILLI-GINGER CABBAGE

Pork shoulder is a very tasty part of the pig and as it has a little fat it brings a lovely flavour to this dish. Although I think the secret to the success of this recipe lies in the cabbage! I have used a pointed cabbage, also called sweetheart, which is braised in a delicious combination of chilli, ginger and honey that gives it a wonderful balance of flavours.

SERVES 4
PREPARATION TIME 10 minutes
COOKING TIME 20 minutes

2 tbsp sunflower oil
4 pork shoulder steaks, about 150g/5½oz each
90g/3¼oz unsalted butter
1 pointed or sweetheart cabbage, quartered lengthways, stem removed and shredded
2 long red chillies, deseeded and finely chopped
50g/1¾oz piece of root ginger, peeled and cut into julienne strips
2 tbsp clear honey
1 tbsp roughly chopped flat-leaf parsley leaves
2 tbsp extra virgin olive oil
sea salt and freshly ground black pepper

1 Preheat the oven to 140°C/275°F/gas 1. Heat a large frying pan (skillet) over a medium heat. Add the sunflower oil and the pork and cook for 3–4 minutes until golden brown underneath, then add one-third of the butter, turn the pork and cook the other side until golden. Transfer the pork to a plate, cover with foil and keep warm in the oven. Leave the frying pan to one side.

2 Bring a saucepan of salted water to the boil, add the cabbage, cover with a lid and return to the boil, then drain immediately. Return the cabbage to the saucepan and add 1½ of the red chillies, the ginger, honey and half the remaining butter and season with salt and pepper. Cover the pan with a lid, put over a very low heat and braise gently for 2–3 minutes until just tender. Remove from the heat, cover with a lid and leave to one side while you finish making the sauce.

3 Return the frying pan (skillet) to a high heat. When the juices are bubbling, add 100ml/3½fl oz/scant ½ cup of water and cook for 2 minutes until reduced by half. Reduce the heat to medium, add the remaining butter to the pan, a little at a time, whisking to incorporate it into the sauce. Add the remaining chilli and half the parsley and stir through. Check the seasoning, adding more salt and pepper to taste. Remove the pork from the oven and pour any resting juices into the sauce, stirring one last time.

4 Stir the remaining parsley into the cabbage. Scoop the cabbage out of the pan with a slotted spoon into a warm bowl, making sure that any residual liquid stays in the pan. Return the pan to a high heat and cook the liquid until reduced and slightly syrupy. Add the extra virgin olive oil, season with salt and pepper to taste, then spoon the sauce over the cabbage. Serve the pork with the buttery sauce spooned over the top and with the honey-coated cabbage.

MEDALLIONS OF PORK WITH CORIANDER & GARLIC

I often make this dish for myself at home, partly because it's so quick but also as I love the mix of flavours, and I always use good-quality pork to make sure the results are really tender. The garlic, sautéed in its skin until soft, perfectly complements the nuttiness of the crushed coriander seeds, then both combine with the buttery pork juices and fresh coriander (cilantro). And all this served with succulent slices of pork tenderloin. Fantastic!

SERVES 4
PREPARATION TIME 5 minutes, plus at least 1 hour marinating and making the stock
COOKING TIME 15 minutes

2 pork tenderloin fillets, about 300g/10½oz each, trimmed and cut into 2.5cm/1in slices
1 tbsp olive oil
½ tsp coriander seeds, crushed
8 garlic cloves, unpeeled, lightly crushed
1 tbsp vegetable oil
100g/3½oz unsalted butter
100ml/3½fl oz/scant ½ cup Chicken Stock (see page 24)
1 small handful of coriander (cilantro) leaves, roughly chopped
sea salt and freshly ground white pepper
boiled, mashed carrot, to serve

1 Put the pork in a large dish, pour over the olive oil and sprinkle with the crushed coriander seeds. Cover with cling film (plastic wrap) and leave to marinate in the refrigerator for at least an hour, or until ready to use.

2 Bring a small saucepan of water to the boil over a high heat, add the garlic, then turn the heat down to low and simmer for 5 minutes until softened (taking care to simmer and not boil, so the skins stay attached to the garlic). Lift out with a slotted spoon and drain on paper towel.

3 Heat a large sauté pan over a medium-high heat. Add the vegetable oil and 20g/¾oz of the butter, then add the pork and when it has just started to brown, add the garlic. Cook the pork and garlic for 2–3 minutes on each side until both are golden brown, taking care not to burn the garlic. Remove the pork and garlic from the pan and leave to one side on a plate, covered with foil to keep warm.

4 Discard the fat in the pan, then return it to a medium heat, making sure the pan does not get too hot. Pour in the stock and deglaze the pan by stirring to remove any caramelized bits stuck to the bottom. Add the remaining butter to the pan, a little at a time, whisking to incorporate it into the sauce. When all the butter has been added, add the unpeeled garlic and the resting juices from the pork and heat through.

5 Just before serving, add the fresh coriander (cilantro) leaves to the sauce and season with salt and pepper to taste. Spoon the sauce over the pork and serve with mashed carrot.

PORK LOIN WITH MUSHROOMS, FIGS & CHESTNUTS

Not only is autumn the mushroom season, but it is also the best time for figs and chestnuts. They all have an 'earthy' quality but with different textures. Remember to look out for ready-cooked and peeled chestnuts, which are really good and save a lot of time, too! I have given you the option of cooking the pork in different ways and I hope you'll try both methods to appreciate the differences in flavour, colour and texture.

SERVES 4
PREPARATION TIME 20 minutes, plus making the stock
COOKING TIME 20 minutes

4 pork tenderloin fillets, about 150g/5½oz each, trimmed
80g/2¾oz unsalted butter
2 tbsp sunflower oil
200g/7oz mixed wild or cultivated mushrooms
12 cooked whole chestnuts
4 tbsp sherry vinegar
2 medium-firm figs, quartered
200ml/7fl oz/scant 1 cup Chicken Stock (see page 24)
1 tbsp chopped chives
sea salt and freshly ground black pepper
boiled rice (optional), to serve

1 Season the pork fillets with pepper, then tightly wrap each one in cling film (plastic wrap). Twist and secure each end with a knot, pushing out any air. Put a large saucepan of water on to simmer, with a steamer insert on top. Put the pork parcels in the steamer, turn the heat down to low, cover and cook for 12 minutes, then remove and leave to rest for 1 minute until cool enough to handle. Remove the cling film and pat the pork dry with paper towel.

2 Heat a frying pan (skillet) over a medium-high heat. Add 20g/¾oz of the butter and 1 tablespoon of the oil and when the butter is foaming, add the pork and cook for 3–4 minutes, turning occasionally, until browned all over. The pork should still be slightly pink in the centre, which is perfect. (Alternatively, brown in an ovenproof frying pan as above, instead of steaming, then transfer the pork to an oven preheated to 140°C/275°F/gas 1 for 7–9 minutes. Remove and leave to rest for 1 minute.)

3 While the pork is cooking, heat 20g/¾oz of the butter and the remaining oil in a frying pan (skillet) over a medium-high heat. When the butter is foaming, add the mushrooms and fry for 2 minutes until they have released all their juices and are golden. Add the chestnuts and cook for 2 minutes. Add the sherry vinegar and deglaze the pan by stirring to remove any caramelized bits stuck to the bottom. Add the figs, pour in the stock and cook for 3–4 minutes until reduced by one-quarter, then add the remaining butter. Cook for a further 2 minutes until the sauce has reduced and is thick enough to coat the back of a spoon. Season with salt and pepper to taste and stir in the chives.

4 Cut each pork fillet into diagonal slices and spoon the mushroom mixture over the top before serving with rice, if you like.

CHAPTER 7
FROM KITCHEN & PANTRY

When you change countries and languages it is not always easy, especially when writing in a different language. It can be confusing but, after a while, you get used to the spellings and words. "Pantry" is an English word that I have grown to love. The pantry is a sort of mystery place where you keep your secrets, next to your kitchen. This is exactly what happened at home: somewhere for all those lovely jams, marmalades, conserves, pickles, and all the dry herbs, fruit and spices. The pantry was often a spare room, cool and dark, or a big cabinet, never too far away from the kitchen, always easily accessible.

LENTIL & BACON SOUP WITH MUSHROOMS & THYME CREAM

Where I'm from in the Haute-Saône region of France we use lentils a lot, particularly the slate-green-coloured Puy lentils. The first record of the famous *lentilles vert du Puy* dates back to 1643, and the Puy lentil was awarded Protected Designation of Origin status (PDO) in 2009. Known as the "caviar of the poor", the earthy flavour of these lentils blends beautifully with the pancetta, mushrooms and thyme.

SERVES 4
PREPARATION TIME 25 minutes, plus making the stock
COOKING TIME 30 minutes

1 tbsp olive oil
100g/3½oz thick pancetta or streaky bacon, cut into small lardons
1 shallot, finely sliced
1 carrot, peeled and diced
1 bouquet garni, made with 1 thyme sprig and 1 parsley sprig, tied together with kitchen string
200g/7oz/1 cup Puy lentils, picked over and rinsed
1.2l/40fl oz/4¾ cups Vegetable Stock (see page 25)
150ml/5fl oz scant ⅔ cup whipping cream
leaves from 2 thyme sprigs
40g/1½oz unsalted butter
100g/3½oz Paris, chestnut (cremini) or button mushrooms, thickly sliced
sea salt and freshly ground black pepper
crusty bread, to serve

1 Heat a saucepan over a medium heat. Add the oil and pancetta and fry for 3–4 minutes, stirring occasionally, until golden brown. Add the shallot and carrot and cook for 2–3 minutes until slightly softened, then add the lentils, bouquet garni and stock. Bring to the boil over a medium-high heat, then turn the heat down to low and simmer for 8 minutes. Pour in 100ml/3½fl oz/scant ½ cup of the cream, return to a simmer and cook for a further 7–8 minutes until the lentils are tender. Discard the bouquet garni.

2 Ladle the soup into a blender and blitz until smooth and creamy. Return the soup to a saucepan and add a little water or more stock to the pan if the soup is very thick. Season to taste with salt and pepper, cover with a lid and keep warm.

3 Whip the remaining cream until soft peaks form, then fold in two-thirds of the thyme and season with a touch of pepper.

4 Heat a frying pan (skillet) over a high heat. Add the butter and when foaming, add the mushrooms and sauté for 3–4 minutes until golden brown. Season with salt and pepper to taste, then add the remaining thyme. Divide the mushrooms into four shallow soup bowls, piling them in the middle and put a spoonful of the thyme cream on top. Finally ladle the soup around the mushrooms and cream and serve with crusty bread.

MORTEAU SAUSAGE & WARM BORLOTTI BEAN SALAD

SERVES 4
PREPARATION TIME 15 minutes,
  plus overnight soaking and 30
  minutes infusing
COOKING TIME 2½ hours

3 tbsp olive oil
6 garlic cloves, 3 unpeeled, lightly
  crushed, plus 1 whole and
  2 chopped
250g/9oz cherry tomatoes, cut
  in half crossways and gently
  squeezed
1 tsp icing (confectioners') sugar
leaves from 1 thyme sprig
150g/5½oz/¾ cup dried borlotti
  beans, soaked overnight, drained
  and rinsed
1 large carrot, peeled
1 shallot
1 flat-leaf parsley sprig, plus 1 tbsp
  chopped leaves
2 morteau sausages or other
  smoked sausage, about
  300g/10½oz each, pricked
  with a knife
3 tbsp French Dressing (see
  page 26)
sea salt and freshly ground black
  pepper

The town of Morteau gave its name to this famous sausage and it comes from the same part of France as I do, which is Franche-Comté to the east of the country next to the Jura mountains. Local cooks only use pork from the region because the animals are fattened traditionally. In addition, to be permitted to use the label *saucisse de morteau*, the sausage must be smoked for at least 48 hours over sawdust from conifer and juniper trees. In this recipe, the borlotti beans bring a nuttiness, which is complemented by the sweet flavour of the oven-dried tomato. Throw in some garlic and herbs and a drizzle of French dressing and this dish is sure to impress!

1 Preheat the oven to 110°C/225°F/gas ½. Put the oil and the whole unpeeled garlic in a small roasting tray in the oven for 30 minutes to infuse. Remove and leave the garlic to one side. Add the tomatoes to the tray, cut-side up, then sprinkle with the icing (confectioners') sugar and season with salt and pepper. Scatter the thyme over the top and roast for 2½ hours until the tomatoes are dried and wrinkly.

2 After the tomatoes have been cooking for 1 hour, put the soaked borlotti beans in a saucepan and cover with plenty of cold water. Bring to the boil over a high heat, then skim off any foam that rises to the surface. Add the carrot, shallot, parsley sprig and the peeled whole garlic clove. Turn the heat down to low, partially cover and simmer gently for 30 minutes. Add the sausages to the pan and simmer for a further 30 minutes until the beans are tender and the sausages cooked through.

3 Lift the sausages out of the beans into a bowl and cover with cling film (plastic wrap). Strain the beans, reserving the cooking liquor in a separate pan. Tip the beans into a bowl. Discard the garlic clove and parsley sprig, then cut the carrot into small dice and add to the beans. Return the cooking liquor to the heat, bring to a the boil, then cook for about 5 minutes, uncovered, until reduced by half. Whisk in one-third of the French dressing.

4 Add the oven-dried tomatoes to the beans along with the remaining chopped garlic, chopped parsley and another one-third of the dressing and mix gently. Discard the skin from the sausage and cut the sausage into thick slices. Spoon the sausage on top of the beans and drizzle with the remaining dressing to serve.

BUTTERNUT SQUASH & SAFFRON RISOTTO

Butternut squash is a very popular vegetable that is harvested between September and the end of winter. Its colour and flavour are striking: orange flesh that's tasty and delicate. The saffron-infused stock and mashed roasted squash intensify the flavour of the risotto. If you are using carnaroli rice, my grain of choice, follow the recipe closely and keep the heat low when you add it, otherwise the rice can break down and create a sticky risotto. You could finish it with a sprinkling of crispy butternut squash along with the Parmesan. A small herb salad will also go down a treat.

SERVES 4
PREPARATION TIME 20 minutes,
    plus making the stock
COOKING TIME 55 minutes

1 small butternut squash, unpeeled,
    quartered lengthways and
    deseeded
875ml/30fl oz/3½ cups Vegetable
    Stock (see page 25)
2 pinches of saffron strands
150g/5½oz unsalted butter
1 onion, finely chopped
300g/10½oz/scant 1⅓ cups
    risotto rice, such as Carnaroli
    or Arborio
90g/3¼oz Parmesan cheese, grated
2 heaped tbsp Greek yogurt
1 tbsp chopped chives
sea salt and freshly ground black
    pepper
Dehydrated Pumpkin Crisp (see
    page 17), to serve (optional)

1 Preheat the oven to 160°C/315°F/gas 2½. Put the butternut squash in a roasting tray, cover with foil and roast for 45 minutes until very tender.

2 When the squash has been in the oven for about 30 minutes, start to make the risotto. Heat the stock and saffron in a saucepan and bring to a simmer, then turn the heat down to very low. Melt 75g/2½oz of the butter in a frying pan (skillet) over a low heat. Add the onion and cook for 3–4 minutes, stirring occasionally, until softened. Add the rice and turn the heat down to very low. Mix with a wooden spoon until the rice is well coated in the butter and onion mixture.

3 Add the hot stock to the pan, little by little, stirring continuously until the liquid has been absorbed before adding more stock. Carry on adding the stock, stirring to stop it sticking, for about 20 minutes until the rice has a lovely creamy texture.

4 When the squash is cooked, and while the risotto is still cooking, remove the squash from the tray and leave until just cool enough to handle. Scoop the flesh away from the skin into a bowl and mash roughly with a fork. When the rice is almost cooked, fold in the mashed squash, the Parmesan, yogurt, chives and the remaining butter. If the risotto is a little thick, add a few more spoonfuls of stock to loosen it, then season well with salt and pepper and serve immediately with pumpkin crisp, if you like.

SOFT PAN-FRIED PEARS WITH CARDAMOM & SZECHUAN PEPPER

SERVES 4
PREPARATION TIME 10 minutes
COOKING TIME 35 minutes

1 tsp Szechuan peppercorns
200g/7oz/heaped ¾ cup caster
    (superfine) sugar
1 tsp cardamom pods, lightly
    crushed
juice of ¼ lime
4 large or 8 small, firm pears, such
    as William, Rocha or Comice,
    peeled with the stalks left on
25g/1oz unsalted butter

Pear, the glorious pear! Soft, juicy, tasty, with a hint of summer petals. And yet pears are not used enough in home cooking. I don't know why! The season is September through to January and there are loads of varieties to choose from. In this recipe I have combined the pears with cardamom and Szechuan peppers, and they will gladly take them on to lift themselves to new heights. Yet the right quantity is critical as too much would overwhelm the subtlety of this delicate fruit. You can use the same quantity of syrup and adjust the number of pears according to the size and your guests' appetites! This dessert goes really well with Pistachio Madeleines (see page 215).

1 Put the Szechuan peppercorns in a small, dry frying pan (skillet) over a medium heat and toast for 1–2 minutes, shaking the pan occasionally, until just coloured and aromatic. Tip onto a plate and crush lightly with the flat blade of a knife.

2 Bring the sugar, half the cardamom, the lime juice and 800ml/ 28fl oz/scant 3½ cups of water to the boil in a saucepan over a medium heat. Stir occasionally for about 5–8 minutes until the sugar dissolves and starts to turn syrupy.

3 Add the pears to the pan with the syrup. You need to cover the pears with a *cartouche* (see page 232). Turn the heat down to very low and simmer for 8 minutes, or until the pears have softened very slightly. To check the pears, insert the tip of a knife into the thickest part – there should still be a little resistance. Put the pears on a clean dish towel to drain. Return the pan to the heat and simmer for 8–10 minutes until the syrup has reduced by about three-quarters.

4 Meanwhile, melt the butter in a large, non-stick frying pan (skillet) over a medium heat. When the butter is foaming, add the pears and the remaining cardamom and cook for 3–4 minutes, turning occasionally, until they are slightly golden all over.

5 Add 4 tablespoons of the reduced syrup to the pan and cook the pears for 4–5 minutes, basting them occasionally with the syrup, until tender but not mushy. Baste the pears again with the syrup and add the crushed Szechuan pepper. Serve the pears with the syrup poured over the top and any remaining syrup served separately.

PISTACHIO MADELEINES WITH CHOCOLATE SORBET

This makes for a perfect combination, but you may also like to serve the madeleines with a simple vanilla ice cream or even a dessert pear. They go well with the strawberries (see page 155) too instead of the lime shortbread. So many flavours seem to be made for madeleines – vanilla, cinnamon, star anise, hazelnut, orange, honey – but, for me, the one thing you certainly can't beat is when they are served warm straight out of the oven.

SERVES 4
PREPARATION TIME 30 minutes, plus overnight resting and making the *beurre noisette*
COOKING TIME 15 minutes

FOR THE CHOCOLATE SORBET
125g/4½oz/heaped ½ cup caster (superfine) sugar
50g/1¾oz/scant ½ cup good-quality dark cocoa powder
125g/4½oz dark chocolate, 60% cocoa solids, broken into small pieces

FOR THE PISTACHIO MADELEINES
unsalted butter, for greasing
140g/5oz/heaped 1 cup plain (all-purpose) flour
¾ tsp baking powder
2 eggs
90g/3¼oz/heaped ⅓ cup caster (superfine) sugar
3 tbsp milk
25g/1oz light clear honey
145ml/4¾fl oz/scant ⅔ cup warm Beurre Noisette (see page 30)
25g/1oz/scant ¼ cup pistachio nuts, toasted and chopped

1 First, prepare the madeleines. Lightly grease a 12-hole madeleine tray. Sift the flour and baking powder into a mixing bowl and leave to one side. Whisk together the eggs and sugar in a large mixing bowl, using an electric whisk, for about 10 minutes until the mixture is pale, thick and doubled in volume.

2 Heat the milk and honey in a saucepan until just melted. Fold the flour mixture into the egg mixture, then pour in the milk and honey, stirring until combined. Add the warm *beurre noisette* and mix slowly until fully incorporated, then fold in the pistachios. Spoon the mixture into the prepared madeleine tray, half-filling each hole. Cover with cling film (plastic wrap) and leave to rest in the refrigerator overnight.

3 To make the sorbet, pour 300ml/10½fl oz/scant 1¼ cups of water into a small saucepan. Mix together the sugar and cocoa powder, then add to the water and bring to the boil, whisking continuously. It's very important not to let the cocoa powder sink to the bottom of the pan and burn.

4 Put the chocolate pieces in a heatproof bowl. When the cocoa mixture has reached a boil, pour the hot liquid onto the chocolate pieces and whisk until the chocolate has melted. Pass the mixture through a fine sieve (strainer) into a 500ml/17fl oz/2 cup freezerproof container and freeze until hard.

5 When the sorbet is hard, cut the mixture into pieces and blitz in a food processor until smooth. Return to the freezer container and freeze for at least 3 hours until firm.

6 The next day, preheat the oven to 200°C/400°F/gas 6. Bake the madeleines for 5 minutes, then turn the tray around in the oven, front to back, and cook for a further 5 minutes until light golden and slightly firm to the touch. Insert a skewer into a madeleine and if it comes out clean, they are ready. If not, bake for a further 2 minutes. Remove from the oven and leave to cool for 5 minutes until lukewarm before turning out and serving with the chocolate sorbet.

PAIN DE GÊNES WITH ROSEMARY AND TONKA BEAN CRÈME ANGLAISE

I have loved *pain de gênes* since I was a boy. It was an afternoon cake at home, often served when we had visitors, and is similar to a genoise sponge but with toasted flaked almonds on top. For an exotic twist, I'm serving it with a chilli, rosemary and tonka bean crème anglaise and sprinkling it with hazelnuts. Tonka beans, by the way, are wrinkled black seeds with an aroma reminiscent of vanilla and almond – you can buy them online if they are not available in your supermarket.

SERVES 4–6
PREPARATION TIME 40 minutes, plus 30 minutes infusing and cooling
COOKING TIME 50 minutes

FOR THE PAIN DE GÊNES
60g/2¼oz unsalted butter, softened, plus extra for greasing
50g/1¾oz/scant ½ cup strong white flour, sifted, plus extra for dusting
200g/7oz good-quality soft marzipan, ideally 50:50
3 eggs
1 tbsp baking powder, sifted
2 tbsp blanched hazelnuts, toasted and chopped

FOR THE ROSEMARY AND TONKA BEAN CRÈME ANGLAISE
125ml/4fl oz/½ cup full-fat milk
125ml/4fl oz/½ cup whipping cream
leaves from 1 small rosemary sprig
1 small red chilli, deseeded and finely chopped
1 tonka bean or 1 vanilla pod, split in half lengthways and seeds scraped out
3 large egg yolks
50g/1¾oz/scant ¼ cup caster (superfine) sugar

1 Preheat the oven to 150°C/300°F/gas 2. Grease and flour a deep 20cm/8in loose-bottomed cake tin.

2 To make the *pain de gênes*, put the marzipan and butter in a food mixer fitted with a paddle, or use a bowl with an electric hand whisk, and beat for 5 minutes until soft and light. Add the eggs, one at a time, making sure that they are properly incorporated before adding the next one. When all the eggs have been added, continue to beat for at least 20 minutes until white and fluffy. Add the flour and baking powder and fold in very gently with a large metal spoon. Pour the mixture into the prepared cake tin and sprinkle the hazelnuts over the top. Bake for 35–40 minutes until risen and golden. To check the cake is ready, insert a skewer through the deepest part and if it comes out clean then it is cooked. If not, bake for a further 5 minutes and check again. Remove from the oven, put on a wire rack to cool slightly, then turn out of the tin and leave to cool completely.

3 While the cake is baking, make the rosemary and tonka bean crème anglaise. Put the milk and cream in a saucepan over a medium heat, bring to a simmer, then remove from the heat. Add the rosemary leaves, half the chilli and the tonka bean, stir to combine, then cover and leave to infuse for 30 minutes.

4 Put the egg yolks and sugar in a bowl and whisk until the sugar dissolves. Return the pan of infused cream and milk to a medium-high heat and bring to a simmer, then pass through a sieve (strainer) onto the egg mixture, whisking continuously. Discard the solids in the sieve. Return the mixture to the pan and cook over a medium heat for 5–8 minutes, stirring continuously with a wooden spoon (otherwise you'll get scrambled eggs!) until it starts to thicken. You will be able to tell when the crème anglaise is ready if, when you run two fingers down the back of the spoon, the two lines don't immediately join. Stir in the remaining chilli. Serve the *pain de gênes* cut into wedges with a generous spoonful of the crème anglaise.

PARIS-BREST WITH CHICORY & COFFEE CREAM

This is a twist on the beautiful, classic Paris-Brest choux pastry dessert, which I've given a whole new dimension by filling it with a delicious mixture of chicory and coffee cream. You will find chicory and coffee online or in specialist coffee shops.

SERVES 4
PREPARATION TIME 45 minutes, plus
    cooling and 35 minutes resting
COOKING TIME 40 minutes

FOR THE CHOUX PASTRY
180g/6¼oz unsalted butter
¾ tsp salt
¾ tbsp caster (superfine) sugar
250g/9oz/2 cups plain
    (all-purpose) flour
8 small eggs
a few drops of vanilla extract
1 tsp granulated chicory and coffee

FOR THE CHICORY & COFFEE CREAM
270ml/9½fl oz/generous 1 cup
    full-fat milk
2 tsp granulated chicory and coffee
3 eggs
100g/3½oz/scant ½ cup caster
    (superfine) sugar
25g/1oz/scant ¼ cup cornflour
    (corn starch)
150g/5½oz unsalted butter,
    softened

1 To start the chicory and coffee cream, put the milk in a small saucepan over a medium heat and bring almost to the boil. Stir in the chicory and coffee until dissolved. Cover and set aside to cool.

2 To make the pastry, put the butter, salt, sugar and 500ml/17fl oz/2 cups of water in a large saucepan and bring to the boil over a medium heat. Remove from the heat and whisk in the flour. Return to the heat and stir with a wooden spoon until the mixture starts to come away from the sides of the pan and falls off the spoon easily. Remove from the heat and whisk in the eggs, one at a time, until incorporated. Stir in the vanilla, cover and rest for 35 minutes.

3 Meanwhile, using an 8cm/3¼in biscuit (cookie) cutter or cup as a template, draw eight circles on a large sheet of baking paper. Turn the paper over and put on a large baking sheet. Preheat the oven to 180°C/350°F/gas 4.

4 Spoon the choux pastry dough into a piping bag, snip off the end to a 2cm/¾in diameter, then pipe eight circles using the rounds drawn on the baking paper as templates. Sprinkle the granulated chicory and coffee on top and bake, with the door ajar by 5cm/2in, for 30 minutes, or until a medium golden brown. (Leaving the door open allows the pastry to dry as it cooks and makes it very light.)

5 While it is cooking, complete the chicory and coffee cream. Whisk together the eggs, sugar and cornflour (corn starch), using an electric whisk, for about 5 minutes until light and fluffy. Strain the chicory-coffee milk onto the egg mixture and whisk to combine, then return to the pan. Put over a medium-low heat and stir continuously for 10 minutes, or until the mixture starts to thicken. Remove from the heat and continue to stir until the mixture has cooled down and is smooth, thick and slightly trembling. Whisk the softened butter in a separate mixing bowl until very soft, then add the chicory-coffee cream, a little at a time, until incorporated. Continue to whisk for 10 minutes or until you have a very light butter cream.

6 To assemble, halve the choux rings horizontally and spoon the chicory-coffee cream into a piping bag the same size you used for the choux pastry. Pipe the cream over the bases, then gently put on the pastry tops.

CIDER-SOAKED BABAS WITH CINNAMON CHANTILLY CREAM

In my version of the classic rum baba I'm using an infusion of cider and cinnamon to give a welcome, refreshing, tangy flavour. They are served with a cinnamon Chantilly cream, or you could try ice cream – I know which one I would go for, though!

SERVES 4
PREPARATION TIME 25 minutes, plus 50 minutes proving and 10 minutes cooling
COOKING TIME 12 minutes

FOR THE BABAS
200g/7oz/heaped 1⅔ cups strong white flour
a pinch of salt
1 tbsp caster (superfine) sugar
2 eggs
60g/2¼oz unsalted butter, very soft, plus extra for greasing
7g/¼oz fresh yeast or 5g/⅛oz dried yeast mixed with 1 tbsp warm water

FOR THE CIDER AND CINNAMON INFUSION
1.5l/52fl oz/6 cups good-quality dry cider
110g/3¾oz/scant ½ cup caster (superfine) sugar
1 cinnamon stick

FOR THE CINNAMON CHANTILLY CREAM
200ml/7fl oz/scant 1 cup double (heavy) cream
1 heaped tbsp caster (superfine) sugar
a pinch of ground cinnamon or ½ tsp vanilla extract

1 To make the babas, put all the ingredients in a food mixer bowl and, using the dough hook, mix slowly until it forms a soft dough, then remove the bowl from the machine. (Alternatively, put all the ingredients in a mixing bowl and mix using a wooden spoon for 2 minutes until it forms a soft dough. Tip out onto a lightly floured work surface and knead for about 6 minutes until smooth.) Cover the bowl with a clean dish towel and leave at room temperature for 30 minutes until risen by half. When risen, press it down with one hand to knock back.

2 Lightly grease a 12-hole deep muffin tin and put on a baking sheet. Divide the dough into 12 pieces, each about the size of a golf ball. Take a ball of dough in your hand, form a fist and squeeze the dough out through the bottom of your fist into a muffin hole. Repeat with all the dough. (It is important that the muffin holes are only half filled to allow the dough to rise.) Cover with a clean dish towel and leave to rise in a warm place for 20 minutes or until doubled in size.

3 Meanwhile, make the cider and cinnamon infusion. Put the cider and sugar in a large saucepan and bring to the boil over a medium heat. Stir to dissolve the sugar, then remove from the heat. Add the cinnamon stick, cover and leave to infuse for 30 minutes.

4 To make the cinnamon Chantilly cream, whip the cream with the sugar and ground cinnamon, using an electric whisk, until soft peaks form. Cover and put in the refrigerator until ready to serve.

5 Preheat the oven to 190°C/375°F/gas 5. Bake the babas for about 12 minutes, turning the tin once, until golden and cooked through. Remove from the oven and leave to cool in the tin for 5 minutes, then turn out onto a wire rack to cool completely.

6 Remove the cinnamon stick and check that the cider and cinnamon infusion is still warm. If not, reheat it briefly. Carefully dip the babas, two at a time, into the cider infusion, pushing them under until wet and heavy. Serve the babas with the cinnamon Chantilly cream.

CINNAMON & HONEY-BAKED FIGS WITH SWEET GINGER SLICES

SERVES 4
PREPARATION TIME 10 minutes,
  plus freezing
COOKING TIME 40 minutes

about 9cm/3½in piece of ginger
  cake, frozen until almost hard
12 firm purple-black figs, cut into
  quarters from top to bottom but
  not all the way through, so the
  figs are held together
2 tbsp clear honey
½ tsp ground cinnamon
75g/2½oz/scant ⅓ cup
  Greek yogurt
2 egg yolks

I look forward to fig season every year! Figs are at best in the autumn; they are at their most succulent and there are a lot of different types to choose from. They go from beige to brown, purple to black and green. In France, the colours are often associated with a beautiful name: La Noire de Caromb, La Dorée, La Bourjasotte, La Dauphine, La Marseillaise. How charming is that? For me, the best ones are the purple/black; I find they have the best flavour, which makes them perfect for baking. The spiced crisp cake really complements the dish and the addition of the smooth yogurt with honey, well, you'll see just how good it is!

1 Cut the cake into 8 thin slices. Freezing the cake until it is nearly hard makes it easier to slice thinly and also gives a much better crisp. Preheat the oven 140°C/275°F/gas 1, line a baking sheet with baking paper and have another sheet of baking paper and a second baking sheet ready.

2 Put the cake slices on the prepared baking sheet, cover with the second sheet of paper, then the second baking sheet so that the cake is held flat, and bake for 6–8 minutes. Carefully lift off the top sheet and paper, checking that the cake is not too coloured, then put back in the oven for 3–4 minutes to dry out. Remove from the oven and leave to cool. Turn the oven up to 180°C/350°F/gas 4.

3 Put the figs in a baking sheet, cut-side up, drizzle over the honey and 4 tablespoons of water and sprinkle with 2 pinches of the cinnamon. Roast for 12–15 minutes until they are soft. There will be a lovely liquid left in the baking sheet. Pour half into a large, heatproof bowl and leave to one side, and the other half into a serving bowl with the yogurt and mix well. Preheat the grill (broiler) to medium.

4 Add the egg yolks to the juices in the heatproof bowl and mix together. Rest the bowl over a saucepan of simmering water, making sure the bottom of the bowl does not touch the water. Beat the mixture for 8–10 minutes, using an electric whisk, until it turns pale, thickens and forms ribbon-like shapes when you lift the whisk out of the mixture. Spoon straight over the figs, then put under the grill (broiler) for a few minutes until just browned. You don't want it too close to the top of the grill, just until it is light golden brown.

5 Sprinkle the yogurt with the remaining cinnamon. Serve the figs hot with the spiced crisp slices to dip into the yogurt.

ROSEMARY-INFUSED CRÊPES SUZETTE WITH GRAPEFRUIT & ROSEMARY SYRUP

Created in the late 19th century, both the name and origin of this dish are disputed, although everyone does agree that a girl called Suzette was involved! In my new twist on this classic, we will make a syrup with grapefruit juice infused with rosemary, and you will see how different and delicious it is.

SERVES 4
PREPARATION TIME 20 minutes, plus 45 minutes infusing
COOKING TIME 25 minutes

FOR THE ROSEMARY-INFUSED CRÊPES
300ml/10½fl oz/scant 1¼ cups milk
2 rosemary sprigs
125g/4½oz/1 cup plain (all-purpose) flour
2 tbsp caster (superfine) sugar
a pinch of salt
2 eggs
25g/1oz unsalted butter, melted, plus extra for frying (optional)

FOR THE GRAPEFRUIT & ROSEMARY SYRUP
100g/3½oz/scant ½ cup caster (superfine) sugar
100g/3½oz unsalted butter
grated zest of 1 and juice of 2 pink grapefruits (150ml/5fl oz/scant ⅔ cup juice)
leaves from 1 small rosemary sprig, finely chopped

1 Bring the milk to the boil in a saucepan over a medium heat. Add the rosemary sprigs, then remove the pan from the heat, cover with cling film (plastic wrap) and leave to infuse for 45 minutes until just cool. Discard the rosemary.

2 While the milk infuses, make the syrup. Put a frying pan (skillet) over a low heat, add the sugar and cook gently for a few minutes until it turns to a light golden caramel. Add the butter and when it is foaming, add the grapefruit zest and juice, mix well and bring to a simmer. Cook for about 3 minutes until it forms a syrup, then remove from the heat, toss in the chopped rosemary and leave to infuse in a warm place.

3 Put the flour, sugar, salt, eggs and 125ml/4fl oz/½ cup of the rosemary-infused milk in a bowl. Add the melted butter and whisk, using an electric whisk, until smooth, then whisk in the remaining milk until smooth, quite runny and lump free. Adding the milk gradually means there is no need to rest the batter.

4 Heat a 15–18cm/6–7in non-stick pancake or frying pan (skillet) over a medium heat. If you use a non-stick pan, you won't have to add butter, though it can make flipping easier if you do. If you are not using a non-stick pan, add a little butter first to keep the pancake from sticking.

5 Using a ladle, pour enough batter into the pan to cover the base thinly, swirling the pan around to spread the batter, then cook for 1–1½ minutes until the underside is golden. Now comes the fun part: try to flip it over, or turn it with a spatula. Cook for a further 1–2 minutes until the other side is golden. Remove the pancake from the pan and keep it warm, then repeat with the remaining batter, adding more butter if necessary.

6 Fold the warm pancakes in half one at a time, pick them up with tongs and dip them into the syrup, swirling them around to make sure the pancake is coated, then fold over into quarters and serve immediately. Repeat with the remaining pancakes and syrup. If you're really lucky the last one will be for you.

GLUTEN-FREE CHOCOLATE & GINGER FONDANT

Chocolate fondant is often served in restaurants in many different ways with many different flavours or spices added to it or infused into it. The main idea is always the same – when cooked and turned out, the warm chocolate must find its way out, running slowly like lava coming down the slopes of a volcano. That is a must, but there is also no compromising when it comes to the chocolate you are using – it must be good quality, not too sweet, not too bitter, and it must be dark. In this recipe it is scented with ginger confit, which I love. If that is not to your taste, try it with star anise, cinnamon, cardamom or Szechuan pepper, but whatever the spice, you just want a hint of it, so do use it carefully.

SERVES 4
PREPARATION TIME 25 minutes, plus 30 minutes resting
COOKING TIME 8 minutes

100g/3½oz unsalted butter, plus extra for greasing
a little good-quality dark cocoa powder, for dusting
100g/3½oz dark chocolate, 70% cocoa solids, broken into pieces
3 eggs
4 tbsp caster (superfine) sugar
4 tbsp cornflour (corn starch)
1 ball of stem ginger, finely chopped
Chilli Crème Anglaise (see page 31), to serve

1 Butter four small ramekins or pudding moulds and dust with cocoa powder. Put the chocolate and butter in a heatproof bowl and rest it over a pan of gently simmering water, making sure that the bottom of the bowl does not touch the water. Heat, stirring occasionally, until the chocolate has melted. Alternatively, melt very gently in short bursts in the microwave, stirring regularly. Remove from the heat.

2 Whisk together the eggs and sugar, using an electric whisk, for at least 15 minutes until they are almost white in colour, very shiny and almost forming soft peaks. This will give a really light, crusty outside to the fondant, but the inside will be meltingly soft. Pour the melted chocolate and butter into the mix and whisk to combine. Sift the cornflour (corn starch) over the top and fold in, then finally fold in the stem ginger, taking care not to overmix at this point. Divide the mixture into the prepared ramekins, filling them only three-quarters full. Put on a baking sheet in a cool place to rest for 30 minutes.

3 Preheat the oven to 220°C/425°F/gas 7. Bake the chocolate fondants for 5–6 minutes until the fondant has risen above the moulds and has formed a light crust on top and around the edges. Remove from the oven and turn out straight onto a serving plate, then serve immediately with chilli crème anglaise.

CHOCOLATE, CHILLI & LEMONGRASS TART

Infused with lemongrass and chilli and made with the finest cocoa, this superb chocolate tart has a rich texture, a silky silhouette and lovely crisp pastry, which is a combination bound to make you happy. I almost decided not to give any of the details away, but it was just too good to keep to myself!

SERVES 4–6
PREPARATION TIME 15 minutes, plus 50 minutes chilling and 1½ hours setting
COOKING TIME 15 minutes

FOR THE CHOCOLATE PASTRY
90g/3¼oz/¾ cup plain (all-purpose) flour
1 tbsp good-quality dark cocoa powder
60g/2¼oz unsalted butter, softened, plus extra for greasing (optional)
30g/1oz/¼ cup icing (confectioners') sugar
a pinch of salt
1 large egg yolk

FOR THE CHOCOLATE FILLING
250ml/9fl oz/1 cup whipping cream
1 large really fresh lemongrass stalk, cut in half lengthways and bruised
2 small red chillies, deseeded and roughly chopped
200g/7oz dark chocolate, 70% cocoa solids, roughly chopped
20g/¾oz unsalted butter, softened

Orange, Cardamom and Thyme Salad (see page 168) made with ordinary oranges, to serve

1 To make the sweet pastry, sift the flour and cocoa powder into a bowl. In a separate bowl, beat together the butter, sugar, salt and egg yolk until light and fluffy. Sift in the flour mixture, then fold it through gently until it just begins to form a dough, then stop! You don't want to work this pastry at all. Wrap in cling film (plastic wrap) and put in the refrigerator for 20 minutes.

2 Grease an 18cm/7in non-stick, loose-bottomed flan tin with a little butter, if necessary. Roll out the pastry between two sheets of baking paper until 3mm/⅛in thick, then roll the pastry over the rolling pin and lift it over the flan tin. With one hand, lift the pastry edge and with the other, gently tuck the pastry into the bottom and sides of the tin so that it fits tightly. Don't overstretch it or it will break, and press down gently to push out any bubbles. Trim off any excess pastry by rolling the pin over the top edge. Prick the base with a fork and chill for 30 minutes to prevent the pastry shrinking during baking.

3 Meanwhile to make the filling, put the cream in a saucepan over a medium heat and bring just to a simmer. Remove from the heat, add the lemongrass and chilli, cover with cling film (plastic wrap) and leave in a warm place to infuse for 30 minutes.

4 Towards the end of the infusing time, preheat the oven to 180°C/350°F/gas 4. Line the pastry case with baking paper and cover with baking beans. Bake for 6 minutes, then remove the paper and baking beans, turn the oven down to 160°C/315°F/gas 2½ and bake for 3–4 minutes more, until the pastry is cooked through and light brown.

5 Put the chocolate and butter in a heatproof bowl and rest it over a saucepan of gently simmering water, making sure the bottom of the bowl does not touch the water. Heat, stirring, until the chocolate has melted. Remove the cling film (plastic wrap) from the cream and strain to discard the lemongrass and chillies. Pour the cream slowly into the chocolate mix, whisking all the time until you have a soft, shiny, chocolate ribbon. Pour it into the pastry case and leave to one side in a cool place for 1½ hours until just set. Do not put it in the refrigerator as this will take the shine off the chocolate. Serve sliced with the orange salad.

THYME-INFUSED CHOCOLATE POTS WITH BISCOTTI

I love the subtle hint of thyme in this rich chocolate dessert – it adds an elegant and unexpected touch that will surprise your guests. Serving the chocolate with your favourite biscuit (cookie) provides a welcome contrast.

SERVES **8**
PREPARATION TIME **15 minutes, plus 10 minutes infusing and 3 hours chilling**
COOKING TIME **1 hour**

250ml/9fl oz/1 cup full-fat milk
250ml/9fl oz/1 cup whipping cream
1 thyme sprig
70g/2½oz clear honey
4 egg yolks
250g/9oz dark chocolate, 70% cocoa solids, roughly chopped
Almond Biscotti (see page 163), Pain de Gênes (see page 216) or Pistachio Madeleines (see page 215), to serve

1 Preheat the oven to 150°C/300°F/gas 2 and line a deep baking dish with baking paper to direct the bubbles away from the pots, making the cooking process more gentle so the custard won't curdle. Have ready eight 150ml/5fl oz/scant $^2/_3$ cup ovenproof glasses or pots. Bring the milk and cream to a simmer in a small saucepan over a medium heat. Remove from the heat, add the thyme, cover with cling film (plastic wrap) and leave to infuse for 10 minutes.

2 Whisk together the honey and eggs in a bowl for 1–2 minutes until the sugar has dissolved. Put the chopped chocolate in a separate heatproof bowl. Remove the thyme from the cream mixture, return the pan to a low heat and bring to a simmer. Pour the hot infused milk over the chocolate, whisking all the time until the chocolate has melted, then add the egg mixture to the chocolate and whisk together.

3 Divide the mixture into the glasses and put them in the prepared baking dish, then pour enough warm water into the dish to come halfway up the sides of the glasses to create a bain marie. Bake the glasses for 10–12 minutes, or until just trembling. If necessary, return to the oven and cook for a further 5–10 minutes. Remove from the oven and transfer the glasses to a wire rack to cool completely. Cover with cling film (plastic wrap), then chill in the refrigerator for 2–3 hours. Serve the chocolate pots with biscotti, *pain de gênes* or warm madeleines.

CHOCOLATE MARBLE CAKE WITH CITRUS FRUIT GLAZE

SERVES 6–8
PREPARATION TIME 25 minutes,
    plus 5 minutes cooling
COOKING TIME 30 minutes

FOR THE MARBLE CAKE
175g/6oz/1⅓ cups strong plain
    (all-purpose) flour, plus extra
    for dusting
½ tsp baking powder
4 eggs
200g/7oz/heaped ¾ cup caster
    (superfine) sugar
a pinch of salt
6 tbsp double (heavy) cream
60g/2¼oz unsalted butter, melted,
    plus extra for greasing
2 tbsp good-quality dark cocoa
    powder

FOR THE CITRUS SYRUP
juice of 1 orange
juice of 1 pink grapefruit
juice of 1 lime
2 tbsp caster (superfine) sugar

When I was younger, I always wondered how the pattern on a marble cake was created! It looked so pretty when it was sliced, and the chocolate aroma used to pervade the room. As always, quality ingredients are crucial, so do make sure the cocoa powder is of great quality, as the success of the final result will depend on it. You may need a little practice to perfect the technique of folding and swirling the mixture, but the chocolate aroma will make it all worthwhile. Don't forget to drizzle over the citrus syrup while the cake is still warm so the liquid gold can gently find its way down this beautiful cake.

1 Preheat the oven to 160°C/315°F/gas 2½ and butter and flour a 1kg/2lb 4oz loaf tin or use a silicone cake mould.

2 Sift the flour and baking powder into a bowl. Put the eggs, sugar and salt in another large bowl and whisk, using an electric whisk, for a good 8–10 minutes until really light, thick and foaming. Fold in the cream, then add the sifted flour and baking powder and fold gently together. Finally fold in the melted butter. Remove one-third of the mixture into a small bowl. Sift the cocoa powder into the remaining mixture and mix gently until all the cocoa is combined.

3 Put half the cocoa mixture into the bottom of the prepared cake tin, add the reserved plain cake mix, then finish with the rest of the cocoa mixture. Put the handle end of a spatula into the mixture at the left-hand side of the tin at a 45 degree angle. Using a folding action, gently pull the handle round the edges of the mixture, then down through the centre, making three 'folds' while moving from left to right down the length of the cake tin. This will give you a great marbled effect.

4 Bake for 25–30 minutes until a skewer inserted into the centre comes out clean. If the cake is not quite ready, then slide it back into the oven and bake for a further 5 minutes, then check again.

5 Meanwhile, put all the syrup ingredients in a small saucepan over a low heat and heat gently until the sugar has dissolved, then turn the heat up to medium and cook until there is about 2 tablespoons of syrup, which is thick enough to coat the back of a spoon. Remove from the heat and leave to one side.

6 Remove the cake from the oven and put the tin on a wire rack to cool for 5 minutes. Turn the cake out of the tin and drizzle the citrus syrup over the top. Leave to cool a little before slicing and serving.

PRUNE, RAISIN & APRICOT CLAFOUTIS INFUSED WITH GREEN TEA

Ahh, clafoutis. This is a famous French recipe that my mother often made when she was young. Of course, the classic way would be with cherries, which remains a favourite, but because I love apricots, prunes and raisins, I have created this alternative. It's infused with green tea, which lifts it a note higher and brings something new and fresh to the recipe. Make sure you use a high-quality green tea to get the best flavour.

SERVES 6
PREPARATION TIME 20 minutes, plus
    1 hour marinating time
COOKING TIME 12 minutes if in
    ramekins, 25 minutes if using
    larger dish

90g/3¼oz soft dried apricots,
    roughly chopped
40g/1½oz soft raisins
90g/3¼oz soft prunes, roughly
    chopped
40g/1½oz soft dried figs, roughly
    chopped
1 green tea bag, plus 1 tbsp loose
    green tea
280ml/9½fl oz/generous 1 cup
    full-fat milk
60g/2¼oz unsalted butter, half
    softened and half melted
90g/3¼oz caster (superfine) sugar
80g/2¾oz/generous ½ cup plain
    (all-purpose) flour
a pinch of salt
1 large egg
2 large egg yolks

1 Put the dried fruits into a bowl with the green tea bag. Just cover with warm water and leave for a good hour or two so the fruits soak well. Add the loose green tea to the milk and leave to infuse while you make the clafoutis mixture.

1 Preheat the oven to 180°C/350°F/gas 4.

2 Strain the fruits, which should be nice and plump. Set aside. Discard the liquid and the tea bag.

3 Grease a 24 x16 x 6cm (9½ x 6 ⅓ x 2 ⅓in) baking dish or clafoutis dish (an oval earthenware dish) or 6 individual ramekins with the softened butter and sprinkle with 3 tablespoons of the sugar. Carefully shake the sugar around the dish or dishes to make sure it coats the inside.

4 Sift the flour and salt into a mixing bowl. In a separate bowl, whisk together the egg, egg yolks and remaining sugar, then slowly add this to the flour and mix until incorporated, silky and smooth.

5 Strain the green tea-infused milk through a sieve (strainer) and slowly add to the mixture, stirring until the batter has the consistency of a crepe mix. Add the melted butter and mix until combined.

6 Tip the fruits into the baking dish or clafoutis dish, or divide among the individual ramekins. Spread out evenly, then carefully pour over the batter. Bake in the preheated oven for 25 minutes until set and golden brown, or until a skewer inserted into the centre comes out clean. Remove from oven and serve.

RHUBARB TART WITH LEMONGRASS & ROSEWATER

Rhubarb tart. What can I say about it other than good things? I love the sharp acidity coming through, I love the scent of lemongrass and the waft of rose water. What a difference these ingredients make to this classic. This tart is so delicious that it will leave you wanting more. So, who's baking the next one?

SERVES **8**
PREPARATION TIME **30 minutes, plus making the pastry and chilling it**
COOKING TIME **35 minutes**

100ml /3½fl oz/scant ½ cup double (heavy) cream
1 lemongrass stalk, bruised
1 tbsp rose water
butter, for greasing
sweet short pastry (see page 30)
plain (all-purpose) flour, for rolling out the pastry
50g/1¾ oz caster (superfine) sugar
1 egg, plus 1 egg yolk
50g/1¾ oz ground almonds
1 tbsp dry rose petals, crushed to dust
500g/1lb 2 oz rhubarb, cut into large cubes

1 Put the cream in a small pan over a low heat and add the rose water. Heat gently until the cream is just starting to simmer, then remove from the heat and set the pan aside, covered with clingfilm (plastic wrap) for 15 minutes to allow the flavours to infuse. .

2 Grease a 24cm (9½ inch) loose-bottomed tart pan with butter. Roll out the pastry on a lightly floured surface until it is about 3–5mm thick, then roll the pastry over the rolling pin and line the prepared tart pan. Do not overstretch it or it will break. Tuck the pastry into the bottom and sides of the pan, pressing down gently to push any bubbles out.

3 Trim off any excess pastry, prick the base all over with a fork, cover with cling film (plastic wrap) and chill for 30 minutes. Towards the ends of the chilling time, preheat the oven to 180°C/350°F/gas 4. Strain the cream through a sieve (strainer) into a bowl, add the sugar, egg and egg yolk and whisk with an electric mixer or electric whisk for about 3-4 minutes until pale and fluffy.

4 Take the tart pan out of the refrigerator. Mix the ground almonds with the rose petal dust and sprinkle over the tart base, then arrange the rhubarb on top. Pour the egg mixture over the rhubarb, making sure the whole surface is covered and there are no gaps.

5 Bake in the oven for 25–30 minutes until pale golden. Remove from the oven and leave to cool a little. Serve when it's still warm, as that's when it's most delicious!

KITCHEN TERMINOLOGY

I hope you find this short glossary useful when you are using the recipes. Many of the terms may be familiar, others less so, and there are some that you may take for granted but not really know the precise details.

Bain marie: Literally a water bath, the food is cooked very gently, on the stove or in the oven, in a dish surrounded by hot water in a larger pan.

Bake blind: To cook a pastry case without the filling, lined with baking paper and covered with baking beans to keep it flat, for about 10 minutes, then without the paper and beans for a further few minutes to finish.

Beignet: A fritter.

Blanch: Briefly immersing food in a pan of boiling water to barely cook it, before lifting out the food and submerging it briefly in iced water to stop further cooking.

Bouillon: A broth or stock made with meat and vegetables.

Boulangère: A dish made of layers of sliced vegetables, usually potatoes, and meat.

Bouquet garni: A small bunch of mixed herbs – usually made up of a bay leaf, thyme, parsley and celery leaves – used to flavour a soup, stew or sauce.

Braise: To roast or brown a piece of meat, poultry or vegetable in fat, then add a small amount of liquid and simmer gently in a covered pot.

Bruise: To gently crush an ingredient, such as a lemongrass stalk, to release the flavour.

Caramel: A rich golden brown syrup made by heating sugar and water together.

Cartouche: A circle of baking paper with a small hole in the centre used to cover foods while they cook.

Ceviche: Raw fish marinated in citrus juice in order to 'cook' the fish without heat.

Clarify: Gently melt butter so that the solids separate from the liquid and can be discarded.

Confit: The French word for 'preserved', this most usually refers to pork, goose, duck, chicken or turkey, cooked in its own fat and stored, covered in fat, in a pot, but it can also refer to foods preserved in syrup.

Coulis: A thick sauce of purée made from fruit or vegetables.

Cure: To preserve food, usually by salting, smoking or drying.

Deglaze: Adding liquid to a pan in which meat or vegetables have been cooked and stirring to dissolve the caramelized brown bits on the bottom of the pan to incorporate them into the liquid, and then boiling to reduce the liquid.

Dehydrate: Dry out a food in order to preserve it and intensify the flavours.

Emulsify: Combine two ingredients, like oil and water, that don't usually mix by gradually whisking them together.

En cocotte: Eggs individually baked in cream or butter in small ramekin dishes.

En papillote: Food cooked in a parcel made of baking paper or kitchen foil.

Farci: The French word for 'stuffed', often referring to stuffed vegetables.

Flambé: To pour a measure of alcohol, often brandy, over hot food in a pan and briefly set it alight to burn off the alcohol.

Fold in: To combine two mixtures very gently, using a large metal spoon in a figure-of-eight movement, in order to knock out as little air as possible.

Fricassée: A dish of small pieces of meat, often chicken, served in a thick white sauce.

Gratin: A dish with a topping, often including cheese and breadcrumbs, browned under a hot grill (broiler).

Julienne: Cutting vegetables or fruit zest into thin sticks, 2 x 30mm/$\frac{1}{16}$ x $1\frac{1}{4}$in, using a knife or a mandolin.

Macerate: To soak and soften before cooking or serving.

Marinate: To soak in a spiced liquid to impart flavour before cooking.

Mandolin: A manual slicer with different blades so that you can use it to slice very thinly, grate or cut into strips.

Pithivier: A round double-crust pie made with puff pastry.

Poach: To cook food gently in a very hot but not bubbling liquid, keeping it just below a simmer.

Ragoût: A stew made from meat, poultry, game, fish or vegetables cooked with herbs and spices.

Reduce: To boil in an uncovered pan to evaporate some of the liquid and, by doing so, to reduce the quantity of liquid and thereby strengthen the flavours of a finished stock or sauce.

Refresh: To quickly immerse cooked food in iced or very cold water to stop the cooking process and set the colour.

Rémoulade: A mayonnaise-based sauce seasoned with various ingredients, sometimes including chilli, capers or paprika.

Rillettes: Cooked, shredded meat preserved in fat.

Sabayon: A light, frothy sauce made by whisking egg yolks with liquid in a bowl set over a pan of simmering water.

Sauté: Cooking in a little fat in a shallow pan over a medium to high heat to brown or cook ingredients, keeping the food moving around the pan.

Sous-vide: To cook food in a vacuum pack, either by boiling or steaming.

Steam: To cook food in the heat from the steam from boiling water.

Tian: A dish made of alternate layers of various sliced vegetables and other ingredients, such as seafood, flavoured with herbs and seasoning.

Velouté: One of the basic sauces in classic French cuisine, a rich sauce made from chicken, fish or veal stock thickened with a roux, a blend of butter and flour.

INDEX

almond milk chicken scented with
lemongrass, garlic & thyme 186

almonds
cherry and almond cream tarts 167
chicken & cucumber en papillote with
toasted almonds 191
pan-fried plums & almond biscotti
with amaretto cream 163

apples
apple, raspberry & thyme puffs 92
celeriac & apple rémoulade with
crystallized celeriac leaves 60
glazed chicory & thyme 138
langoustine or prawn ceviche 103

apricots
caramelized apricots with pistachio
nuts & peach sauce 164
prune, raisin & apricot clafoutis
infused with green tea 230

artichokes
goats' cheese, summer vegetable &
herb quiche 182
Provençale salad with courgette
flowers tempura 132
spring vegetables with watercress
dressing 145

asparagus
asparagus, parsley & chestnut
mushroom risotto 78
Jerusalem artichoke velouté with
truffle oil & chive cream 53
ragoût of summer vegetables with
vanilla beurre blanc 141
spring vegetables with watercress
dressing 145
warm white asparagus salad with
grapefruit zest vinaigrette 62
wild asparagus, wild garlic & potato
soup 86

babas: cider-soaked babas with
cinnamon chantilly cream 218

bacon
game, chestnut & sultana terrine 39
lentil & bacon soup with mushrooms &
thyme cream 207

balsamic vinegar
balsamic & lime raspberries with
goats' milk ice cream 90
reduced 27

beans
fennel-smoked cod with warm bean
salad 21
morteau sausage & warm borlotti bean
salad 208
pan-fried cod loin with white bean
purée & garlic crisps 118
ragoût of summer vegetables with
vanilla beurre blanc 141
spring vegetables with watercress
dressing 145

beef
beef carpaccio with beef tartare &
wasabi cream 49
beef stock 24–5
braised ox cheeks with crushed
potatoes 74
slow-roast beef rib eye with carrot &
horseradish purée 73

beetroot/beets: heirloom beetroot
'tagliatelle' & carpaccio 50

Belgian endive: see chicory

beurre noisette 30

blackberries: Earl Grey rice pudding
with blackberry marmalade 94

bread
cocoa-infused pain perdu with roasted
peaches 147
croûtons 27
brioche: spiced autumn fruits with
pan-fried brioche 156

butter: beurre noisette 30

butternut squash
butternut squash & saffron risotto 211
butternut squash soup with mussels &
saffron cream 108
casserole of autumn vegetables with
pears & ceps 44
swede & squash soup with
caramelized chestnuts 54

cabbage
lime-leaf poached chicken 185
pork shoulder with chilli-ginger
cabbage 199
stuffed chicken breasts with cabbage
& chestnuts 188

cakes
caramelized pear & rosemary cake
169
chocolate marble cake with citrus fruit
glaze 228
lemon & chilli cake with chilli glaze
151

lemon, wild thyme & dandelion flower
cake 93
orange & tarragon gâteau with
candied orange 152
pain de gênes with rosemary and
tonka bean crème anglaise 216

carrots
casserole of autumn vegetables with
pears & ceps 44
chicken & lemongrass broth 174
goats' cheese, summer vegetable &
herb quiche 182
pancetta-wrapped monkfish with
carrot & mandarin purée 114
poached chicken with lemon zest &
black olives 194
prawn & plaice soup 109
ragoût of summer vegetables with
vanilla beurre blanc 141
slow-roast beef rib eye with carrot &
horseradish purée 73
spring vegetables with watercress
dressing 145
vegetable pot-au-feu with kohlrabi 76
venison bourguignon with dark
chocolate & star anise 40
casserole of autumn vegetables with
pears & ceps 44
casserole of lamb & pomegranate
molasses 69

cauliflower
lemongrass & saffron-scented
cauliflower gratin 146
ragoût of summer vegetables with
vanilla beurre blanc 141
scallops with cauliflower purée &
hazelnut dressing 102

celeriac/celery root
casserole of autumn vegetables with
pears & ceps 44
celeriac & apple rémoulade with
crystallized celeriac leaves 60
partridge with celeriac, turnips &
chestnut boulangère 64
plaice with celeriac & pancetta galette
117

chard
goats' cheese, summer vegetable &
herb quiche 182
Provençale with courgette flowers
tempura 132

cheese
crushed pea & mint tortellini with pea
shoots 142

AUTHOR ACKNOWLEDGEMENTS

For Heston: A special thank you to Heston Blumenthal who has, since the late nineties when he first walked into Harvey's restaurant, been someone very special to me. Since then, he has remained a friend and I have so much respect for the man, the chef, and his genius forward thinking. Merci Heston, for, once again, writing a wonderful foreword for my book!

For Raymond: I met Raymond Blanc a long time ago, during a gala dinner, not long after when I had just earned my first Michelin star. We soon discovered that we were from the same region and that our upbringings were very similar, so we clicked straight away. Because of where we come from, Raymond understands me the most, and I have huge admiration for what he has done, and what an extraordinary chef he is. Respect!

I also want to thank the Watkins team who helped me along the way to make this a beautiful book!